Local Religion in Colonial Mexico

A series of course-adoption books on Latin America

FRONTIS: Flyers

Taken from Francisco Javier Clavijero, Storia antica del Messico *(Cesena: Gregorio Biasini, 1780). Courtesy of Mandeville Special Collections Library, University of California, San Diego.*

Local Religion in
Colonial Mexico

❧

edited by

MARTIN AUSTIN NESVIG

UNIVERSITY OF NEW MEXICO • ALBUQUERQUE

LIBRARY OF CONGRESS CATALOGING-IN-PUBLICATION DATA

Local religion in colonial Mexico /
[edited by] Martin Austin Nesvig.— 1st ed.
p. cm. — (Diálogos)
Includes bibliographical references and index.
ISBN-13: 978-0-8263-3402-2 (PBK. : ALK. PAPER)
ISBN -10: 0-8263-3402-4 (PBK. : ALK. PAPER)
1. Catholic Church—Mexico—History.
2. Christianity and culture—Mexico—History.
3. Mexico—History—Spanish colony, 1540–1810.
I. Nesvig, Martin Austin, 1968–
II. Diálogos (Albuquerque, N.M.)
BX1428.3.L63 2006
282'.72 — dc22

2005028926

Book design and type composition by Kathleen Sparkes.
This book is typeset using the Janson family, 10/13.5; 26P.
Display type is Bernhard Modern.

For my students, past, present, and future

Contents

List of Illustrations

~≥

Acknowledgments

Numerous people helped with the production and completion of this book. First and most importantly, this volume would not have been possible were it not for the support of Lyman Johnson, who agreed that a discussion of the role of religion in colonial Mexico would make an interesting contribution to both professional historiography and the classroom. I have been lucky to work with such a careful editor, valued colleague, and friend. The editorial staff at the University of New Mexico Press—David Holtby, Kathy Sparkes, Alex Giardino, and others—offered crucial logistical support every step of the way. The contributors to this volume offered me a tutorial in style and method. Bill Christian Jr. was gracious in allowing a group of Mexicanists to appropriate his terminology as well as in offering reflections on his conception of popular religion and his own critical observances on style and method. The many Mexicans who showed me just how far and deep religious sentiment still runs—women completing a pilgrimage on bloody knees, the young man who explained the intricacies of Santa María Tonanzintla, the liberality of the Jesuits and father Salvador Treviño, who accepted an unbeliever into their excellent libraries, the boys who sell Malverde potions or the herb sellers in the Mercado Sonora—deserve praise for reminding me that I will always be a student myself.

Finally, this collection was conceived as a way to provoke debate and discussion among students. My first year out of graduate school, I completed a visiting professorship at New Mexico State University and had the good fortune to work with a dynamic group of students who challenged me on numerous levels. They combined an admirable distrust of professorial authority with a genuine love of learning. I learned much more from them than they ever could from me while they dared me to understand the role of interlocutor, to think about the way that culture adapts in historical contexts, and to make sense of the myriad expressions of religion in Mexico and the rest of Latin America. In particular my thanks go to Catherine Comer, Nancy Donde, Theresa Esparza, Eilleen García, Lori Gonzales, Mark Harben, Jarma Jones, Natalia Lira, Carla Martínez, Audra Mitchell, Abdullah Orozco, Oscar Pérez, and Katie Swank, as well as to those students, not formally mine, whose linguistic expertise or personal connections to Latin American religion helped me so much: Lilia Campos, Marcelo Fajardo Cárdenas, Ray González, Jorge Porrata, Iana Quigley-Phillips, and Claudia Quintana.

FIGURE 1. Cortés before Charles V

This is a highly symbolic print of Cortés presenting the world to king and emperor Charles V. Designed to reinforce a regal view of Mexico as part of the Spanish empire, one notes the attempt by editor Archbishop Lorenzana to incorporate important elements of the very early days of Spanish Mexico: Indian nobles, Franciscan friars, as well as the symbol of the empire in the form of a globe. Taken from Historia de Nueva España, escrita por su esclarecido conquistador Hernán Cortés, aumentada con otros documentos, y notas, por el ilustríssimo señor don Francisco Antonio Lorenzana *(Mexico: Joseph Antonio de Hogal, 1770). Courtesy of Mandeville Special Collections Library, University of California, San Diego.*

Introduction

Martin Austin Nesvig

On Holy Saturday (the day before Easter), 2004, in the town of Yuriria, Guanajuato, on the southern edge of the Bajío, hundreds of Catholic faithful throng to the town's various churches to receive a benediction from the reposed Christ before the altar. In the Church of the Christ of the Precious Blood (Iglesia de Nuestro Señor de la Sangre Preciosa), the crowds are so thick that the sacristan has to remind the faithful every couple of minutes to form two lines in the nave so that the foot traffic will not overwhelm the church itself. In some churches, women shuffle to the altar on their knees in a show of devotion to the crucified Christ. In the Augustinian church to the right of the main altar is a shrine to martyred saints, but it is not to these martyrs that the crowds turn. Rather, it is to venerate the Augustinian friar and priest, Miguel de Zavala, known also as padre Zavalita. Neither beatified nor canonized, ex-votos of innumerable quantity crowd around pictures, drawings, and notes dedicated to Zavala, all beneath an imposing portrait ten feet high that hangs above the entrance to the martyrs' chapel. Many ex-votos thank "padre Zavalita, santo," or simply Saint Zavala, for miracles performed or fulfilled, contrary to all official proscriptions of the church.

Four hundred eighty-five years after the arrival of the Spanish, 237 years after the expulsion of the Jesuits, more than a century and a half after the promulgation of strict reforms of the church, and nearly a century after a revolution brimming with anticlerical sentiment, Mexico and Mexicans remain profoundly Catholic. Yet a cursory review of North American scholarship on Mexican culture and history reflects relatively little of this vast religious significance in Mexican society, politics, and everyday life. And if more than a century of secularization attempts by the Mexican state have whittled away significant amounts of the church's power, in retrospect, given the current state of Mexican culture, one cannot but be struck by the impact the church and Catholicism had in prenational Mexico as part of New Spain.

Yet for all the vast power of the church in colonial Mexico two distinct dilemmas face the North American practitioner of Mexican history. First, there is the tendency among North Americans to lend broad credence to the progression of secularization in the nineteenth and twentieth centuries as something implacable, irreversible, and inevitable. What is generically called a Whiggish vision of history—that all history is forward moving, diachronic, and linear—has exercised immense influence among Mexicanists and Latin Americanists who viewed in the Reform projects in Mexico the final blow to church control of various segments of the state and society. Yet a brief visit to Mexico cures even the most jejune observer of this view. Tepeyac, in the northern end of Mexico City, with its shrine to the Virgin of Guadalupe, has now surpassed all other sites as the world's most visited Catholic pilgrimage site outside Rome.

The second dilemma, broadly stated, is a kind of reverse corollary to the first. If many North Americans have bought into the anticlerical positivism of Mexican reform and revolution, too often other historians have viewed the church as monolithic and unstoppable in its power in the pre-Reform era. That is to say the rubric of "Spiritual Conquest," formulated by Robert Ricard in 1933, posits that with the arrival of the Spaniards and their peculiar brand of triumphant Catholicism came the victorious and oppressive superimposition of orthodox Catholicism in New Spain. Yet as late as the eighteenth century Indians in both the Spanish-dominated Valley of Mexico and the farther-flung regions like rural Michoacán, San Luis Potosí, and Oaxaca continued to celebrate pre-Hispanic, autochthonous religious ceremonies. The Black Christs of Michoacán, which the faithful kissed in Yuriria, are black because people believe they drink the venom of poisonous animals like scorpions, snakes, and beetles in order to protect whoever offers them propitiation.

This book of essays, *Local Religion in Colonial Mexico*, challenges the student as well as the professional historian to look beyond, or indeed perhaps even scuttle forever, these twin formulae of North American scholarly discussion of religion in Mexico. The collective thrust of this book is to offer, by way of vignettes, broad-ranging discussions of the challenges to the view that religion in Mexico is either now extinct and thus deserves no scholarly attention, or that its colonial precedent was so ruthlessly oppressive and unmitigated that it went unchallenged, unrelieved, and blindly obeyed until the 1850s.

The title of this book and the thread that holds it together is a concept elucidated by William Christian Jr., in his justly notable 1981 book, *Local Religion in Sixteenth-Century Spain*. Just as the title of Ricard's best-known work took on a methodological significance beyond the book, so too has Christian's work on Spain. According to Christian's conceptualization, Catholicism developed specifically local and popular traditions side by side with the universal and official aspirations of the church. These two strands do not lie in direct contradiction but rather overlap, sometimes officially tolerated, other times officially ignored, still other times formally prosecuted.

Christian emphasized the locally specific and determined nature of "popular" religion in early modern Spain in ways that came to represent a new method of looking at historical religious devotion. For Christian religion in sixteenth-century Spain was about community-centered devotions, locally specific saints, pilgrimages, shrines, and customs. Although some scholars have taken Christian to task for what they view as a too heavy focus on unofficial and extraliturgical religious practice, Christian was interested in demonstrating the dicey nature of explaining Catholicism, and especially Iberian Catholicism, in terms of universal doctrine, theology, and liturgy. Instead, he demonstrated the multitudinous ways that Catholicism exerted a local character that, so long as it was not at extreme odds with the Vatican or the diocesan authorities, tended to be accepted as legitimate.

A second strand of thinking about religion that is perhaps not so explicit in this volume but whose influence cannot fairly be underestimated is the vision of religion as the accumulation of local custom made into religious doctrine. The anthropologist Clifford Geertz enunciated such a view of religion (as well as law) as the organic outgrowth of custom as opposed to the superimposition of doctrine from a central authority. In recent years what has become known as the "new cultural history" has exerted a tremendous influence on historians and the way they conceive of the past. The study of colonial Mexico and religion is no exception to this trend. Geertz and his organic view of culture have been central to the development of this cultural history. Indeed, when this "new" cultural history was being hashed out by North American practitioners, it was Clifford Geertz and Robert Darnton who explicitly experimented with this methodology and vision of history in their seminars at Princeton University, leading to a revolution within the profession of North American historians.

The conceptualization of Hispanic Catholicism as local and "popular" has in recent years taken on particular interest among many practitioners of Mexican religious history. As historians moved away from the myths of a unidirectional "conquest" they began to challenge the assumptions of the spiritual conquest. Likewise, the recent focus on power as multidirectional and contested has begun to influence scholars of religion in Mexico. The irony is immense. The political historians of Latin America, born of the Old Left and the Old New Left, "discovered" cultural history in the late 1990s. With their epiphany these political historians fused an older model of political economy and material neo-Marxist inquiry, with a study of the culture of politics, the methods of the underdogs (called "subalterns" in their lingo), and the complicated and ever-contested nature of power. In other words, while older models emphasized the top-down or high-level politics of formal parties, revolutions, and policies, the newer cultural history of politics emphasized the role of the peasant, the underrepresented, and the "popular." In similar fashion studies of religion moved toward more prosaic and popular manifestations of religious sensibility. Thus while political historians were discovering the multiplicity and complexity of power among political actors, historians of religion began to see the same potential fruits of a cultural history approach. The result is that North American historians of religion in Mexico are challenging the assumptions of a vast undifferentiated Iberian Catholicism in colonial Mexico.

In a classically Mexican metaphor for these mixed reactions, the chile (autochthonous to Mexico) entered the Hispanic consciousness soon after the conquest. But this led to notorious problems. In 1530s the inquisitor and archbishop of Mexico, Juan de Zumárraga, prosecuted, convicted, and heavily sentenced the first Spanish settler in Guayangareo (present-day Morelia), Gonzalo Gómez. Among his "crimes" was his penchant for hanging chiles up to dry next to his crucifix.[1] Less than thirty years later, in 1561 the diocesan inquisitor of Michoacán prosecuted Hernando de Coca for having compared a meat stew made with chiles with the blood of Christ.[2] The chile, along with cacao, was viewed as a potentially suspect food, leading the faithful to lust, imbalanced thoughts, and in the cases against Gómez and Coca, far too idiosyncratic, and Mexican, visions of local religion.

But if the Spaniards attempted to eradicate or regulate foods related to religious practice like pulque or peyote, just as they imported Spanish wine to administer the Eucharist, Indians and mestizos were little convinced of the necessary connections between universal Catholicism and the eradication of their local traditions. Pre-Hispanic ancestor worship fused with the Catholic celebration of All Saints Day to become the Day of the Dead. Pre-Hispanic deities were subsumed into Catholic saints. Even ecclesiastics themselves borrowed pre-Hispanic traditions in order to make them Catholic. The Nahua symbolism of an eagle atop a nopal cactus sitting on a stone (the glyph itself means Tenochtitlan, or place of the wild nopal cactus, and is seen today most notably on the Mexican flag) was quickly adopted as a symbol of the new religious-political culture of Mexico. Indeed, on the front of the same Augustinian church in Yuriria mentioned above, built in the 1550s, one can see the eagle on a nopal, evidence of the rapidity with which Catholic missionaries adapted to their particular local needs.[3]

It is no accident that chocolate (the word itself is of Nahuatl origin), chiles, and nopales are all inherently linked to Mexican identity. In a now-classic study of cultural interaction, Solange Alberro argued that the cultural mixture of Mexico began not only with the Hispanization and Christianization of Indians but also of the adoption of Indian customs by Spaniards and mestizos.[4] But this complex network and interaction has infrequently been examined from the view of religion. This volume hopes to add a discussion of the specifically religious nature of the cultural fusion that became not Indian, not Spanish, not African, but Mexican, a unique, extremely rich, and dense culture.

The essays offered here intend to provide departure points for discussion and further inquiry into the locally specific character of religion and religious culture in colonial Mexico. To that end this volume does not pretend to offer a comprehensive examination of the church or the processes of Christianization in Mexico. This is not to say that such studies are somehow not worthy or that this volume pretends to offer a "better" analysis. Rather, our hope is that these essays will provoke debates about that wider realm of religion and its role in Mexican culture. Nevertheless, these essays hope to highlight specific themes in that debate that are not as isolated as an initial perusal of the book might indicate. For example, the highly suggestive essay by David Tavárez about continuing pre-Hispanic "idolatrous" practices in late colonial Oaxaca points up several of these broader themes: the complexity of ethnic identity, the interplay of Indian and Spaniard in negotiating a socially conceived religious structure, the relative success or failure of Catholic missionary efforts, and the extent to which self-aware religious belief is a necessary component of religious culture.

Besides offering essays that tend toward locally specific issues and histories, the essays as a whole tend to approach specific methodological and theoretical issues. As noted, the rubric of local religion and local culture unites the essays as a whole. But more specifically, the essays are brought together by an overreaching concern with the ways that formal political, economic, and theological structures inform and interact with what has been termed "mentality." As a staple of the new cultural history, the history of mentality supposes that societies and cultures have complex and interwoven mental, philosophic, and religious structures. On one level there are formal structures, known sometimes as ideology or doctrine, that tend to be worked out in specific areas, whether within government, the law, or the church doctrine. On yet another level there are broad and culturally diffuse meanings that historian Michel Vovelle calls "mentalities" that are more difficult to define and tend to overlap with ideology.[5] Thus we might say that in an official world of ideology or doctrine the veneration of Christ is a broadly accepted form of pilgrimage and worship but that the worship of the Christ of Chalma, southwest of Mexico City, has a much more diffuse cultural pattern that is associated with pre-Hispanic holy spots and with the physical geography in the valleys and streams of that area west of Cuernavaca.

The book offers dialogues between the formal and informal, the universal and the local, the sanctioned and the sometimes only barely tolerated, forms of Catholicism that were woven throughout a very complex Mexican culture. To that end the first essay in the volume is a synoptic overview of this interaction between official and popular religion by Carlos Eire, the historian of early modern Europe. Eire, whose work focuses on the Protestant Reformation and early modern Spanish religious thought, offers an overview of the development of what he conceives broadly as a lengthy tradition that dichotomizes "official" and "popular" religion. He traces the origins of this juxtaposition that continues to bedevil modern historians to the early church itself and a deep-seated distrust of unofficial religion. This dichotomy, in Eire's assessment, derives from a variety of internalized distinctions within the Catholic Church and Western thought: between urban and rural; theology and popular thought; doctrine and heterodoxy; educated and illiterate. Further drawing out these distinctions, Eire explains how modern-day historians of religion and Catholicism have struggled with the burden of a dichotomous view of Catholicism as a cultural and religious pattern.

More regionally focused essays dealing with themes in colonial Mexican religion and culture follow Eire's essay. Antonio Rubial García explains the broad patterns of the use of saints in colonial Mexico. Dividing his essay into the use and appropriation of saints in colonial Mexico between Indian and Spanish/mestizo culture, Rubial García demonstrates that the integration of Catholic saints into the society of New Spain had different trajectories divided on an ethnic fault line. For Indians the introduction of Catholic saints was associated with the substitution of the gods of the military victors, the Spanish—a tradition that he demonstrates predated the arrival of the Spaniards. But in the case of Catholic saints the issue was amplified by the radically different vision of the utility of saints between Indian and Spanish thought. For Spaniards, a deeper problem was the relative lack of saints from New Spain itself.

This relatively functional emphasis is contrasted in my essay on the debate on Indians, their humanity and intellect, and the ordination of Indians as priests. Rather than view religious thought and theological discussions as outgrowths of broader sociopolitical issues, I emphasize the specific philosophical debates surrounding the so-called Indian question. In the case of Mexico, vigorous debates on the relative intelligence of Indians occurred at the level of diocesan law and provincial councils as well as within the broader missionary priesthood. My essay on the "Indian question" focuses on these debates about the nature of the sacraments, their applicability to recent Indian converts, and the ultimate question of whether Indians could or should be educated for the priesthood. The result is a focus on a formal theological debate that concerned a locally specific issue. In Mexico especially, the Franciscan effort to train an Indian clergy at Tlatelolco had repercussions throughout the Spanish Catholic world because it continued a debate about the relative humanity and intelligence of Indians, of conversion practices, and of the overall imperial project in the Indies. These debates took place among the highest-ranking members of the Spanish Catholic intelligentsia. My essay examines the thought of intellectuals placed high in the Spanish imperial and academic world, individuals such as Francisco Vitoria (holder of the highest theological university position in Spain) and Alfonso de Castro (confessor to the king), both of Salamanca. In sum, the essay is an effort to highlight the ways that local concerns in Mexico (administration of the Eucharist to new believers, Indian priesthood training) became debates of deep political significance on the other side of the Atlantic within the same religious system.

The following three essays offer detailed discussions of locally specific manifestations of Spanish-Indian cultural and religious encounters in the later colonial period. These three essays tend to offer the most detailed examinations of the effects of the detailed cultural "encounters" that made colonial Mexico such a dynamic society. William Taylor's essay examines the way that a late colonial Spanish Franciscan struggled to make sense of a largely Indian parish and its unique traditions. Taylor lays in relief the continuing complex attitudes toward Indians, their culture, and adaptation of Catholicism that continued well into the end of the colonial era. He elucidates an important theme for the development of both universal and local religion: the role of the priest—in this case the "accumulated local religion and networks of authority, power, and knowledge [that priests brought with them into] pastoral service." Indeed, in the early modern period in Europe as well as Latin America, contemporaries from the upper ranks of the church frequently commented (often bitterly) that the lower, local clergy, less educated and frequently less orthodox than bishops, cardinals, and popes, tended to retain a good deal of local "superstition" and religious custom. Taylor's essay offers a tightly woven example to demonstrate that local religion sprung not only from the laity but also was often the result of priests whose religious conceptions were every bit as "local" and "popular" as the local laity.

Tavárez's essay is a kind of "thick description" of events in late seventeenth- and early eighteenth-century Oaxaca. Drawing an analytical description of trials against Indians for idolatry, Tavárez argues that such criminal procedures reveal a great deal about both the persistence of native religious practice as well as community identity. To that end the essay demonstrates that for Indians and mestizos in Oaxaca religion was an important component of local community identity. Edward Osowski likewise examines the ways the religion promoted locally specific identity. In this case, however, it was the ways that Indians adapted Catholic religio-cultural traditions into their own local cultures. Examining the ways that Indian communities near Mexico City engaged in alms collection, Osowski demonstrates that there were considerable admixtures of a Spanish-Catholic tradition—bearing saints on alms-collection journeys—and a pre-Hispanic tradition that afforded women a greater role in public religious activity.

Brian Larkin offers the strongest critique in this volume of Christian's vision of locally specific Catholicism in Hispanic culture. Larkin focuses on the *cofradía* (confraternity) as a unit of social cohesion, emphasizing the inherently religious value associated with the cofradía. Accordingly, for Larkin, previous discussions of cofradías and of religious mentality as found in the work of Christian have heavily emphasized their extraliturgical nature. Larkin views this as drawing attention away from the liturgical value that Spaniards placed on their social religious activities. Larkin's essay, then, argues that Spaniards had a deeply imbued sense of the liturgy that is usually absent from discussions of popular religion that tend to argue that Spaniards were more interested in unofficial celebrations of religion than in a religion that was guided by formal structures of the church.

Larkin's essay provides a foil for the essay by Nicole von Germeten on men of African descent and their integration within cofradías in New Spain. Although von Germeten does not specifically reject Larkin's thesis of the liturgical nature of cofradías and religious sociability, her analytic focus is social, economic, and cultural. Examining the careers of two men of African descent, one in Mexico City and one in current-day Morelia, she analyzes the ways that Africans used cofradías to integrate themselves into Spanish colonial society. To that end von Germeten demonstrates that in colonial Mexico religion possessed a heavy element of political structure, since by adopting Spanish Catholic social bonds and emphasizing their integration into Catholic social activities, men of African descent were more effective in their ascent of the sociopolitical ladder.

Whereas von Germeten tends to emphasize the successful use of the political structure of Catholicism within Spanish colonial society, Javier Villa-Flores discusses the ways that black slaves used the concepts of Christian charity and blasphemy for material purposes. Focusing on a case study of an *obraje* in Coyoacán, Villa-Flores argues that black slaves often purposefully committed acts of blasphemy in the hopes of drawing attention (to harsh conditions) of the highest religious authority in the church: the Inquisition. In so doing, black slaves attempted to draw in a wide array of religious and criminal investigations into the abuse of power by their owners. The result, as discussed by von Germeten, is a vision of religious structures as fluid but also functional within a broader rubric of colonial society.

Finally, as a kind of coda to the collection, William Christian offers a reflective essay on the notion of "catholicism"—a term that he contrasts with Catholicism (with a capital "C") to underscore what he sees as the inherently local condition of religion. For Christian, local religion and "popular" religion can be understood to a great extent by the concept of catholicism as opposed to Catholicism. In other words locally determined practice and cultural understanding of the church has a long-standing tradition of being tolerated by the official church so long as it is not directly heretical. For this reason in Christian's view, most Catholic practice is locally specific and what most people experience as Catholicism is something unique to their geographic-cultural area. The end result in Christian's view is an inherent entropy, dragging down attempts at universal consensus and tolerant of local versions of Catholicism. If the essays in this volume offer any evidence, Christian's view would appear correct, given the extremely specific local versions of Catholicism in the context of colonial Mexico. So locally determined it seems was this catholicism that the version of it in one location would have been nearly unrecognizable to those in other areas.

Ultimately, Mexico in the colonial period was a society where the church had tremendous authority, wealth, and prestige. Bishops held the power to excommunicate the faithful, placing their salvation in peril. The Inquisition itself was the highest religious court in the Hispanic world and could impose a variety of terrifying penalties. Diocesan authorities as well as peripatetic friars investigated and punished Indian idolatry. But despite all these controls and power of the church, much of the religious history of colonial Mexico is marked not by uniform obedience but by disregard for those rules and authorities and by adapting formal church structures to everyday life. Indeed, public disobedience for the Inquisition and threats of excommunication were not rare. Spaniards often replied with scatological insults for church authorities. For example, in 1569 in Irapuato near Morelia, Pero Muñoz Maesso de Roa received a threat of excommunication from the bishop of Michoacán for having refused to pay tithes from his estates in 1558, 1563, and 1567. When the messenger of the bishop arrived to threaten him, Muñoz replied, "Shit on the notification and for the man who brought the order."[6] Eventually, he was convicted by the Inquisition, but the very fact of his initial disregard goes a long way toward highlighting the complexity of religion, authority, and cultural behavior in colonial Mexico.

NOTES

1. *Gonzalo Gómez. Primer poblador español de Guayangareo (Morelia). Proceso inquisitorial*, intro. by Richard Greenleaf and Benedict Warren (Morelia: Fímax, 1991).

2. Archivo General de la Nación (AGN), Inquisición, vol. 17, exp. 4. (Standard archival abbreviations seen throughout this book include the following: vol. for volumen/volume; exp. for expediente [file]; and f. for foja [sheet].)

3. The Mexica did not use alphabetic language prior to the arrival of the Spanish but used glyph symbols. The glyph for Tenochtitlan, the capital of the Mexica empire, was a nopal cactus on top of a stone in the middle of a lake. Thus *tetl*, for "stone," *noxtli*, for "wild nopal cactus," and *tlan*, a locative formation meaning "place of." These then, like many Nahuatl words, were combined and shortened to make the full word "Tenochtitlan." The eagle atop the nopal was understood to represent the origin mythology of the Mexica who believed that when they found their permanent home (they were nomadic prior to their 1325 establishment in Tenochtitlan) they would see an eagle devouring a serpent.

4. Solange Alberro, *Del gachupín al criollo: O de cómo los españoles de México dejaron de serlo* (Mexico: El Colegio de México, 1992). Alberro developed this theme further in her study *El águila y la cruz: Orígenes religiosos de la conciencia criolla. México, siglos XVI-XVII* (Mexico: Fondo de Cultura Económica; El Colegio de México, 1999).

5. The classic definition of these terms can be found in Michel Vovelle, *Ideologies and Mentalities*, trans. Eamon O'Flaherty (Chicago: University of Chicago Press, 1990). Vovelle's methodological and theoretical frameworks are discussed at length in the essay by Carlos Eire below.

6. AGN, Inquisición, vol. 11, exp. 4, f. 304.

FIGURE 2. Map of Anáhuac (Mexico).

Frontispiece from Francisco Javier Clavijero, Storia antica del Messico *(Cesena: Gregorio Biasini, 1780). Courtesy of Mandeville Special Collections Library, University of California, San Diego.*

CHAPTER ONE

The Concept of Popular Religion

Carlos M. N. Eire

Loud screams filled the parish church of Yebenes, a small town near Toledo, in Castile, just as the priest began to say Mass. It was March 16, 1611, a Sunday in Lent, that season when everyone was supposed to abstain from food, drink, and sex, and to amend their sinful behavior. Suddenly, two women began yelling at each other, drowning out the Latin prayers of the priest at the altar. One of the women, María Fernández, struck the other woman with a wooden plank, gashing her head. The injured woman, Ana Díaz, lunged at María, shrieking, and the two of them began to scuffle, *mano a mano*. As the priest stood frozen at the altar, some men jumped into the fray, separated the two women and took them away, each to her own house. Then the Mass resumed. When Ana and María were hauled into court some days later, they confessed to fighting over a seat in church. Court records tell us that the two women formally pardoned one another and were fined and admonished to keep the peace.[1]

Two women bickering over a seat in church, drawing blood inside sacred space during a sacred season, apparently for reasons of status and privilege; laymen breaking up the fight; a priest passively watching, then returning to his ritual performance: Is this popular religion?

Finding an answer to this question requires caution, patience, and a high degree of tolerance for generalizations. Summarizing and analyzing the concept of "popular religion" is highly problematic, for it is not a well-defined concept, and it remains open to varying interpretations despite at least thirty years of intense research and discussion. The emergence of the subject of "popular religion" during the past five decades stems largely from the ascendancy of social history over intellectual history, and from the growing acceptance among historians of the perspectives offered by anthropologists, ethnographers, and folklorists. Instead of focusing on formal doctrines and the clerical elites who formulated them, as past generations had done, historians have steadily turned their attention to the way in which religion was actually lived out by individuals and societies, and especially by those who were not clerics.[2] This shift in focus has brought forth new insights, and plenty of disagreement.

For instance, among those who specialize in late medieval and early modern religious history—my area of expertise—the spectrum of opinion concerning popular religion is exceedingly broad. Experts on European religion tend to agree on two things: there was a great upsurge in religious devotion in the fifteenth century, and nonclerics became more active than ever in shaping and living out their religion. But this is where agreement ends. Some historians tend to see this increased fervor as hollow and anxious, and ripe for reform.[3] Others see it as robust and satisfying.[4] Some perceive the clergy and their flocks as sharing a common piety.[5] Others detect a great gulf between them.[6] Where some discern genuine Christian fervor, others find far too many surviving pre-Christian elements. Some have gone so far as to argue that much of late medieval religion was "magical."[7] Others propose that Europe was not truly "Christianized" until the sixteenth century.[8] These different points of view can be seen as reflections of ideological differences, some of which date back to the sixteenth century, some of which are more recent. All have something to do with larger questions about the meaning of history and of the relation between religion and culture. Reconciling them is impossible and also perhaps unnecessary.

There are even more fundamental disagreements to contend with. At bottom, the largest problem of all is that the subject of popular religion seems to resemble pornography in one crucial respect: though it is easy to recognize, it is not very easy to define.[9] In the early 1980s Natalie Zemon Davis, one of the leading historians of popular religion had this to say about the subject, invoking in the process the names of two other influential colleagues who had wrestled with it:

> As to the definition of "popular religion," scholars agree
> that it refers to religion as practised and experienced and
> not merely as defined and prescribed. Beyond this there
> is somuch ambiguity that Carlo Ginzburg and William
> Christian, Jr. suggest that historians not employ the phrase
> at all. They may well be right.[10]

Twenty-two years later, little has changed because, in essence, the concept of "popular religion" is inseparable from a certain approach to religion that has long been part of Western civilization. Although most scholars who study "popular religion" are deeply indebted to anthropologists, ethnographers, folklorists, and social and cultural historians who developed analytical tools for the study of non-Christian religions, their focus is predominantly Western. Inseparable from the broader study of "popular culture" and the narrower study of "folk religion" or *religiöse Volkskunde*, the study of popular religion is as much a practical as a theoretical perspective on religious behaviors developed by European and North American scholars in the final decades of the twentieth century, partly out of methodological considerations regarding the study of religion and partly out of ideological concerns raised by Marxist critiques of culture and religion.[11] In fact, it could be argued that the distinction made by Karl Marx between the elite class and "the people"—as in his memorable summation, "religion is the opiate of *the people*"—lies deep within the structures of much of the scholarship on popular religion.

This is not to say that Marx invented the concept or that Marxists were the first to seize it, but rather that interest in Marxist ideology, sometimes of a highly charged practical bent, sometimes inchoate, gave new contours and a whole new life to an already ancient conceit among European Christians and their American descendants. For centuries and centuries, class-conscious Christian clerics and the cultural elite of Europe had been making distinctions between their understanding of religion and that of "lesser" folk. Most often, to make distinctions was also to criticize—to point out where the common masses were in error, or subject to superstition. So, long before Marx became a totemic figure, and also before folklorists and anthropologists invented the study of "religion" in the nineteenth century—chiefly by analyzing colonized non-Christian peoples—Christian clerics had already been passing judgment on the religious life of their flocks for nearly two millennia, usually with a heavy heart and no small measure of suspicion and loathing.

Yet if this dichotomy figures prominently in European studies of "popular religion," much recent work by Latin Americanists has veered considerably away from a focus on Western models. In the case of Mexico the dense and sophisticated work on ethnohistory, native-language studies, and Indian cultures and religious adaptations of Catholicism belies this hard distinction. Important work by numerous individual scholars, as well as the dense output by research institutes like Centro de Investigaciones y Estudios Superiores en Antropología Social (CIESAS) and the Universidad Autónomia Metropolitana, highlights this focus on the ways that Mexico has been, culturally, the result of a deep interaction between indigenous and Spanish forms.[12] In this volume two historians of native language and Indian religious culture, David Tavárez and Edward Osowski, demonstrate the complicated ways that Catholicism was received by Indian communities. Likewise, essays by Martin Nesvig and Antonio Rubial García examine the processes in which Spaniards understood the religious issues facing evangelization.

Popular Religion and the Evolution of Christendom

Already in the fourth century, one can find Saint Gregory Nazianzen, a well-educated upper-class ecclesiastic, distinguishing elites from commoners, attacking fellow Christians who feared all classical culture simply because it was non-Christian, saying:

> Therefore learning is not to be despised because it seems despicable to some people, but we are rather to consider these people to be boorish and uneducated, wishing that everyone would be like them, in order to hide in the commonality and escape reproach for their ignorance.[13]

What was at stake in Saint Gregory's day was not so much a class struggle as an epochal clash of cultures: the battle between a new uncompromising religion, Christianity, and the syncretistic pagan religions of the ancient Mediterranean and Middle Eastern worlds. Given the fact that Christianity would eventually eclipse the ancient religions of the Roman Empire, and that the elites among the Christian clergy would one day have to struggle to weed out remnants of pagan religion from their pastures, there was no small degree of irony in Saint Gregory's defense of classical learning and his diatribe against the lower-class Christian boors who wanted to toss out everything non-Christian, no matter how beautiful or refined. It was precisely this struggle between the old and the new in the formative years of the Christian religion that would give rise to the dichotomies that lay at the very heart of the concept of "popular religion."

This ancient issue of syncretism and the parallel or conflicting religious systems of paganism and Christianity has long been a staple of Mexican historiography and found contemporaneous discussions in the colonial period. Indeed, Spanish Franciscans often compared Mexico to the ancient world as a place to be converted and won over for the universal church. The theorist Alfonso de Castro, discussed by Nesvig in this volume, made frequent comparisons between Indians and the ancient pagans of the Middle East, arguing that they could and should be seen as potential converts and thus future full members of the church and not as inherent unbelievers.

From its earliest days, as recorded in its oldest texts, the Christian religion faced stiff competition from pagan religion and magic.[14] Christians were gaining ground fast in the Roman Empire of the fourth century, but paganism still held its ground, pervading the culture from top to bottom. In Rome and cities throughout its empire the upper crust tended to remain steadfastly tied to the ancient beliefs and rituals. But the urban elites were not alone: in the vast countryside of the ancient world, the old religions were hard to vanquish.[15] Christianity began as an urban religion.[16] It retained its urban character even after the Caesars became Christian. For quite some time lexicographers believed that the fact that the Latin "paganus," meaning "villager, or rustic" came to mean "non-Christian," or "heathen," proved that the ancient pre-Christian religions lingered on in rural areas after Christianity had been widely accepted in the urban centers of the Roman Empire. Although the *Oxford English Dictionary* says that this etymology "has been shown to be chronologically and historically untenable," the fact remains that Christianity, which is centered on clerics and churches, could not penetrate the countryside as thoroughly as the towns and cities.

Christianity was also a religion that almost immediately developed a well-defined authority structure, with a distinct class of religious elites, or clergy, and a hierarchical institutional framework that defined the Christian community as distinct from the surrounding world.[17] It was, by self-definition, the community of those who had been called out, the *ekklesia* in Greek, the lingua franca of early Christianity. This is the word that evolved into *ecclesia* in Latin, *eglise* in French, *iglesia* in Castilian, *kirche* in German, and *church* in English, a word so loaded with meaning that it came to mean three things simultaneously: the universal institution to which all Christians belonged that guarded the faith and passed it on; the clerical hierarchy who guided this institution; and the individual building in which each Christian community assembled and worshiped. In the language of the clerical elite, whatever was not "the church" was "the world." Out of this basic dichotomy other dichotomies unfolded, mirrorlike, each reflecting the others.

Christianity was also a religion that shunned syncretism and brooked no compromises with polytheism, therefore distinguishing itself sharply from all the other religions of the ancient world. Although some degree of borrowing or layering did take place, especially in the case of pagan schools of thought such as Stoicism and Platonism, the clerical elites tried to keep it at a minimum, for the most part, and to stamp it with a distinctly Christian character, to such an extent that exclusivity remained the norm and pagan religions remained an alien and hostile "other."[18] On top of this, from its earliest days, the Christian religion was inclined toward specific definitions of belief and a high degree of universal conformity in ritual— definitions that distinguished sharply between truth and error, the right way and the wrong way, definitions that were in the hands of the clergy.

Much of the history of the first six to seven centuries of Christianity is about the ways in which "falsehood" was identified in belief and ritual, and "false" Christians were cast out of the community.[19] Concepts such as "true belief" (orthodoxy) and "false belief" (heresy or heterodoxy), became part and parcel of Christian identity, along with the concept of "correct religious behavior" (orthopraxis), which applied to worship and ethics. This process of definition, which intensified after Christianity became the religion of the Roman emperors, brought into high relief the boundaries between what was acceptable and what was not, encoding the faith itself with a dichotomous view of reality, of itself, and of its relation to the world around it.

As the ancient world gradually became Christian between the fourth and eighth centuries, it became impossible to keep syncretism totally at bay. As the new faith spread to the northern barbarians, many of whom descended on the collapsing empire, bringing their ancient customs with them, the old pre-Christian beliefs and rituals lingered, sometimes Christianized, sometimes diluted, sometimes thoroughly unconverted, giving rise steadily to the coexistence of two types of religion: that which was sanctioned by the Christian clergy and that which was out of bounds, or somewhere in between.[20] So, alongside Christianity, one could find all sorts of beliefs, symbols, and rituals of ancient lineage and perhaps also recent or evolving or of a hybrid nature, which would eventually be classified by the Christian clergy as error, idolatry, superstition, magic, sorcery, and witchcraft. Such issues would come to the forefront of debates about the nature of religious belief in Mexico, due to the complexity of a society that had long-standing and ancient pre-Christian and pre-Hispanic customs that were often seen as inherently idolatrous, magical, or satanic. For example, chocolate, which is American in origin and widely used as a stimulant both in pre-Hispanic and colonial Mexico, inspired lengthy debates about its role and acceptability in Catholic custom. Many clergy viewed it as harboring the potential to inspire the mortal sin of lust. Others debated whether it was a food or a drink, which in turn led to debates about whether it could lawfully be consumed before the Mass or whether such consumption broke the prohibition on eating before Mass. Likewise, peyote, long a staple in religious ceremonies of the Huichol and other Indians, was viewed originally with suspicion as inspiring visions and destroying reason and was eventually banned by the Mexican Inquisition in the early seventeenth century.[21]

In Europe a fundamental dichotomy had evolved by the fourth century—a binary arrangement that manifested itself in nearly infinite permutations, giving shape to a culture that was at once Christian and something else too. Christendom, or *Christianitas*, was a culture or cluster of cultures with an "official" religion defined and guarded by the Christian clergy and a "popular" religion observed alongside that. This is not to say that European Christians had to choose between one religion and the other, or necessarily conceived of two religions, one imposed from above by the elites and the other springing up from below, from the nonelites. Not at all. On the contrary, during the late antique and medieval centuries, the relation between what was Christian and non-Christian could be fluid and uncertain and somewhat variegated according to time, place, and social class. Religion was imbued with a complex binary structure on all levels. A dialectic was constantly at work, with oscillations between repression and compromise—a phenomenon discerned by Antonio Gramsci long before the subject of "popular religion" had a proper name.[22] Syncretism and antagonism were as intertwined as were the clergy and the laity, the elites and the nonelites, the towns and the countryside, zeal and indifference, the sacred and the profane.

Such was the state of affairs in Christian Europe for centuries. As the new faith aged and continued to spread throughout Europe, even to the most remote corners of the Baltic Sea, to volcanic Iceland, and to the vast Russian steppes, the binary structure remained in place, ever evolving and ever entrenched. And, despite the unceasing complaints of purists and zealots among the clerical elites, and the occasional ferreting out of those who trespassed the boundaries between truth and falsehood most blatantly or of those who challenged the church's authority most impudently, this is how things remained, for the most part, until the fifteenth century or thereabouts.

Then came the Renaissance, and soon afterward the Protestant and Catholic Reformations. Harvest time had arrived: the wheat and the tares had to be separated. Ironically, along with the love of pagan antiquity and the return *ad fontes* to the cultural treasures of Greece and Rome came a heightened awareness of the distinctiveness of Christianity and of the need to purify it. Elite scholars led the way to renewal, and none among them was more able, ardent, or eloquent than the humanist Erasmus of Rotterdam, Europe's first scholarly superstar, who lashed out constantly against popular misconceptions and superstitions among those Christians that Gregory Nazienzen had called "the commonality."

Immersed in antiquity, steeped in the reforming zeal of the spiritual movement known as the Devotio Moderna, Erasmus was quick to point out how medieval religion was shot through with superstitious pagan dross. An orphaned illegitimate son of a priest and no stranger to hardship and hunger, Erasmus was also a genuine precursor of Karl Marx: a member of the intellectual elite who was deeply aware of class distinctions and had little trouble realizing how religion could be manipulated in the service of maintaining or deepening such distinctions. Speaking about the veneration of saints' images and relics by the common people in his own day, a religious behavior he called "an ocean of superstition," Erasmus blamed the clergy for taking advantage of their flocks and perverting their religion: [23]

Truly, I do not condemn those who do these things with a guileless sort of superstition, so much as I despise those who, looking out for their own profit, prey upon the ignorance of the common people and raise things that are barely tolerable to the level of the highest, perfect piety.[24]

Erasmus figures prominently in the development of a binary conception of religion, for he was one of the first Europeans to formulate a history of the religion of the common people, and also one of the first to have conceived of popular religion as a subject worthy of scrutiny. But his history of popular religion was not at all systematic or dispassionate or tinged with folkloric romanticism. Instead, his history was an emotionally charged and sharp-edged critique, which tended to see the piety of the common man and woman as not much different from that of their pagan forebears—a thinly veiled worship of ancient deities. Speaking of the veneration of the saints in his own day, Erasmus laid down an indictment of popular religion that would be picked up by all the Protestant reformers and quite a few twentieth-century historians:

This kind of piety... is hardly a Christian practice. As a matter of fact, it is not very different from the superstitions of the ancients.... The names have been changed, indeed, but the purpose is the same in both cases.[25]

In the case of Mexico such worship was fraught with the difficulty for Spanish priests of the uncertainty of knowing the extent to which indigenous deities were still being worshipped in the guise of Catholic saints. As Rubial García explains in this volume, indigenous deities were rapidly subsumed into the pantheon of Catholic saints as part of the evangelization process. In fact, Indians and mestizos became so heavily devoted to saints locally associated with their towns and lands—and this practice became so deeply imbued in Mexican culture—that by the nineteenth century liberal reformers often saw devotion to the saints as one of the prime obstacles to modernization.

Back in Europe in the sixteenth century, if Erasmus did indeed lay any eggs to be hatched by Luther or other Protestants, as some charged back in the sixteenth century, then this tendency to see the cult of the saints as a remnant of pagan religion is certainly one of them. The essence

of Protestantism was the conviction that the medieval church was corrupt
and that piety had become intolerably unbiblical. Martin Luther led the
way at first, beginning in 1517, but his attempt to purify church and society according to scriptural guidelines was somewhat limited in comparison with those of other Protestant reformers such as Andreas Bodenstein
von Karlstadt and Ulrich Zwingli. Luther was not as concerned with
wiping out idolatry or pagan holdovers in piety as he was with ridding
Christianity of manmade or invented customs that failed to square with
Holy Writ. Consequently, his reform of ritual was somewhat moderate.
Among those Protestants who came to be known as Reformed, the heirs
of Karlstadt and Zwingli, however, much more of medieval piety was
rejected as thinly disguised pagan idolatry and superstition.[26]

It would be up to John Calvin, a second-generation Reformed spiritual leader, to articulate and widely disseminate this aggressive war against
the "idols" of medieval popular religion. Calvin thought in binary terms
too, like Erasmus, seeing a great dichotomy between "true" and "false"
religion, and finding the source of all falsehoods deep within the human
heart, where idolatry was a basic instinct. As he once said, "Every one of
us is, even from his mother's womb, a master craftsman of idols."[27] Over
and against such instincts stood the "true" revealed religion of the Bible,
made manifest by well-trained and correctly inspired clergymen. For
Calvin, what some scholars call the "official" religion, that is, the religion
of the clergy, should always be opposed to the instincts of the people. The
clergy's job was to eliminate popular religion and ensure that the laity
stuck close to official religion.

Like Erasmus, Calvin was convinced that much of what passed for
Christian ritual was actually nothing more than thinly disguised paganism, and he blamed the Catholic clergy for this sorry state of affairs,
accusing them of caving in to the religion of theirs flocks, or, in other
words, of sinking down to the level of popular religion. Calvin's deep distrust of human nature led him to favor a religion so tightly controlled by
the clergy as to leave no room for what was popular, that is, for what came
easiest and most naturally to all humans. His disgust with the religion of
his fellow countrymen shines through in the *Inventory of Relics*, a scathing
critique of the ignorance and misguidedness of popular piety:

> I remember what I saw them do to images in our parish when I
> was a small boy. As the feast of Saint Stephen drew near, they

would adorn them all alike with garlands and necklaces, the
murderers who stoned him (or *tyrants* as they were called in
common speech), in the same fashion as the martyr. When the
poor women saw the murderers decked out in this way, they
mistook them for Stephen's companions, and presented each
with his own candle. Even worse, they did the same with the
devil who struggled against Saint Michael.[28]

Luther, Zwingli, and Calvin were not alone in their quest to purify
Christianity. Catholics, too, decided to put their own house in order in the
sixteenth century, in ways different from those of the Protestants. Those
contemporaries of Calvin who remained Catholic would not go so far as to
reject the veneration of the saints or to think of their own rituals and symbols as idolatrous, of course, but they nonetheless also sought to purify the
church and to rid it of superstition and error. The epochal changes
effected by the Council of Trent gave Catholicism a greater uniformity
than it had ever enjoyed before, a more precise definition of its beliefs and
rituals, and a deeper awareness of the boundaries between religion and
superstition, and between itself and all "others," be they heretics, sorcer-
ers, witches, magicians, or necromancers. After the Council of Trent, the
elites of the Catholic Church turned their attention to popular religion
with as much intensity as their Protestant counterparts and committed
themselves to an equally vigorous assault on all errors, superstitions, and
remnants of paganism. A new phase in the Christianization of Europe had
begun—a phase in which the yet nameless concept of "popular religion"
played a large role.

Debates about the reform of worship and the excesses of saint and
image veneration were taken up quickly in Mexico in the sixteenth century.
Indeed, Erasmus found a wide reading audience in Mexico among the literate laity as well as among numerous Franciscans. Book inventories of the
period reveal the steady presence of Erasmus, both through his accepted
works and also through his forbidden ones, which had been placed on the
Index. These Erasmian texts could be found in most of the Franciscan
convents in central Mexico as well as among even high-ranking judges and
representatives of the Inquisition charged with removing prohibited books
from circulation. Additionally, missionary friars often took up Erasmian
themes in their writings, urging other missionaries to encourage a
Christocentric worship among Indians for fear that promoting the cult of

the saints would only breed secret idolatry. For example, Maturino Gilberti, a Franciscan missionary in Michoacán, ran afoul of the Mexican Inquisition for precisely this advice in his various Purépecha works written for literate Indians and missionary clergy.

The Twentieth Century

In the 1970s, one of the greatest analysts of popular religion, the French historian Jean Delumeau would argue that Europe was barely Christianized at the beginning of the sixteenth century, the time of Calvin's birth. Delumeau's assessment, which has had a profound impact on the historiography of popular religion, is but an eloquent and more finely nuanced echo of complaints of Erasmus and Calvin.[29] Delumeau himself was aware of this, having once argued that Calvin and his fellow Reformers as a whole were among the first armchair ethnographers of the Western world.[30] But Delumeau might have missed identifying other early ethnographers within Catholicism itself. This critical view of the shallowness of the Christian faith was shared by many Spanish clergy of the sixteenth century; Alfonso de Castro, for one, lamented the state of pagan religious practices in his native northern Spain, relating that peasants continued to venerate goats and other animals. Priests in Mexico also complained frequently that the Spaniards who came to the Americas were blasphemous and irreverent and set a poor example of piety for the Indians.

So far as Europe is concerned, when one reads Gregory Nazienzen, Erasmus, Calvin, Castro, Marx, or Delumeau, or when one runs into generalizations such as "the commonality" or "the common people" or simply "the people," it does not take long to realize that one is dealing with a binary understanding of society and religion. Polarity is the key to popular religion, or whatever else one chooses to call the subject: the basic assumption on which the subject rests is the existence of at least two distinct classes or spheres at which religion is experienced and lived out, each in some hierarchical relation to the other. Key to this understanding of religion is the accompanying assumption that all human beings live in distinct, readily identifiable spheres of meaning. Whether the spheres are two or many or whether they intersect or overlap or not, or whether they are static or dynamic is beside the point: the basic structure is always assumed to be binary. Whether the boundaries between the distinct spheres are drawn on the basis of social, economic, cultural, or geographic markers is also beside the point: the basic structure is always assumed to be binary. This pairing of opposites is a natural extension of the broader concept of "popular culture," which includes religion within it.

Know it or not, like it or not, all scholars of popular religion need to acknowledge the work of Robert Redfield. A cultural anthropologist from the University of Chicago and a genuine pioneer in the study of popular culture, Redfield carried out comparative studies of tribal peoples and advanced civilizations. His great contribution to the study of cultural systems was his definition of the "folk-urban continuum." In the 1950s Redfield argued that cultural systems are always comprised of dual, interdependent, ever-evolving symbiotic traditions, which he labeled the "Little" and the "Great." As Redfield saw it, the "Little Tradition" was that of folk society and folk religion, and the "Great Tradition" was that of urbanized civilizations and world religions.[31] Although these categorizations sparked debates among anthropologists, they also provided scholars of Western culture with a useful way of speaking about the binary nature of religion. In 1978 historian Peter Burke adapted Redfield's categories, making them a centerpiece of his pioneering and immensely influential study, *Popular Culture in Early Modern Europe*, in which he argued that culture—and also religion—is a dynamic interrelationship between the two traditions, Great and Little.[32] This tradition is reflected in William Taylor's essay in this volume, which explores the experience of a priest who viewed his station in a small town on the outskirts of Mexico City as a kind of punishment—placed outside the orbit of the urban center of Mexico City and therefore far from the reaches of what he viewed as civilized society. By the same token, the essay by Tavárez demonstrates that in the rural enclaves of colonial Oaxaca there was no small measure of a self-conscious sense of a specific tradition, though rural peoples tended to reject the kind of dichotomy assessed by Redfield.

Binary Structures and Dichotomies: A Survey

No matter what one calls this subject, then, it always seems to be about the relation of one kind of religion to another, of one sphere of existence to another, and about the gap or exchange that exists between the "this" and the "other." At first sight, this structure seems simple enough, but its symmetrical simplicity can be deceptive. The more one probes this concept, the murkier it seems to get. This basic, binary understanding of religion can go by many names. Herein lies a large part of the problem with the subject. A brief foray into nomenclature should be enough to make anyone's head spin faster than Linda Blair's in *The Exorcist*. "Popular religion" has various polar opposites, or antonyms, and it is most commonly contrasted with "elite religion."[33] This has its parallel, of course, in the dichotomous pairing of popular and elite culture.[34] Quite often, though, the opposite of popular religion is dubbed "official religion."[35] The stress placed on "official" or institutional norms in contradistinction to "popular" rests on the assumption that what is formulated by the clerics need not be—or often is not—what is believed or observed by "the people." This assumption leads to another set of pairings: "clerical" versus "lay."[36] One scholar's "popular religion," therefore, can be another's "lay religion."[37] But that is not all. The terms "religion" and "piety" at times seem interchangeable. "Lay religion" can also be called "lay piety."[38] It can also be called "popular piety."[39] But are "religion" and "piety" or "lay" and "popular" fully equivalent and interchangeable terms? And how about "devotion?" Is that the same as "piety" or "religion?"[40] How about "religiosity," which is favored in Romance languages?"[41] Or how about "lived religion?"[42] And how about the fuzziest term of all, "spirituality?"[43] In one way or another, all these terms have ended up being used interchangeably, always in a basic binary dialectic. A case in point is the way the same subject is handled by two recent reference texts: what *The Oxford Encyclopedia of the Reformation* (1996) covers under the nomenclature of "Popular Religion," becomes "Religious Piety" in the *Encyclopedia of the Renaissance* (1999).[44]

Many of these definitions and problems of arranging a scheme of "popular" or "elite" religion recur throughout this volume. For example, Brian Larkin's essay examines the relationship between laypersons and their understanding of components of the liturgy. In this sense he develops a discussion of lay piety through the lens of confraternities and their use of liturgical processes as a method for developing a consciousness of their own spiritual collective identity in the baroque world. Likewise, Nicole von Germeten examines the role of the confraternity, specifically black/African ones. Whereas Larkin's essay focuses on lay understandings of liturgy and their use thereof, von Germeten offers an analysis of the ways that men of African descent adopted Catholic forms of association to integrate themselves into Mexican Catholic culture. Other essays, like those by Nesvig and Taylor, examine the ways that members of the educated elite understood religion and specifically its relation to Indians.

Osowski's essay reverses this focus to analyze how Indian communities adopted Catholic forms of worship to their own unique cultural traditions associated with land and location.

Defining the concept "popular religion" has been an ongoing process of self-reflection on the part of those who work with it. Most of the pioneers were French historians, adherents of the *Annales* school and the "new history," or *nouvelle histoire*.[45] In 1977, Michel Vovelle, one of the most highly esteemed of these pioneers, was among the first to reflect on the development of this subject, saying: "Old, new, or simply revamped; so many definitions have now been proposed that one can step back from them and attempt to group them into families."[46]

Vovelle grouped these definitions of popular religion into six categories. First came the folkloric model: that approach which proposes that there has always been a timeless gulf between the religion of the common people, bubbling up from below, and the religion that is offered to them from above by the elites. This view tends to reduce popular religion to a static body of pagan survivals: myths, magic, witchcraft, and superstitions of all sorts, some thoroughly mixed in with Christian beliefs. One of the most significant characteristics of this view is its tendency to see the popular substratum as bedrock or some static substance trapped beneath the surface, unchanging and enduring.[47] This folkloric approach, as described by Vovelle, comes close to that used by Carlo Ginzburg in *The Cheese and the Worms*, where the miller Mennochio ends up representing the most ancient beliefs of the rural folk of the Friuli region of northern Italy—beliefs that had always been there, hidden from view, suddenly brought to the surface by Mennochio and recorded for posterity by his inquisitors.[48]

Second, Vovelle also identified a structuralist model, citing Michel Meslin as one of its theoreticians. In the structuralist model, popular religion is always pragmatic, anti-intellectual, and emotional. In Meslin's own words, "A religious phenomenon is popular when it manifests hostility to any systematic objectivization of religious belief . . . it humanizes God in order to feel closer to him and in order to capture his power through the use of the techniques which it invents."[49]

Third, there is also the model of religious stratification. According to Vovelle, this model, first proposed by Robert Mandrou in 1961, sees religion as operating on three different levels: elite, urban, and rural.[50] Elite religion is described as individualized and prone to mysticism; urban religion is predominantly focused on practice and narrow definitions of belief; rural religion is a blend of Christian and pagan beliefs and rituals. This definition, though tripartite rather than binary, still posits two basic levels, for the greatest and most significant difference lies between the religion of the rustics in the countryside and that of the urban /elite categories. This model has tended to have a fairly strong pull on Mexican historians of religion who often study rural culture as precisely a mixture of pre-Hispanic and Catholic ritual and belief—a view that seems supported by a good deal of evidence in the colonial period. Indeed, the essay by Tavárez in this volume suggests that pre-Hispanic beliefs and religious systems were still common nearly two centuries after the arrival of Christianity to Oaxaca. Likewise, Taylor's essay here shows how urbanites often viewed the rural world as beyond the limits of civilization. The Franciscan theologian Castro likewise viewed rural Spain as a backwater of pagan superstition.

Vovelle counted himself among the theorists too, claiming a fourth model, citing his work on attitudes toward death in Provence, which tabulated and analyzed requests for prayers and liturgies found in last wills and testaments.[51] Vovelle's approach to popular religion is functionalist at heart, heavily sociological and quantitative. Social status is the key factor: all attitudes and religious gestures are determined by one's place on the social hierarchy, which may or may not be static, but can be fairly accurately discerned by the historian through quantitative data. This approach is taken by Larkin in his essay here, examining how the requests in wills reflect collective religious sensibilities among Spaniards in the late colonial period in Mexico. As in the case of Mandrou's model, this one posits a layering that at first sight seems to transcend or bypass the binary model, but which, on closer examination ends up dwelling on one basic dichotomy, for, as Vovelle himself admits, behind the quantification of gestures there is always "the other religion, the submerged mass of the iceberg of popular religion whose practices and rituals remain invisible."[52]

Vovelle's fifth model is closely related to the folkloric model, perhaps nearly indistinguishable from it. Citing the work of Jean Delumeau, Vovelle argues for the existence of a dialectical model, in which the pagan-Christian syncretism of the Middle Ages, predominantly associated with peasant culture, is seen as being in constant competition with the elite and urban culture, especially after the advent of the mendicant preachers.[53] In this model, the Renaissance heightens the dialectic and both the Protestant and Catholic Reformations—twins at heart—kick it up into high gear. In this model, the elites put a great deal of effort into fully "Christianizing" Europe.[54] This is basically the same thesis that Keith Thomas also proposed in his monumental *Religion and the Decline of Magic*, in 1971, at the same time as Delumeau.[55]

Such issues were germane to the Spanish missionary efforts in Mexico in the sixteenth century. For example, many mendicants lamented the persistence of Hispanic folkloric traditions among the Spanish laity in Mexico. The presence of strong bishops was seen by many as the best way to prevent the "corruption" of the Mexican religious experience by such customs. Indeed, the sexual behavior of Spanish men in Mexico was a frequent subject of debate. Spanish law had long recognized concubinage and Spanish culture viewed cohabitation and the practice of men keeping mistresses as a relatively benign fault. Such "popular" cultural traditions ran squarely into the demographic realities of Mexico where only a very small percentage of Spanish immigrants were women and where Spanish men lived in close social proximity to Indian women, leading to a system where cohabitation was common. Church officials and the Inquisition campaigned against these practices, especially after the Council of Trent, in an effort to "Christianize" domestic life in Mexico.

A sixth model identified by Vovelle is the one proposed in the work of Mikhail Bahktin, which, while remaining close to folkloric sources, does not rely as much on dichotomies between elites and the common people.[56] Bahktin does not see popular culture as the repository of pagan or magical beliefs and practices, but rather as a collection of attitudes and behaviors that are dynamic rather than static and based on the inversion of values and hierarchies. It is the eternal struggle between carnival and lent, laughter and utter seriousness, spontaneity and rigor, riotous excess and penance, scatology and theology. In Bahktin's model, popular culture—and therefore also popular religion—tend to be seen as an ongoing process of inversion: a constant dialectic in which a "constantly demystifiying counter-system is opposed to the established order and the established religion."[57] Although not discussed explicitly in this volume, similar dynamic cultural processes occurred with regularity in Mexico. Numerous Indian religious practices—taking peyote, smoking tobacco, drinking pulque—were in effect "desacralized" by Spaniards who came to adopt such stimulants as essentially nonreligious items. Likewise, the Indian practices of frequent bathing and attendance at social, public bathhouses (*temazcales*) were quickly adopted by Spaniards, much to the horror of theologians who had argued in the

Spanish context that bathing had the potential to incite the capital sin of *lujuria* and should therefore be avoided.[58]

Having completed his typology of approaches to the study of popular religion, Vovelle goes on to say that, of course, there are many historians who combine these approaches, and that the most perceptive among them were the ones who settled neither for the static folkloric models nor for Bakhtin's dynamic thesis. His summary essay on the subject, a pioneering effort that helped give shape to subsequent research, closes with a resounding call for a shift in perspective and for the development of a more precise sociology of popular religion—"a sociology which must go beyond the simplistic dichotomy of people and elite in order to penetrate the realities of social groupings; something which would also permit a more supple definition of the idea of 'popular' religion."[59]

Such an approach was already being taken by several historians at the time that Vovelle's essay first appeared.[60] By the time it was published in an English translation, it was almost old hat. Few other historians pushed this approach more enthusiastically than the late Robert Scribner, who also took a stab at summarizing and analyzing the subject of popular religion in a seminal essay, "Ritual and Popular Religion in Catholic Germany at the Time of the Reformation."[61]

The way Scribner sees it, the study of popular religion can be broken down into four basic definitions or categories, each involving dichotomies. The most basic definition, says Scribner, identifies "official" with institutional religion and "popular" with any practices at variance with institutional norms. A second definition proposes instead an opposition or antithetical relation between theory and practice. In this case, "popular religion" is religion as lived, or practical religion, which embodies the religious outlook of the ordinary churchgoer. Its antithesis is religion as conceived by the elites, that is, theological or philosophical religion. A third definition identified by Scribner is social-historical. In this case, popular religion becomes the religion of the vast majority of the people, which is distinct from and even in opposition to the religion of the elites who belong to "learned culture." The fourth and final definition identified by Scribner is a combination of all of the three above, with a derogatory value judgment thrown in for good measure. In this case popular religion becomes an inferior and deformed version of a "higher" or "superior" religion. This would appear to be the oldest view of all, perhaps, for, as Scribner points out, it tends to link popular religion with superstition.

Dissatisfied with all these approaches to popular religion, Scribner instead proposes a more supple definition, precisely of the type that Vovelle envisioned. Scribner approaches popular religion through ritual rather than through stark dichotomies. Ritual is at the heart of religion, as Scribner sees it, especially in medieval Christendom. But ritual is not a monolithic whole. On one level, the church had a rich and carefully ordered liturgical life, with the Mass as its centerpiece—a liturgical life that included all sorts of rituals and that was performed largely through the agency of the clergy. The laity in Mexico, for example, demonstrated considerable knowledge of liturgy, as Larkin's essay reveals. This "official" aspect of ritual, which the clerical elites recognized as "correct," was only part of the whole picture, however. There was yet another level, closely related to this one. Employing a corporeal metaphor that did not draw explicitly on the image of the church as the body of the faithful or the body of Christ, but which nonetheless fit that image rather well, Scribner calls the "official" ritual "only a skeleton" on which was built "a fuller and more complex body of observances which may be called the 'popular' side of ritual life."[62] Scribner argues that this side of religion could rightly be called "popular" because its observances developed among lay people and granted them a greater participation in the ritual life of the church. Some of these observances were "paraliturgical" and granted the laity a role in established "official" liturgies, as in the case of processions or reenactments of Christ's final entry into Jerusalem; others, however, extended beyond the liturgy proper, as in the case of the observance of certain feasts in the hopes of obtaining specific results. Some of the paraliturgical practices were eventually accepted by the clergy and became part of the "official" ritual life of medieval Catholicism; the other type tended to be viewed with a measure of suspicion by the clerical elite or were sometimes rejected and outlawed.

Scribner calls the paraliturgical practices that were eventually accepted "folklorised ritual." The other practices—the ones that extended beyond the liturgy and were often rejected—he dubs "magical ritual." Scribner cautions that these categories had permeable boundaries and that both kinds of "popular" ritual had an ambivalent relation with "official" ritual. Some of those rituals where the line between popular devotion and magical ritual were not all too clear—such as the blessing of candles on Candlemass—were not rejected at all and instead became official.

The tension or dynamism between liturgical and paraliturgical practices forms a thread woven through William Christian's work and is reflected here on various levels. Christian's eponymic work on local religion stressed the role of paraliturgical or extraliturgical practices of shrine building, pilgrimages, and saint veneration outside of the Mass. Larkin, for one, sees this emphasis as detracting from the important role that the liturgy played for the laity in baroque Mexico. In his essay here Larkin argues that members of confraternities had a clear understanding of the role of the liturgy not only in their spiritual life but also in the social sphere, through their view of confraternal observances as a set of social and public activities. Von Germeten, by contrast, emphasizes the ways that men of African descent used confraternities for largely socioeconomic purposes with relatively little attention to the liturgical or spiritual role. Other essays, like that by Rubial García, show how practices like saint veneration remained strong extraliturgical components for colonial social identity for Indians and criollos alike.

Fluidity, dynamism, and dialectical relations between binary sets: these are the hallmarks of Robert Scribner's definition of "popular religion." Dichotomies and antitheses almost disappear, but not entirely. As he put it:

> Popular religion is not a fixed category or set of practices, but something which has a continuing dynamic which occurs in two ways: both as developing practice and in relationship to the institutional Church.[63]

Scribner's dynamic model has popular devotions being continually developed from below, as it were, by the people, and continually scrutinized from above by the clergy. Some devotions end up being accepted, others remain somewhat suspect, and others are rejected outright. In this scheme of things, clergy and laity participate in the same "official" religion and many of the clergy also participate in the "nonofficial" religion of the laity. Scribner goes on to provide diagrams of these relationships, which gives his definition a definite aura of empirical and sociological precision, fulfilling Vovelle's expectations.

Does Scribner's more finely nuanced and dynamic definition of popular religion finally manage to capture the subject's full complexity for good? Does it manage to transcend dichotomies and binary structures? Not really. Scribner's definition, for all its focus on dynamic relations and its introduction of a corporeal metaphor—the skeleton of official ritual and the body of popular devotions—certainly lends a new perspective on the subject. But when push comes to shove, this is a definition that still relies on binary structures, especially on distinctions between "official" and "nonofficial," "folklorised ritual" and "magical ritual," and especially between clergy and laity. In the long run, Scribner's dynamic model has at its core, as its skeleton (if one may employ his own metaphor), a series of dichotomies, the most crucial of which is that between clergy and laity, and, as he lays out the alignment of these two classes, it does not take much effort to see that this ends up being an asymmetrical relationship, with the clergy always holding the trump card.

Conceptual Problems

Bypassing a binary interpretation of popular religion seems impossible, and discerning which of the dichotomies to employ can be difficult. Take the basic lay/clerical dichotomy, central to so many studies of popular religion, including Scribner's.

First: What does the term "lay" mean? Since the first century, Christian societies have made a distinction between the clergy who performed specific duties as spiritual leaders—the bishops, priests, monks, and friars— and the rest of society, known as the "laity," or "lay" people. The original meaning of the term "lay," in fact, is simply "people" (Latin: *laicos*; Greek: *laos*, *laikos*). The distinction between clerical and lay, though somewhat blurry and controversial at times, dominates much of religious life in the West, in theory as well as in practice. Whether they performed key rituals deemed necessary for salvation, or defined and guarded beliefs, or simply prayed for society at large, the clergy were supposedly in charge of "the people," leading them to salvation. In the practice of religion, the clergy were the professionals—a truism confirmed by the fact that clerics were known as *religiosi*, that is, "the religious." But this was not as simple a distinction as it seems, for "the people," or laity, defined the very existence and purpose of the clergy. Because the laity and clergy were symbiotically linked and shared the same myths, rituals, and symbols, the religious life of the laity was never distinct from or totally independent of the clergy, or vice versa. In medieval and early modern Europe, lay Christians could indeed take the lead in the observance of religion, but the clergy were always somehow involved, directly or indirectly. Any religious practice that excluded the clergy ran the risk of being judged by them as heterodox, or, as in the case of witchcraft, even demonic.

Anyone who speaks of "lay religion" or "lay piety," then, needs to keep in mind that the clergy and the laity are joined at the hip, so to speak, and that neither of these two classes can do much or make any moves without the other. It should also be kept in mind that the category "lay" applies to a wide spectrum of people, from the monarch at the apex to the beggar at the bottom of the social hierarchy. To speak of "lay" piety or "lay" religion, then, is to gloss over significant social, political, and cultural differences in the stratified society of Europe: though all the laity shared in a common religion, it should never be assumed that the piety of literate nobles who had family chapels, for instance, could ever be exactly the same as that of illiterate peasants who lived miles from the nearest church.

What about women, that half of the human race that could never join the clergy? Women are problematic in more ways than one for those who try to define popular religion or lay piety. Is the religion of all women, by definition, "popular," in the sense that women were always subservient to men and especially to male clerics? But what about nuns, where do they fit in? Do they count as clergy or as laity? Or are they a *tertium quid*? What about queens, princesses, and other ladies of noble rank? What about the wives and daughters of rich merchants and the emerging bourgeoisie? Is their religion "elite" because they belong to the ruling class or "popular" because they tend to have less power than their male cohorts and can never become priests?

Murkiness seems as unavoidable as the dichotomies themselves, and the search for terminology adds to the murkiness. Is this subject made more precise when one speaks of "piety" instead of "religion?" One has to ask, then, what "piety" is, and more specifically, what "lay piety" is if one is to overlay these terms or suggest them as a substitute or synonym for "popular religion." "Piety" is most often understood as the observance of religion, in public as well as in private, both communally and individually: "piety" refers any human activity that involves the myths, rituals, and symbols of religion and that aims to transcend the mundane and commune with the divine.

In a fundamental way, then, "piety" seems identical to "religion." But can "popular religion" and "lay piety" be the same thing? In some respects, yes, but in others, no: clerics and lay people shared in the same piety to some extent, but not entirely and not always to the same extent. More definitional problems arise when one considers that the observance of the Christian religion by clerics and nonclerics alike encompassed a wide array of practices, from liturgies, processions, and pilgrimages, to private prayer and devotional reading at home, along with the occasional or perennial observance of rites that were of questionable origin or even outside the boundaries established by the church. Are these various practices all to be lumped together into the same category?

Another murky area in the study of popular religion—and its definition—is that which refers to questions of quality and quantity. Are fervor and intensity to be taken into account? Should historians try to measure this invisible, interior dimension of religion? On this there is no agreement: some have tried to appraise the quality of devotion; others have not. The question is far from settled, but it cannot be avoided. While any definition of religion that focuses on outward practices cannot exclude questions of sincerity or fervor from its purview, it also cannot consider them in an absolute way, as quantifiable or measurable, especially in a culture such as that of medieval and early modern Europe, where all ultimate values were officially and self-consciously framed in religious terms, and where the sacred and the profane could be—and often were—inseparably intertwined. Anyone who deals with piety in premodern Europe needs to keep in mind that everyone in that world became a Christian at birth by compulsion and that the observance of religion was an inevitable fact of life, as much a burden and a threat to the scoffers as a blessing to the devout. This is not to say that popular religion was necessarily hollow, then, but simply to acknowledge that saints and blaspheming hypocrites could partake of the same devotions. Moreover, in a culture in which much of life was sacralized, and in which many traces of pre-Christian religion survived, the boundaries between devotion and superstition, or godliness and magic could be awfully blurry.

Could the concept and the subject get any murkier?

Structuring the Concept and the Subject

Fortunately, there is a way of making sense of all of this apparent confusion. First, one must realize that the profusion of terms and models in the study of popular religion stems from the fact that the concept and the subject are both exceedingly complex and that the scholarship has not evolved from a single source, but rather from multiple sources. In many ways, the study of popular religion could be compared to a territory that has been settled all at once by peoples from various backgrounds and cultures, with about as much order as the stampede of the "Sooners" who rushed into Oklahoma when Congress opened two million acres of land for settlement on April 22, 1889. Years later, sorting through the resulting hodge-podge and making sense of it is quite a challenge. A tough challenge, yes, but not at all an impossible task. In essence, one can see the concept and the subject as stratified into four interdependent levels.

At the first level, that of nomenclature, we can find various tongues spoken, that is, various terms used, sometimes without clear definitions, sometimes interchangeably. At this level, scholars speak at each other, and sometimes past each other by employing terms for their subject such as "popular religion," "piety," "devotion," "religiosity," "spirituality," and even "ritual."

At the second level, that of methodology, we can find various approaches being taken, among which the most significant could be identified as folklorist, functionalist, structuralist, phenomenological, and historical. Some combine and mix and match from more than one approach. Each of these approaches, in turn—whether of a pure sort or a blend—can be found in various permutations. For instance, among those who take a historical approach, we find some wielding the tools of functionalists as *cultural* historians and others wielding the same tools as *social* historians, or a combination of the two. And so on with all the possible permutations, which do, in fact, give rise to a web of interlocking, interdependent interpretations, as vast in its proportions as it is intricate in its complexity.

At the third level, that of the most basic framework of interpretation, which all scholars take for granted, we find agreement on one thing: the binary structure of religion itself—and also of culture—in which there is always a "this" and an "other" within a single religion or culture. This is perhaps the sole point at which there is utter simplicity: the basic twinning of an entity, be it cultural or religious. There is a "this" and there is a "that." But beyond the simple twinning, scholars disagree on the relation of the "this"—however defined, named, or approached—to the "other." The disagreement stems from the fact that anyone who deals with a binary structure has to determine how the two parts relate to one another in terms of the passage of time and also in terms of the amount of tension between them. The twinning or pairing, therefore, leads to questions about two kinds of relations: that which could be called the *static-dynamic*, and that which could be called the *dialectical-oppositional*.

The first of these two questions, the static-dynamic, takes into consideration rates of change over time and attributes "static" and "dynamic" qualities to the relation between the "this" and the "other." How stasis and dynamism are defined or related to one another, or how these attributes end up being identified in either the "this" or the "other," or to what extent the attributes themselves are made relative or flexible remains a matter of choice and opinion among scholars.

The same is true of the second of these questions, the dialectical-oppositional, which takes into consideration the issue of the tension between the "this" and the "other." Are the two halves of the pair in an oppositional relation to one another, marked by confrontation, or are they in a dialectical relation, partaking of each other to some extent or influencing one another in the very process of defining one another, no matter how much tension exists between them? So far as this question is concerned, we find a broad spectrum of opinion, from scholars who set up fairly rigid categories to those who prefer sliding scales.

So far as the relation between the two questions is concerned, there is really no symmetry or any apparent need for it in the existing scholarship on popular religion. We find some scholars paying more attention to one question than the other, or ignoring one of them altogether. All of this, of course, makes for plenty of disagreement and no small amount of confusion on the part of novices and seasoned experts alike. But the basic structure of the various opinions, no matter how varied or how much at disagreement with one another, is at bottom a fairly simple one at this third level: the "this" and the "other," facing each other over time.

This brings us to the fourth level, which is where the "this" and the "other" are given names, the level where pairings are made and dichotomies are identified. At this level we find the wildest profusion of terms and opinions. Fortunately, though the number and types of pairings and opinions can seem bewildering, they are fairly easy to classify. Dichotomies can be broken down into four basic types: (1) social and cultural; (2) spatial and dimensional; (3) typological and structural; and (4) historical and qualitative. Within each of these basic types we find numerous pairings and dichotomies—the ultimate list, as it were, of all that is identified as "this" or the "other."

When the four types of dichotomies are laid out in columns, side by side, it becomes clear immediately how they are broken down, and how it is that the dichotomies themselves relate to each other within each type

and across types. It helps to keep five things in mind about these dichotomies: (1) they are not mutually exclusive and do not cancel each other
out necessarily; (2) there are many parallel and complimentary relationships among them, as in the case of lay/clerical, below/above, piety/
theology, and superstition/religion all of which may be employed in the
analysis of exactly the same phenomenon; (3) there is a certain level of
fluidity to these relations within each type and across types; (4) scholars
tend not to chain themselves too tightly to any single dichotomy or even
to any single type of dichotomizing; and (5) the list of dichotomies provided here is by no means exhaustive, but rather a point of departure. The
relation between these individual parts may bespeak a certain messiness
and fuzziness in the scholarship, but the larger whole is itself fairly tidy,
even graced with no small measure of beauty. And, as every Platonist
knows, beauty is never far from truth and goodness.

The four types of dichotomies can be broken down as follows:

Social and cultural dichotomies think of religion in terms
of structures that have to do with differing levels of rank,
status, power, education, or any other markers of identity in
sociopolitical structures, such as lay/clerical, folk/learned;
or suppressed/oppressor.

Spatial and dimensional dichotomies take into account the big
picture, almost on a metaphysical level, breaking down the basic
pairings in terms of relational and geographical space, and of
hierarchical relations, such as local/universal, below/above, and
ancient/new.

Typological and structural dichotomies break down religion in
terms of humanly devised structures and terms that relate to
categories of human experience. These dichotomies have their eye
fixed on the axis between what could be termed flexible and rigid,
such as lived religion/doctrine, piety/theology, or riot/order.

Historical and qualitative dichotomies take the structure of
history into account and also invest it with value, thinking
in terms of what came first / what displaced it, such as
pagan/Christian, superstition/religion, magic/religion.

Of course, this is not the only way to "skin this cat." These are merely suggestions for imposing a greater degree of order and cohesion on a concept and subject that has long seemed as indefinable as it was exciting and alluring.

Beyond Europe, Beyond Simplicity

In many ways, the conquest of the New World by Europeans and their missionary efforts throughout the world after 1492 brought the binary structures and dichotomies of European religion into even higher relief. Now, in addition to all of Europe's interwoven dichotomies, a new set surfaced: those between Europeans and the peoples they sought to Christianize.

Wherever one looks, it is easy to find the new polarities: between colonizers and natives, missionaries and converts, Christianity and native religions, and so on. Europe's already binary religion now stood in relation to a whole new set of complex dichotomies, in which mirrored reflections and distortions abound. "Popular religion" in the colonized parts of America included not only the already ancient European layers of dichotomies, but also those that were created by the conversion of non-Europeans who were all Christianized in different ways, according to time and place, and who already had their own indigenous layers of elite and popular culture. In those colonies where the natives were converted forcibly, the parallels with the earlier conversion of Europe to Christianity were most intense. In areas where a minority of the population converted to Christianity, such as China and Japan, the parallels were still there, but in different guise, with added complications, due to the controversies that arose over the adoption or Christianization of native, or "popular" rites, such as the veneration of ancestors.[64] As European clerics fretted over "pagan" holdovers and hunted down witches at home, they also worried about native "heathen" holdovers in their colonies and mission fields. False religion and the devil were everywhere, in new permutations.[65]

In some circles in the Hispanic world, the word "Indies" came to mean any place where Christianity was nonexistent or merely a thin veneer over heathenism—precisely the same kind of situation that Jean Delumeau has suggested for all of Europe at the dawn of the modern age. European clerics could be keenly aware of this: some of them accepted the dichotomy between "official" and "popular" or "clerical" and "lay" as one between Christianity and something less than Christian. Reflecting on this fact, many European elites came to realize that Europe, too, was full of Indies of its own, and of dichotomies not much different in extent than those found overseas. "Experience has shown that within Spain there are Indies, and mountains in this case of ignorance," said Felipe de Meneses in 1554. Sixty years later, one could hear the same complaint being voiced by a Spanish nobleman, in his letter to the Jesuit superior in Andalusia: "I really don't know why [you] fathers . . . go to Japan and the Philippines to look for lost souls, when we have here so many in the same condition who do not know whether or not they believe in God."[66]

What is one to make of this? Whether one is dealing with Mayan natives in Yucatán who were suspected of practicing idol worship and human sacrifice or Mexican natives who venerated the horse of Saint James rather than the saint's image, or Chinese mandarins who still revered their ancestors and Confucius far too intensely, what one finds in Europe's colonies and mission fields is both an extension of Europe's own dichotomies and new permutations of them. In brief, one comes face to face with something new, yet quite familiar—something recognizable, yet very hard to define—popular religion.

One must ask if a concept so seemingly vague and ill-defined is of any real import, perhaps even ask whether it is valid at all. This is rhetorical question, of course. The richness of the scholarship on popular religion speaks for itself and provides the best answer of all. The difficulties involved in defining the concept and in marking out the subject's boundaries in no way deny its existence or lessen its significance. It could be argued that the complexity of the concept is itself an argument for its validity, especially in light of its appeal to researchers and readers alike. Occam's razor notwithstanding, the simplest argument is not always the best one: logical simplicity does not guarantee anything but simplicity itself. Truth is often complex and not easily reduced to simple or neat definitions

Perhaps the time has come to stop looking for a single definition of "popular religion," or for a single approach to the subject; perhaps even the competition for a single name should also stop. The fact is that there are many ways to approach the binary structure of religion in the West, and no single approach can do justice to the phenomenon. If the study of religion itself cannot be reduced to a single methodology or one type of approach, why should the study of popular religion be any different? Perhaps the time has come for scholars who work on this subject to own up to the fact that the basic binary structure of much of Western religion can best be viewed through various lenses and perspectives. Perhaps the time has also arrived for scholars of popular religion to take several approaches to the subject all at once, taking into account the inexhaustible richness and complexity of the subject.

Historians no longer need to stumble over their terms and get tangled in a web of dichotomies when it comes to defining the concept of popular religion. What they need to do is define their approach up front and measure the boundaries of their subject, fully conscious of the pluses and minuses of whatever perspective they choose to take, fully aware of the fact that to admit limitations is also to acknowledge complexity. No one has yet denied the existence of the concept or the phenomenon, despite a seemingly frantic search for definition. No one is likely to do so in the future either, no matter how many limitations we scholars own up to, for it is a weighty and often intriguing subject.

As intriguing as two women fighting over a seat during Mass.

NOTES

1. Archivo Municipal de Toledo, CC, Y leg. 1611, "Querella María Gómez Ana Díaz," cited by Scott Taylor, "Honor and Violence in Castille, 1600–1650" (Ph.D. dissertation, University of Virginia, 2001), 192.

2. See the essays in *Religion and Society in Early Modern Europe*, ed. Kaspar von Greyerz (London: German Historical Institute, 1984).

3. Jacques Toussaert, *Le sentiment religieux en Flandre à la Fin du Moyen Âge*, preface Michel Mollat (Paris: Plon, 1963); Johan Huizinga, *The Autumn of the Middle Ages*, trans. R. J. Payton and U. Mammitzsch (Chicago: University of Chicago Press, 1996); Bernd Moeller, *Imperial Cities and the Reformation*, ed. and trans. H. C. E. Midelfort and M. U. Edwards Jr. (Philadelphia, PA: Fortress Press, 1972); Steven Ozment, *Protestants: The Birth of a Revolution* (New York: Doubleday, 1992).

4. Eamon Duffy, *The Stripping of the Altars* (New Haven, CT: Yale University Press, 1992); John Bossy, *Christianity in the West* (New York: Oxford University Press, 1985).

5. William A. Christian Jr., *Local Religion in Sixteenth-Century Spain* (Princeton, NJ: Princeton University Press, 1981).

6. Carlo Ginzburg, *The Cheese and the Worms: The Cosmos of a Sixteenth-Century Miller*, trans. John and Anne Tedeschi (Baltimore, MD: Johns Hopkins University Press, 1980); Philippe Ariès, *The Hour of Our Death*, trans. Helen Weaver (New York: Alfred A. Knopf, 1981).

7. Keith Thomas, *Religion and the Decline of Magic* (New York: Scribner, 1971), 49.

8. Jean Delumeau, *Catholicism Between Luther and Voltaire: A New View of the Counter-Reformation*, intro. John Bossy (London: Burns and Oates, 1977).

9. Supreme Court Justice Potter Stewart once expressed his frustration with a pornography case by saying, "I shall not today attempt further to define this kind of material . . . but I know it when I see it."

10. Natalie Zemon Davis, "From 'Popular Religion' to Religious Cultures," in *Reformation Europe: A Guide to Research*, ed. Steven Ozment (St. Louis, MO: Center for Reformation Research, 1982). See also Davis's earlier summary of the subject: "Some Tasks and Themes in the Study of Popular Religion," in *The Pursuit of Holiness in Late Medieval and Renaissance Religion* (papers of the Conference on Late Medieval and Renaissance Religion, University of Michigan, 1972, ed. C. Trinkaus and H. Oberman [Leiden: Brill, 1974]), 307–36.

11. See Rainer Neu, *Religionssoziologie als kritische Theorie: Die marxistische Religionskritik und ihre Bedeutung für die Religionssoziologie* (Frankfurt: Lang, 1982); Hans Bosse, *Marx, Weber, Troeltsch. Religionssoziologie und marxistische Ideologiekritik* (Munich: Kaiser, 1970); Michèle Bertrand, *Le statut de la religion chez Marx et Engels* (Paris: Éditions sociales, 1979).

12. The scholarship runs far and wide and even a brief sampling would be vast. Readers may wish to consult from the following short sampling: Solange Alberro, *El águila y la cruz: Orígenes religiosos de la conciencia criolla. México, siglos XVI-XVII* (Mexico: El Colegio de México; Fondo de Cultura Económica, 1999); Louise M. Burkhart, *The Slippery Earth: Nahua-Christian Moral Dialogue in Sixteenth-Century Mexico* (Tucson: University of Arizona Press, 1989); S. L. Cline, *Colonial Culhuacan, 1580–1600: A Social History of an Aztec Town* (Albuquerque: University of New Mexico Press, 1986); Serge Gruzinski, *Colonisation de l'imaginaire: Sociétés indigènes et occidentalisation dans le Mexique espagnol, XVIe–XVIIIe siècle* (Paris: Gallimard, 1988); James Lockhart, *The Nahuas after the Conquest: A Social and Cultural History of the Indians of Central Mexico, Sixteenth Through Eighteenth Centuries* (Stanford, CA: Stanford University Press, 1992); Matthew Restall, *Maya World: Yucatec Culture and Society, 1550–1850* (Stanford, CA: Stanford University Press,

1997); Susan Schroeder, *Chimalpahin and the Kingdoms of Chalco* (Tucson: University of Arizona Press, 1991); William B. Taylor, *Magistrates of the Sacred: Priests and Parishioners in Eighteenth-Century Mexico* (Stanford, CA: Stanford University Press, 1996); and Kevin Terraciano, *Mixtecs of Colonial Oaxaca: Ñudzahui History, Sixteenth Through Eighteenth Centuries* (Stanford, CA: Stanford University Press, 2001).

13. Quoted by Boniface Ramsey, *Beginning to Read the Fathers* (New York: Paulist Press, 1985), 211.

14. Hans–Josef Klauck, *Magic and Paganism in Early Christianity: The World of the Acts of the Apostles*; trans. Brian McNeil (Edinburgh: T&T Clark, 2000); Keith Hopkins, *A World Full of Gods: Pagans, Jews, and Christians in the Roman Empire* (London: Weidenfeld and Nicholson, 1999).

15. Ramsay MacMullen, *Christianizing the Roman Empire, A.D. 100–400* (New Haven, CT: Yale University Press, 1984); Arnaldo Momigliano, ed., *The Conflict Between Paganism and Christianity in the Fourth Century* (Oxford: Clarendon Press, 1963).

16. Wayne A. Meeks, *The First Urban Christians: The Social World of the Apostle Paul*, 2d ed. (New Haven, CT: Yale University Press, 2003).

17. James S. Jeffers, *Conflict at Rome: Social Order and Hierarchy in Early Christianity* (Minneapolis, MN: Fortress Press, 1991); Hans von Campenhausen, *Ecclesiastical Authority and Spiritual Power in the Church of the First Three Centuries*, trans. J. A. Baker (Stanford, CA: Stanford University Press, 1969).

18. Charles Norris Cochrane, *Christianity and Classical Culture: A Study of Classical Thought and Action from Augustus to Augustine* (Oxford: Clarendon Press, 1940); Gerald L. Ellspermann, *The Attitude of the Early Christian Latin Writers toward Pagan Literature and Learning* (Washington, DC: Catholic University of America, 1949); E. R. Dodds, *Pagan and Christian in an Age of Anxiety: Some Aspects of Religious Experience from Marcus Aurelius to Constantine* (Cambridge: Cambridge University Press, 1965); R. C. Smith and J. Lounibos, eds., *Pagan and Christian Anxiety: A Response to E. R. Dodds* (Lanham, MD: University Press of America, 1984).

19. See W. H. C. Frend, *Orthodoxy, Paganism and Dissent in the Early Christian Centuries* (Aldershot, Eng., and Burlington, VT: Ashgate, 2002); and W. H. C. Frend, *Orthodoxy, Heresy, and Schism in Early Christianity*, ed. with intro. by Everett Ferguson (New York: Garland, 1993).

20. See Ramsay MacMullen, *Christianity and Paganism in the Fourth to Eighth Centuries* (New Haven, CT: Yale University Press, 1997); and M. L. W. Laistner, *Christianity and Pagan Culture in the Later Roman Empire; together with an English Translation of John Chrysostom's* Address on Vainglory and the Right Way for Parents to Bring up Their Children (Ithaca, NY: Cornell University Press, 1967).

21. See Alberro, *El águila y la cruz.*

22. Antonio Gramsci (d. 1937) argued in his *Prison Notebooks* and in "Observations on Folklore" that there were two cultural forces at work in Christian Europe, intertwined in a dialectical relationship. For a discussion of this, see Michel Vovelle, "Popular Religion," in Vovelle's own *Ideologies and Mentalities*, trans. E. O'Flaherty (Cambridge: Cambridge University Press, 1990), 82. This essay first appeared as "La religion populaire, problèmes et méthodes," *Le Monde Alpin et Rhodanien*, vols. I–IV (1977).

23. *Praise of Folly*, trans. H. H. Hudson (Princeton, NJ: Princeton University Press, 1969), 58.

24. Erasmus von Rotterdam, *Enchiridion*, in *Ausgewählte Schriften*, ed. W. Welzig, 8 vols. (Darmstadt: Wissenschaftliche Buchgesellschaft, 1967–80), 1:178–80.

25. Ibid., 1:178.

26. Carlos M. N. Eire, *War Against the Idols: The Reformation of Worship from Erasmus to Calvin* (Cambridge and New York: Cambridge University Press, 1986).

27. *Commentary on the Acts of the Apostles*, in *Ioannis Calvini opera quae supersunt omnia*, 59 vols., ed. W. Baum, E. Cunitz, and E. Reuss (Braunschweig: C.A. Schwetschke, 1863–1900), 48: col. 562.

28. *Inventory of Relics*, in *Ioannis Calvini opera quae supersunt omnia*, 6:452. In Enlightenment Scotland, the Calvinist heritage would be further modernized. See, for example, Robert Millar, *The History of the Propagation of Christianity and Overthrow of Paganism: Wherein the Christian Religion is Confirmed, the Rise and Progress of Heathenish Idolatry is Considered*, 2 vols. (Edinburgh: Thomas Ruddiman, 1723).

29. Delumeau, *Catholicism Between Luther and Voltaire.*

30. Jean Delumeau, "Les Réformateurs et la Superstition," in *Actes du colloque sur l'Admiral de Coligny* (Paris: Societé de l'histoire du protestantisme français, 1974), 471.

31. Robert Redfield, *The Little Community: Viewpoints for the Study of a Human Whole* (Chicago: University of Chicago Press, 1955); Robert Redfield, *Peasant Society and Culture: An Anthropological Approach to Civilization* (Chicago: University of Chicago Press, 1956).

32. Peter Burke, *Popular Culture in Early Modern Europe* (Cambridge: University of Cambridge Press, 1978), 23–29.

33. As in Magdalena Chocano Mena, *La fortaleza docta: Élite letrada y dominación social en México colonial, siglos XVI-XVII* (Barcelona: Ediciones Bellaletra, 2000); and Gregory Hanlon, *L'univers des gens de bien: Culture et comporte-ments des élites urbaines en Agenais-Condomois au XVIIe siècle* (Talence: Presses universitaires de Bordeaux, 1989).

34. As in Robert Muchembled, *Popular Culture and Elite Culture in France, 1400–1750*, trans. Lydia Cochrane (Baton Rouge: Louisiana State University, 1985).

35. As in Willem Frijhoff, "Official and Popular Religion in Christianity," in *Official and Popular Religion: Analysis of a Theme for Religious Studies*, ed. P. H. Vriujog and J. Waardenburg (The Hague: Mouton, 1979).

36. As in Fiona Somerset, *Clerical Discourse and Lay Audience in Late Medieval England* (Cambridge: Cambridge University Press, 1998).

37. As in *Parish, Church and People: Local Studies in Lay Religion, 1350–1750*, ed. S. J. Wright (London: Hutchinson, 1988).

38. As in Claire S. Schen, *Charity and Lay Piety in Reformation London, 1500–1620* (Aldershot, Eng., and Burlington, VT: Ashgate, 2002).

39. As in Peter Burke, "Popular Piety," in *Catholicism in Early Modern History: A Guide to Research*, ed. John O'Malley (St. Louis, MO: Center for Reformation Research, 1988).

40. As in Daniel E. Bornstein, *The Bianchi of 1399: Popular Devotion in Late Medieval Italy* (Ithaca, NY, and London: Cornell University Press, 1993). See also Robert Whiting, *The Blind Devotion of the People: Popular Religion and the English Reformation* (Cambridge and New York: Cambridge University Press, 1989).

41. As in *Muerte, religiosidad y cultura popular, siglos XIII XVIII*, ed. Eliseo Serrano Martín (Zaragoza: Instituto "Fernando El Católico," 1994); and José María Tavares de Andrade, *Approche anthropologique de la religiosité populaire au Brésil* (Cuernavaca: Centro Intercultural de Documentación, 1973).

42. As in *Lived Religion in America: Towards a History of Practice*, ed. David D. Hall (Princeton, NJ: Princeton University Press, 1997).

43. See Philip Sheldrake, *Spirituality and History: Questions of Interpretation and Method* (London: SPCK, 1991); and Carlos M. N. Eire, "Major Problems in the Definition of 'Spirituality' as a Distinct Discipline," in *Modern Christian Spirituality*, ed. B. Hansen (Atlanta, GA: Scholars Press, 1991).

44. *The Oxford Encyclopedia of the Reformation*, ed. Hans J. Hillerbrand (New York: Oxford University Press, 1996); *Encyclopedia of the Renaissance*, general ed. Paul F. Grendler (New York: Scribner's, published in association with the Renaissance Society of America, 1999).

45. For interviews with top practitioners, see Maria Lucia Pallares-Burke, *The New History: Confessions and Conversations* (Cambridge: Polity, in association with Blackwell Publishers Ltd., a Blackwell Publication, 2003).

46. Vovelle, "Popular Religion," 81.

47. Protestant polemicists, of course, had taken this approach since the Reformation and kept it alive until it was adopted by social scientists. See, for example, W. J. Wilkins, *Paganism in the Papal Church* (London: S. Sonnenschein, 1901); and J. M. Wheeler, *Paganism in Christian Festivals* (London: Issued for the Secular Society Ltd., by the Pioneer Press, 1932).

48. See Don Yoder, "Toward a Definition of Folk Religion," in *Western Folklore* 33 (1974).

49. Cited by Vovelle, "Popular Religion," 82.

50. Robert Mandrou, *Introduction à la France moderne, 1500–1640: Essai de psychologie historique* (Paris: A. Michel, 1961).

51. Michel Vovelle, *Piété baroque et déchristianisation en Provence au XVIIIe siècle; les attitudes devant la mort d'après les clauses des testaments* (Paris: Plon, 1973).

52. Vovelle, "Popular Religion," 83.

53. Though not cited by Vovelle, an example of this approach is Jean-Claude Schmitt, *The Holy Greyhound* (Cambridge: Cambridge University Press, 1983).

54. Delumeau, *Catholicism Between Luther and Voltaire*.

55. Thomas, *Religion and the Decline of Magic*.

56. Mikhail Bakhtin, *Rabelais and His World*, trans. Hélène Iswolsky (Cambridge, MA: MIT, 1968).

57. Vovelle, "Popular Religion," 86.

58. For a discussion of this, see Alberro, *El águila y la cruz*.

59. Vovelle, "Popular Religion," 113.

60. A great example is Natalie Zemon Davis, "Strikes and Salvation at Lyons," in her *Society and Culture in Early Modern France* (Stanford, CA: Stanford University Press, 1975).

61. In *Popular Culture and Popular Movements in Reformation Germany*, ed. R. W. Scribner (London: Hambledon Press, 1987).

62. Scribner, "Ritual and Popular Religion," 23.

63. Ibid., 44.

64. See George Minamiki, *The Chinese Rites Controversy: From Its Beginning to Modern Times* (Chicago: Loyola University, 1985); J. S. Cummins, *A Question of Rites: Friar Domingo Navarrete and the Jesuits in China* (Brookfield, VT: Ashgate, 1993).

65. See Inga Clendinnen, *Ambivalent Conquests: Maya and Spaniard in Yucatan, 1517–1570* (Cambridge and New York: Cambridge University Press, 1987); Fernando Cervantes, *The Devil in the New World* (New Haven, CT: Yale University Press, 1994); and Robert Ricard, *The Spiritual Conquest of Mexico*, trans. Lesley Byrd Simpson (Berkeley: University of California Press, 1966).

66. Both quoted by Henry Kamen, *The Phoenix and the Flame: Catalonia and the Counter Reformation* (New Haven, CT: Yale University Press, 1993), 85, 378.

FIGURE 3. San Miguel del Milagro

Woodcuts of saints were extremely common and popular in colonial Mexico. Printers gave them out as promotions for books, and people placed them in their homes as makeshift minishrines. In this image the use of a European saint in a specifically Mexican geographic context, in Puebla, is particularly intriguing. Taken from Devocionario mexicano. Pequeños grabado novohispanos, *introducción de Alicia Gojman (Mexico: Backal Editores, 1998). Courtesy of Backal Editores.*

CHAPTER TWO

Icons of Devotion

The Appropriation and Use of
Saints in New Spain

Antonio Rubial García

Translated by Martin Austin Nesvig

The linkage of the political and the religious is expressed through the complex weaving of saints and idols in colonial Mexico, an overlapping of pre-Hispanic deities with superimposed Spanish and European saints, the importation of those same saints, and their use for social and political ends. One observes this in the Spanish rule of Cholula, one of the principle pre-Hispanic cities in central Mexico, a city replete with innumerable religious temples and sites. In the sanctuary of the Mexica god Quetzalcóatl, the Franciscans, according to the chronicler Agustín de Vetancurt, endeavored "that wherever there were so many pagan temples made to the Devil, there would be dedicated an equal number of chapels and churches to the cult of the saints."[1] In the new religious conception, the ancient gods of Mexico (Tlaloc, Tezcatlipoca, Mola) also occupied a place in the postconquest culture, but they were associated with demons. Some friars fought a fierce battle with them and supposedly confronted their manifestations in the form of idols, speaking with and defeating them.[2]

The term *icon* today has taken on a more and more extended use to denote someone who has marked a certain activity with his or her presence in our globalized planet. We might speak of personalities like Madonna or Michael Jordan as icons, symbols or archetypes that have been popularized by the media and in which aesthetic or emotional values have been concentrated, if always apart from the moral, political, or religious. By contrast the word icon, to designate a religious image, has lost the implication of its Greek and Christian origin that it always had. It was precisely in Byzantine and the eastern part of the Roman Empire where the new Christian religion adapted the rich Hellenistic tradition of iconography to its own needs of missionary expansion. Although born of a Judaism obsessed with idolatry and the negation of the cult of images, Christianity realized quickly that the only way to penetrate the pagan soul would be to employ icons of Christ, the Virgin, and the saints, substituting them little by little for the cult of the ancient gods. Only by way of these images—vectors of the new emotional charge that Christianity wished to impose—and with the official help of later Roman emperors was the cult of the saints transformed into an effective tool for introducing the new religion into all areas of life.

In the West the use of images, which was restricted until the eleventh century to the illustration of monastery books, began to be extensive, by way of Byzantine influence, as a method of mass communication. In the medieval period the propagation of images occupied a central role in the evangelization of the rural and urban masses and the images of Christ and the Virgin Mary returned as human and their cult was made ever more emotional. Moreover, the devotion to saints and their images and relics was extended considerably in this period.

For the church, saints were models of virtue that the faithful could imitate; for individuals, they were transformed into beings that could grant property, wealth, and children. Cities and their inhabitants considered them, in addition to being protectors against plagues and disasters, their heroes; as such, saints offered social cohesion and a chance at collective identity. During baptism every child was given the name of a saint under whose protection the infant was placed. Families, guilds, confraternities, cities, and countries placed themselves under the protection of one or various celestial patrons. Dates of celebration throughout the liturgical year were conceded to saints, as was the dominion over diverse agricultural activities. As such saints were converted into patrons of the bloom, vintage, harvest, rains, and sowing of fields. Thus by relating them with the forces that ruled the cosmos, saints were little by little substituted for the older, pagan gods.

In the sixteenth century, Protestant attacks on the cult of images provoked an unprecedented reaction within the Catholic Church as part of the general movement known as the Counter Reformation. The images of the saints had a double function. On the one hand, they served to narrate effectively the lives of male and female saints and thereby teach moral behavior. On the other hand, saint images were used, along with relics, as objects to which people gave offerings, lit candles, and solicited favors. This cult was fomented even more by the appearance of the printing press that spread written lives of the saints and woodcuts with their images.

During the sixteenth century an important part of the Americas was integrated into the Western Christian culture. Along with the imposition of new mental structures to a millenarian indigenous tradition, which the Christian tradition attempted to destroy, the Europeans brought with them their beliefs and practices, their values and symbols. The process as such resulted in a unique version of the Christian culture in which the Western elements took on autochthonous, Mesoamerican traits.

Most studies have emphasized the adaptation of Catholicism in the environment of Mexico and the Indians, whose cultural patrons were forced to accept the norms of the conquistadors. Yet, it has been little emphasized or studied that the Europeans and mestizos adjusted their Catholicism to the necessities and circumstances of the new, Mexican society, mostly because that religion was born in distant lands and had developed in a distinct cultural environment. Thus we stand before the dilemma of interpreting how the messages of a Western culture were received, perceived, and interpreted in Latin America. This essay deals specifically with the cult of images and relics of saints, and not that of Christ and the Virgin Mary, which have been much studied recently in other places.

The Images of the Saints in the Indigenous Realm

The cult of the saints and their images was transmitted to indigenous communities by friars as part of the evangelization mission. Although recent investigations have insisted that the religion taught to the Indians was essentially Christocentric—from which was derived the source in

Mexico for the cult of the Cross and to symbols of the Crucifixion—and purified of "superstitions," with few miracles and ceremonies, chronicles and other sources tell a different story, in which such a "purified" message was not so radical.

It is undeniable that, concerning ceremonies, community practices formed a central part of the apparatus of Catholic diffusion in Mexico. Yet the majority of friars felt that the faithful were incapable of comprehending abstractions and therefore needed festivals and visual teaching to feel attracted toward the new religion that they preached. One can see the same attitude concerning the cult of relics of those religious men who died in the "odor of sanctity." The friars encouraged the Indians to venerate the mortal remains of the recently departed and the objects belonging to them. For example, the Franciscan friar and founder of the Franciscan mission in Mexico in 1524, Martín de Valencia, whose uncorrupted corpse was venerated in the monastery at Tlalmanalco, in the foothills of the western base of Popocatépetl, was removed from its tomb by Indians and disappeared mysteriously. To this day the cave outside Amecameca, near Tlalmanalco, where Valencia had performed his ritual "discipline" (or self-flagellation) is venerated by Mexicans. A short drive east to the base of Popocatépetl from that cave brings one today to a thriving cult of animism and pre-Hispanic spirit worship overlain with Catholic saint images, reflecting the profound overlapping of religious cultural sensibilities that continue unabated five centuries later.

But it is perhaps in the cult of European saints that one can see with greatest clarity that the attitude of the friars was not contrary to such practices. As occurred in the Roman world, the new faith was accompanied by political dominion, and it was necessary to provide the neophytes with emotional vehicles by which Catholicism would penetrate their everyday lives. The first image offered for veneration was that of the Virgin Mary, brought by Cortés as a standard and used afterward by the friars with such profusion that the Indians referred to the cross and even God as Holy Mary.[3]

This diffusion of the cult of and devotion to the saints quickly spread thanks to the hagiographic texts that circulated in indigenous languages. The Franciscan friar Juan de Ribas, for example, composed a *Flossanctorum* (Lives of the Saints) in Nahuatl and his fellow Franciscan, fray Maturino Gilberti, introduced a series of hagiographies in his *Diálogo de Doctrina Cristiana* in Purépecha (or Tarascan), the language of Michoacán. There also circulated a life of Saint Francis composed in Purépecha at this time.[4] In these saints' lives, as well as in the images that decorated their monasteries, the friars promoted the patron saints of their own order: Saints Francis, Bernard of Siena, and Anthony of Padua among the Franciscans; Saints Domingo de Guzmán, Vicente Ferrer, Catherine of Siena, and Jacinto among the Dominicans; and Saints Augustine, Nicholas Tolentino, and William among the Augustinians. Along with these, various apostles were promoted by all the orders, especially Saints Peter and Paul, Bartholomew and Andrew. Others were among the most widely spread by the missionaries: the parents of the Virgin Mary, Saints Joaquín and Anne, Saints John the Baptist, Mary Magdalene, Catherine of Alexandria, Christopher, Martin, and Sebastian. In general, and above all among the Franciscans, the friars insisted a great deal on the apostolic and biblical saints and in the ancient martyrs as clear proof for their evangelism.[5]

Nevertheless, the promotion of warrior saints was not ignored. The apostle Santiago, the patron saint of Spain and of the Reconquest of the Iberian Peninsula against Islam, the martyr Saint Hipólito, on whose feast day, August 13, the city of Tenochtitlan-Mexico was taken by Cortés, and the archangel Michael, the celestial force that defeated the Devil, idolatry, and the ancient gods, all appeared in a spectacle in Tlaxcala in 1539 that was designed by the Franciscans along with the participation of Spaniards and Indians. The grand public event lasted the entire day of Corpus Christi and recorded the retaking of Jerusalem by Christian armies. Throughout the representation of this historic event those warrior-saints, dressed as conquistadors, announced to the besieged and the armies that the fall of Jerusalem was near as was the imminent baptism of the Muslims.[6]

Soon after the conquest of Mexico, saints' names were given to towns and peoples, rivers and mountains, neighborhoods and churches. Each religious order promoted its own saints and images as a method of propaganda and part of its preaching. Thus in the moment in which a religious community was transferred to a different church and monastery, the new group took possession of its new territory by placing images of its saints wherever it could. In San Juan Teotihuacán, for example, the Franciscans ceded a monastery to the Augustinians in 1557. In their first act of possession, the Augustinian friars ordered painted on the entrance the images of the order's founder and the various members who had been canonized. The Indians, who did not agree with this transfer, demonstrated their opposition by refusing to obey the new officials and erasing the images of the Augustinian saints on the entrance, resulting in various violent disturbances.[7]

Behind the anecdote of Teotihuacán appear two important facts: on the one hand, the political use by the friars of their saints; on the other hand, the acceptance or negation that Indians manifested for the use of these religious symbols. In the same context, Indians openly appropriated Catholic images. Consider the following narration by Jerónimo de Mendieta concerning the habit (or robe) and cord of Saint Francis:

> On the eve of the feast day of Saint Francis, in all the monasteries of his order... more than eight hundred men keep vigil... and a thousand children with their mothers and other parents and friends came there as godfathers and godmothers of that occasion.... They bring their humble robes and cords so that they might be blessed and dressed, as well as their candles of white wax and many other offerings of bread and fruit.... [I]t is customary in our houses to have an old cord in the entrance that the friars had discarded.[8]

The narrative presents an apologetic tone; nevertheless, one can detect an indubitable fact: the Indians accepted the religious codes of the conquistadors in a rather spontaneous way. Does not the cord of Saint Francis recall the *malinalli*, representing an intricately woven cord by which the cosmic forces circulated and which was associated with birth? Additionally, the visually rich Mexica cultures of symbolism recalled a daily sense of visual representation, the most famous of which is the nopal cactus atop a stone in a small lake—a glyph that was the prealphabetic symbol for Tenochtitlan.

In addition to missionary success one must recognize that in the pre-Hispanic world it was common that a conquered pueblo received the gods of the conquerors as a symbol of submission. Indians viewed Catholic saints as part of that imposition and as one of the elements that the new political regime brought with it. But the Spanish conquest also had demonstrated that the Christian gods were extremely powerful. Indeed, this power was demonstrated in the warlike uniforms of the conquistadors modeled on Santiago and Saint Michael the Archangel. As such for the Indians, the alien god could be propitiated in order to ask him for benefits such as liberation from harm. The only difference from pre-Hispanic times was that the new overlords had an exclusive attitude and did not tolerate the coexistence of their gods with those of the ancient religions.

Despite this lack of flexibility, the Indians created points of communication between both cultural worlds, which led them to form a syncretic or parallel religion. Christian saints were integrated as divinities. They substituted for the protector gods of the neighborhoods and covered the principal functions of the cosmos superimposing on their attributes those that the lords that previously ruled natural forces once possessed. Saint Michael and the Devil defeated were seen as only a single figure that symbolized the cosmic forces in battle—forces that were not exclusive but complementary and that showed the fight between opposites on which depended the same existence of the universe: the eagle and the serpent, day and night, light and darkness, life and death.

As a result of his association with water, Saint John the Baptist occupied a place in the indigenous pantheon and like Tlaloc, god of rain, the Christian saint was converted into the lord of the east. Indians celebrated his feast day, which also coincided with the summer solstice, with theatrical representations narrating scenes of the life of his predecessor (Tlaloc), and this performance had to be associated with a propitiatory ritual.[9] Like Huitzilopochtli, Tlaloc and other Mexica deities were addressed with propitiation for specific goals—in this case, rain. Other pre-Hispanic gods were similarly transformed. The parish priest Jacinto de la Serna said that fire, considered an ancient god, was called Saint Simon or Saint Joseph, represented as ancient men, "and thus with these names [the Indians] dissimulate and conserve the ancient name that they gave to fire, Huehuetzin, which means old man." [10]

On other occasions there existed an association between the occurrences of the feast days of the saints with those of the ancient gods, being the result of a common agricultural tradition. In February, the feast of the Virgen de las Candelas corresponded to the propitiatory rites to the goddess of water, Chalchiuhtlicue. Holy Week (or Easter Week), coincided with the rites to Tezcatlipoca, associated with sacrifices like that of Christ. The god Xipe Totec, celebrated when nature drew new strength and bloomed, was assimilated as the ancient Saint Joseph, the father of Christ. The celebration of Saint Francis in the first week of October, by his association with animals, represented a reworking of the festivals of Mixcoatl, god of the hunt.

These celebrations and feast days were also reinforced with a ceremonial apparatus that allowed these associations to operate even more freely. Processions with images were organized by confraternities. Triumphal arches, decorative wreaths of flowers, incense, autochthonous dances, and the representations of battles between Moors and Christians, songs, and bell ringing all formed part of a ritual that had as its goal the protection of celestial forces and the solution of daily problems—just as had been done earlier with ancient gods. For the Indians saints were the relatives of Christ and existed since the creation of the world. As the gods craved things and sought those who would satisfy them, so too it was necessary to make offerings to them of food and the first fruits of the harvest. Jacinto de la Serna showed that the Indians made sacrifices to saints (to those whom they revered like gods), hiding behind the cult of the saints their idolatrous rites:

> Their mitigation and dissimulation goes so far that they make offerings to the saints . . . sacrificing hens and animals, spilling pulque in their presence, offering them food and drink and attributing to them any sickness that befalls them, asking them for help and succor and giving them thanks if they obtain what they ask.[11]

Saints and demons were integrated thus as cosmic forces both positive and negative, but not necessarily within the codes of the European culture. The Indians understood Catholic saints as both good and evil much in the same way they understood pre-Hispanic deities. Indeed, many such deities confounded efforts of the missionaries who often lumped many such deities into the generic category of Satan or the devil. For Indians, saints had power to grant benefits but also were beings with a destructive potential. Mendieta recounts, for example, that at the beginning of the evangelization the Indians called Saint Francis "the cruel," because his feast day, the fourth of October, coincided with the traditional end of the rainy season and the beginning of the cold season in central Mexico when the Indians lost maize and vegetables with this change.[12]

The saints were not, however, abstract entities, but their strength was present in their images that were considered *ixiptla*, or receptacles of a power, presences that possessed strength.[13] Some anthropologists have insisted in this magic character of images in present-day communities. For example, in Ihuatzio, Michoacán, the different sculptures of Saint Francis are considered different saints.[14]

Clearly such phenomena of assimilation were possible thanks to the existence of parallels between the pre-Hispanic and Catholic religions. Christianity presented the Indians a formal catalogue that offered them various images of children, women, men, old men, winged beings, and demons with which they could fulfill the necessary superimpositions of their ancient gods. Moreover, the enormous quantity of representations associated with martyrdom and with blood, including that of Christ, must have constituted for the Indians a rich arsenal of images similar to the sacrifices offered to their gods. In this process of assimilation they even came to integrate animals that served as attributes of the saints and that were identified as their *tona* or protective entity. The Third Mexican Provincial Church Council in 1585 not only banned popular festivals that could lend themselves to the resurgence of idolatry but also the representations of animals, demons, and stars together with saints to prevent the faithful from venerating them and by which "especially the old people suck in idolatry with their milk."[15]

This process of assimilation was nothing new in Christianity. It occurred just the same in the early centuries of Christianity when the early church rules assimilated pagan gods into Christian saints as the indigenous religion integrated its gods with the saints that the evangelizers brought. In the previous essay, for example, Carlos Eire outlines this process by which the early church incorporated pagan gods into the Christian pantheon of saints—a process much like that in early colonial Mexico. For many historians, indeed, indigenous religion as practiced in Mexico differed little from that of European peasants. The adaptation of the Indians to the saints was so successful that, along with rites associated with death, the cult to these celestial beings was undoubtedly the aspect of Christianity that had the greatest impact in their communities. For example, after the evangelization, every indigenous dwelling had a space dedicated to the "house of the saint," sometimes even an entire bedroom. To maintain this space and conserve the image of the saint within the household symbolized the identity and continuity of that same saint because images of saints were family property and associated both with that family and its household.[16]

Among this familial use existed the use of saints' images in the collective realm, above all in fiestas and processions. The Augustinian chronicler Juan de Grijalva recounts:

> An Indian who is unprepared to spend even two reales for
> his food and clothing, happily spends a thousand on an image.

As a result he has nothing more than a room for his dwelling . . .
and makes another more fitting room into an oratory. These
oratories are so highly esteemed among them that they make
them into mansions.[17]

The passage from Grijalva speaks of a cult to the saints that had become basic for the community. In fact, not only could the images of a
church be given over to a private house, but those of each house had to
make a ceremonial visit to the patron saint of the pueblo that was established in the principle church. This image was the center of the community cult, often associated with a confraternity, and its importance became
so great that around it developed an entire system of positions, above all
mayordomo (or, superintendent of religious ceremonies) and *fiscal* (an Indian
official who worked with Spanish authorities to regulate doctrinal compliance). Indeed, in indigenous communities in Mexico, the cult of the saint
lay at the center of social, political, and even agricultural life. Pre-Hispanic
traditions of communal landholding were integrated into the Catholic concepts of the confraternity, and frequently the distinction between confraternity and community property was blurred completely. So central was this
cult that when the liberals of the nineteenth century insisted on scaling back
religious communalism, many indigenous communities viewed the liberals
as enemies of the Indians. It was important that organizing the fiestas of the
patron saint, and above all the ritual meal, was one of the principle functions of the indigenous authorities of the *cabildo* (town council).

Such an apparatus created the need to strengthen institutions such as
confraternities and *mayordomías* (the cult of religious ceremonies over
which the mayordomo presided). The first—the confraternities—were
founded to cover the costs of the fiestas. In some regions they even appropriated community lands and goods that were worked by all. As a result
the saints were converted into owners of extensive properties and saved
such lands from the plunder of Spaniards. The mayordomías, although
they had the same festival purpose, did not receive community funding
but instead the costs of maintaining them fell to a single family, whose
social prestige increased on receiving the honorific office.

Along with the friars, these authorities—the confraternities and mayordomías—had a central role in the election of the patron saints of the
pueblos. Sometimes the election could be related to the necessity of substituting the ancient guardian deities, using appearances similar between

the attributes of the saints and those of the ancient gods. Other times, such elections occurred by making assimilations related to place names. In various pueblos in Veracruz, for example, priests and Indian caciques, on electing the patron saints of the villages, assimilated some characteristic of the indigenous toponymy (or place names) and the protector god to the saint on which they imposed such characteristics. Tlaquilpa, the place of rich vestments, was placed under the patroness of Mary Magdalene. Mixtla, the place dedicated to Mixcoatl, the lord of the Chichimecas, was placed under the tutelage of Saint André, evangelist of the barbarian Escitas, north of the Black Sea.[18] In some parts of Tlaxcala, Saint Anne, the grandmother of Christ, was named patroness of the pueblos where there existed a sanctuary to the goddess Toci, grandmother of the gods. Saint Bartholomew, whose name means "son of he who keeps the rains from falling," could be placed in those places where the Indians venerated one of the gods of the rains.[19]

By the end of the seventeenth century, the Indians had so thoroughly integrated the cult of the saints that their presence appeared an active part in the foundation myths of pueblos. The primordial title of Santiago Sula, for example, narrates the apparition of the warrior saint (Santiago) to two indigenous caciques, who asked the caciques that they elect him patron of their town because he was extremely powerful and close to God.[20] The argument that a saint was close to God was a powerful one, since this meant that the saint could intercede for the community more effectively, having, as it were, the ear of God. The presence of a Christian saint as founder of a village shows not only the rapid process of penetration that Christianity had among Indians but also offers proof of the important role that religion played as vehicle for integrating the two worlds.

What appears certain is that some indigenous groups did not view the conquest as rupture but as continuity. The communal Christian elements were adapted to the pre-Hispanic ones. The patron saint, the cabildo, and the confraternity functioned as new factors of cohesion and substituted for the tribal god and the clan organization prior to the conquest. Thanks to those protector gods and patron saints, the recently congregated pueblos, often formed with groups from very different origins, could reconstruct their spiritual world. With these new saints they created bonds that facilitated integration and cohabitation.[21]

Through their conversion as protector gods of the pueblos, saints also became elements of resistance and behind them were hidden many indigenous concepts held over from before the conquest. However, in their acceptance one can also find processes of adaptation to Western rules and codes. In fact, the relation between celestial forces became more direct and the communication with them closer still, since undoubtedly the Christian saints had many more human traits than had the ancient bloody divinities.

In those processes of substitution it is difficult to know what role the Spanish missionaries played and what role was played by indigenous communities, but it is most likely that both contributed and reached agreements. Some friars, conscious of the necessity of supplanting paganism, made use of similarities between the two religions. The Indians, for their part, by lack of sufficient familiarity with the Christian world, interpreted Christianity as a function of their own traditions. The Christian saints were assimilated, but the campesinos continued with their agricultural rites, their traditional medicinal practices, and domestic religion. Despite the prohibition of the Catholic priests and their attempts at eradication, these practices lived side by side with the cult of the saints.

The Saints and the Spanish and Mestizo Realms

On the feast of All Saints in 1578 the Jesuits organized a festive reception of 214 relics of European saints that the pope had sent them to be distributed in the churches in Mexico City. In order to guard them, eighteen sumptuous reliquaries of gold, silver, and precious stones were ordered constructed, which were taken in procession from the cathedral to the College of the Society of Jesus. For the occasion the streets were decorated with arches and banners and a theatrical representation, *El triunfo de los santos*, was performed. The procession was accompanied by indigenous dances and in them was carried as a standard the eagle on a nopal devouring a serpent—the symbol of the foundation of Mexico City that the Jesuits associated with the sacrifice of Christ. It was represented by a triumphal arch for the first time when a noble indigenous woman, dressed in a *huipil* (the traditional dress of Indian women), representing New Spain, accompanied a young man also attired as a native of the kingdom of Peru. The celebration gave the Jesuits great prestige just six years after their arrival in Mexico. For the inhabitants of New Spain, those relics converted their land into a sacred and sanctified space and above all associated them with their most beloved emblems.[22]

During the sixteenth, seventeenth, and eighteenth centuries, an infinity of bones, objects, and even complete corpses of saints arrived from Europe in Mexico to be placed in the innumerable churches that were raised all around. For all Catholic Christendom, the consecration of a church had to be made by placing on its altars a reliquary. But these objects not only sacralized the interior space of the church but their presence in cities assured celestial protection against illness and catastrophes. Therefore, it was necessary to obtain, whether by purchase or donation, all those relics available on the European market. The phenomenon did not diminish with the arrival of the famous rationalism of the eighteenth century. When the Mexican Jesuits were expelled from the Spanish empire by Charles III in 1767 and placed in Italy, they had as one of their principal sources of income negotiating the shipment of relics to New Spain, not only for churches, but also to be placed in the domestic chapels of families who did business with the Jesuits in relics.

The Jesuits were active agents in promoting a cult of relics. In this surprising manifestation of publicity surrounding relics one can observe that, as was the case in the indigenous realm, the inhabitants of cities were seen as charged with realizing adaptations to the cult of European saints. Nevertheless, continuity with the Western practices was much more immediate. Take, for example, the early cult to Saint Hipólito in New Spain, especially in Mexico City. In the act of the Mexico City cabildo of July 31, 1528, there had already appeared regulations for the festivities of that saint that (with the name of "passage of the standard") was made in Mexico City to celebrate the Spanish martyrs of the conquest of Mexico.[23]

Conforming to the consolidation of society in colonial Mexico, the European saints began to take on central roles in all aspects of urban life. Since the second half of the sixteenth century, the diocese and the secular clergy (as opposed to the friars) promoted a politics of racial openness and integration that was inherently opposed to the concept of an indigenous world closed to external forces favored by the friars. In such a process the presence of Episcopal and papal saints, like Saint Gregory, was basic to the veneration of the faithful. The late arrived orders—Jesuits, Mercedarians, Carmelites, and Dieguinos—along with nuns, were also influential in the process of introducing new saints and new devotions. Finally, the provincial councils—above all, the Third Mexican Provincial Council in 1585—commanded the new rules concerning the cult of images and the veneration of the saints and adopted the principles of Trent—principles that had proclaimed the value and indeed necessity of saint veneration in the face of Protestant attacks on that same cult of the saints.[24]

The new attitude was reinforced by a corporate conscience in which the cult of the saints played a central role. In such organisms, the veneration of the images of their protectors came accompanied with an impressive apparatus of ostentation. The guild corporations, for example, were placed beneath the protections of the traditional saints unique to each skill and job: shoemakers beneath Saint Crispin; tailors beneath Saint Homobono; carpenters beneath Saint Joseph; smiths beneath Saint Eloy; and notaries beneath Saint John the Evangelist.

The religious orders fell within this same corporate spirit, advancing an ostentatious cult to their own founding saints. Every urban monastery had a series of paintings that narrated their lives in numerous scenes. For their part the secular clergy placed on the walls of the parish churches and cathedral pictorial scenes that represented the apostles, converted in emblematic figures of priests who did not live in a separate community but, along with bishops, who were the heads of their dioceses, were seen as inheritors of the twelve founders of the church. In this context after 1700 the image of Saint Peter, emblematic figure of Episcopal power, received a wide distribution.

The saints as corporate symbols and as elements of institutional cohesion were also used by the third orders (groups of laypersons associated with the promotion of a mendicant order), confraternities, congregations, the university, the cathedral chapters, municipal cabildos, and the commercial consulate, as well as by the viceregal bureaucracy (such as the Inquisition or the Audiencia). The images of the saints, as a fundamental part of the apparatus of corporate representation of those bodies, went along in processions in the streets during the feast of Corpus Christi and, as symbols of each social group, were adorned with jewels and accompanied by their standards.

The principal function of these celestial protectors was to attend to the necessities of the faithful united beneath the insignia of a corporation. In this sense the cities were also considered juridical entities that had the obligation to watch over their inhabitants by means of submission to various patrons. Those entrusted with such activities were the urban municipalities that elected their celestial advocates after a catastrophe by means of drawing lots or an election. Once the protector saint was obtained, the cabildo of the city performed a ceremony in which an oath was made: the elected saint would protect the populace from certain mishaps, and in return the city would celebrate the saint on his/her feast day with prayers, masses, and fiestas, place the image of the saint in the principal church, and, if possible, obtain some of its relics. Mexico City swore to Saint Joseph (San José) as patron of conversions and of the church of New Spain in 1555. Saint Nicholas Tolentino was named patron against earthquakes in 1611. At the end of the seventeenth century, Saint Bernard was made the official protector of the capital city against epidemics. And in 1723 Saint Antonio Abad was made patron against fires. The fiesta of Saint Gregory Taumaturdo, protector of the city against floods, often appears mentioned in the Mexico City cabildo and cathedral chapter acts, above all in the seventeenth century, when this type of problem was especially severe.

Indeed, it was the miraculous character of saints and their ability to free society from catastrophes and return individuals to health that made them venerated. The faithful repaid their benefactors with ex-votos, candles, alms, and pilgrimages. When a cult did not demonstrate its efficacy, it declined until it disappeared.

The patronage of San José over New Spain is one of the most interesting examples of the appropriation of a "European" saint in the service of a specific goal. The Franciscans dedicated a chapel to him in their major monastery in Mexico City, used for Indians, with the name San José de los Naturales, and they considered him a collaborator in the process of evangelization. By the eighteenth century, the criollos had associated him with the biblical Joseph, viceroy of the Egyptian pharaoh, and they often represented him with the viceroy of New Spain. San José was often painted in the so-called patronage pictures, in which he held a crown and shawl beneath his cloak protecting the faithful. San José did not function only as the ideal intercessor between his son Jesus and men; he was also a saint seen as a familial model, along with Saint Joaquín, the father of the Virgin. The church of the eighteenth century engaged in the diffusion of an intimate and familial morality in the Catholic sphere and insisted on saints as more than just procurers of miracles. In the popular mind-set the most important aspect was intercession; hence, there was an enormous diffusion of biographies of San José and prayers directed to him above all to solicit a "good death."[25]

For a society obsessed with the afterlife, a good death meant suffering or agonizing sufficiently long to obtain the repentance and pardon of sins, which allowed the soul freedom from the eternal penalties of hell.

However, except for saints, the majority of the faithful could not go to heaven directly and had to pass through a period of purification in purgatory as a place of suffering. In order to minimize the penalties there, the faithful also counted on the help of the Virgin and the saints, especially those who had visions of the souls suffering in purgatory, like Saint Gertrude and Saint Teresa. For remission of purgatorial time, the faithful also relied on objects related to the rescue of souls, such as the cord of Saint Francis, the escapulario of Saint Ramon, or the belt of Saint Nicholas Tolentino. In the eighteenth century people painted enormous canvases called "of souls," in which they represented in the lower part the souls in purgatory and in the upper part those intercessors saints that advocated for them before a God who, for people of the eighteenth century, became more and more tolerant with sinners and more inclined to pardon their faults.

Along with pictures and sculptures, the cult of the saints was reinforced also above all by the festival apparatus in which physically circulated the arrival of relics and the notice of canonizations from Rome. This was the case of Saint John of God (San Juan de Dios), whose canonization was published on October 16, 1700, and which stimulated festivities in Mexico City that lasted eight days with processions, fireworks, sermons, ephemeral altars, *mascaradas* (masked balls or parades), allegorical carriages, music, and poetry contests.[26]

It is important to note the attachment of the citizens of New Spain to the saints of recent canonizations, a result of the enormous publicity of the religious orders moved by a corporate sentiment in which they associated with their brethren of the habit on the other side of the Atlantic. Thus, the Carmelites exported the cult of Saint Teresa de Jesús far beyond the frontiers of Spain, as they did likewise with Mary Magdalene of Pazzi, the reformer of the Italian Carmelites. The Jesuits, in order to publicize their extensive missionary activity in the entire world, expanded the cult of Saint Francisco Javier, the evangelist (and martyr) of Asia.

In order to promote a cult to new saints in America, the religious orders located in New Spain developed publicity campaigns on a wide scale. To propagate their curative powers and attract people to their chapels, the religious ordered the publication of hagiographies that described their lives and broadcast their biographies in sermons during masses and ordered their relics brought to Mexico. In Mexico City the Dominicans, for example, imported a bit of the earth from the sepulcher of Saint Raymond of Peñafort (patron saint of canon lawyers), after he was canonized in 1601. Their order's chronicler, fray Alonso Franco, narrated that this earth, dissolved in water, cured many sick people of their diseases in a hospital.[27]

Sometimes these campaigns were politicized, as was the case with the figure of Saint John Nepomuceno, the saint promoted by the Czech Jesuits in the first decades of the eighteenth century and who had been received by oath in Mexico as the patron of the Audiencia, the cabildo, the Jesuit colleges, and the university. The new saint was converted into a banner of dissidence after the expulsion of the Society of Jesus in 1767. He had been a victim of an unjust monarch in Bohemia in the fourteenth century, thus he returned as an emblem, for the pro-Jesuit criollos, against Charles III, considered a despot for having expelled their countrymen. In a scene dated to 1782 and painted by José de Alcíbar, the saint was depicted with his tongue in his hand, a symbol of the secret of confession, and trampling underfoot the monster of libel and calumny next to a bird thundering forth from a beam of light, as an allusion to the situation in which lived the dissolved Society.[28]

Parallel to this public cult promoted by corporations, the private cult of images of the saints (painted or sculpted) extended in all social sectors. Canvases and sculptures that represented saints appeared with frequency in wills, inventories, testaments, and acts of dowry as part of the wealth of individuals and families. The domestic cult, constructed with kisses and petitions, orders and obsequies, demonstrated an emotive religiosity that had integrated the image within the family and which was considered a living being. In the realm of monasteries (known most by the numerous chronicles and biographies) the possession of and cult to such objects was converted into a factor of competition and envy. Those testimonies reflect that the treatment the images received was often so human that the saints were changed into advocates, given last names, or were assumed to have movement, tears, sweat, and emissions of blood as if they were real human beings. In this respect the case of a Marian sculpture owned by sister (*sor*) Agustina de Saint Teresa in the convent of La Concepción in Puebla is especially interesting. Sor Agustina transformed an image of the Virgin of Carmen into a Saint Gertrude by changing the saint's features. In other words the nun (Agustina) had physically altered the image to make it appear like a Saint Gertude instead of a Virgin. This act earned her a rebuke from her friend, the venerable nun María de Jesús. Confusing

matters further, to complement the attributes of the Virgin of Carmen, sor
Agustina placed on the same statue an image arrived from Spain that
received the nickname "el gachupín" (the name given in New Spain to people of Iberian peninsular origin).[29] So while Agustina had made the image
appear more like a Gertrude, the addition of a child made the image look
more like a Virgin. The nun Agustina had compiled multiple images from
various saints and Virgins to create a composite Gertrude with similarities
to Carmen.

By contrast, in the homes of the rich and poor, there existed familial
altars with numerous printed images. These were also worn among the
clothing like amulets, or placed at the head of the bed, in chests and arm-
oires, and outside doors to protect places from evil and to bring fortune and
health. Even midwives placed images of Saint Ignacio or Saint Ramon above
the womb of a woman in labor to help her with a safe childbirth. The great
use and consumption of images provoked printers to use the original
engravings with which they had made the frontispieces of books to produce
loose impressions that they sold as images to the faithful. Sometimes even
shopkeepers gave away images in the form of printed pages along with the
purchase of merchandise. Similarly printed religious images were used in a
vast range: in novenas (guides of prayers that were supposed to be used during a nine-day period); patents, contracts, and summaries of graces and
indulgences of confraternities (leafs that recounted the spiritual privileges
that they offered); as well as in popular poetry, hymns, verses, and gossip
sheets; and in escapularios (pieces of cloth to place on the chest and back
that bore images of the Virgin or a saint).[30]

But such a diffusion of printed or engraved images was only one part
of a parallel process: the great impulse that devotional literature had
thanks to the printing press. There is no doubt that hagiography, sermons, theatrical works, and novenas were the major instruments in the
distribution and promotion of the cult of the saints and in the multipli-
cation of their images. For example, in 1605 the first lives of saints were
published in Mexico in the printshop of Diego López Dávalos—those of
Saint Anthony of Padua by fray Juan Bautista and of Saint Nicholas
Tolentino by Francisco de Medina. In fact, during the entire seventeenth
century and in the first third of the eighteenth more than half of the
works of devotion printed in Mexico were dedicated to saints.[31] Along
with hagiographies, between 1680 and 1720 the printing of novenas
(prayer cycles) increased considerably in the presses of Mexico City and

Puebla. In time these guides for prayer were published more than sermons, since, thanks to their small format and devotional purpose and practice, they reached a broader public and audience. The sermon was a limited publication that was destined for academic consultation within silent studies and libraries. The novena, by contrast, was a pedagogical instrument that invited the faithful to enact intimately in their hearts the fight between good and evil and to take part in this battle.[32]

In all this New Spain behaved in appearance like the rest of the Catholic countries of the world. Nevertheless, there existed in its realm of representation of the saints some manifestations that took on specific and peculiar traits and that marked its differences compared to Europe. On the first level there appeared the need to situate the saint within a known space, representing it within Mexican scenery. It was common, for example, in the pictures that narrated the birth of Saint Francis or Saint Domingo de Guzmán, to dress their parents and relatives in the sartorial styles of the seventeenth century and to locate their environments with furniture and other objects from the criollo domestic world. Other times, saints occupied the plaza or street of the baroque capital of New Spain, with its balconies full of rich cloth, its racket and bustle and its houses and cultivated chapels, as was the case in a painting by Cristóbal de Villalpando in Guatemala that described the return of Saint Francis from the mountain Alverna, mounted on a burro and received like Christ on Palm Sunday.[33]

In all these manifestations the official cultural codes remained intact, and, in fact, these processes of adaptation took place in Europe as well. However, a second level of representation existed in which, along with conventional attitudes, symbolic elements of patriotic pride were introduced along with the religious codes. Such examples began to appear in the sixteenth century in Mexico City, with the depiction of the emblem of its mythical foundation, an eagle on top of a nopal cactus devouring a serpent in the middle of a lagoon. "January 19 of 1565," recounts the diary of the Indian Juan Bautista, "on the feast of Saint Sebastian, the image of his entire body appeared, with his hands tied to a nopal."[34] This was a reworking of the standard image of Saint Sebastian tied to a tree and impaled with arrows. Saint Sebastian was an early Christian martyr who, refusing to take part in Roman pagan rituals as a military man, was shot with arrows as a form of torture; legend has it that he survived, escaped, and was later beaten to death. But the image of Saint Sebastian tied to a tree, arrows piercing his body, remained constant. The use of a nopal in place of a tree reflects the syncretism in the Mexican context. For his part, the indigenous chronicler Chimalpáhin recounted that on October 4, 1593, a painting of Saint Francis was shown with the saint riding on an eagle above a nopal.[35]

The use of that pagan symbol passed quickly from the indigenous realm to the criollo and became a generalized reference, often associated with the saints. In the eighteenth century Saint Hipólito was represented mounted above an eagle perched on a nopal and venerated by the conqueror Pedro de Alvarado and by the emperor Moctezuma, whose weapons rested next to his knees. This was an extremely unlikely pair, since Alvarado was the Spaniard responsible for the massacre in Tenochtitlan during Cortés's absence that led to the Spanish retreat during the *noche triste*. Later, Alvarado would be the principle conquistador and *encomendero* of Guatemala, while Moctezuma was the defeated Mexican emperor (or *tlatoani*) who today is revered as a symbol of resistance to Spanish imperialism. The patron of the conquistadors was converted thus into an emblem that inserted indigenous and Spanish elements as a sign of the synthesis of both worlds and the new identity that New Spain held for its ideologues. The most interesting aspect is that the representation was ordered painted by an indigenous cacique.

But perhaps the most interesting such case was that of Felipe de Jesús, a missionary to Japan who had been born in Mexico to Spanish parents and who sought a life of converting the Japanese to Catholicism. While the Spanish could count many martyrs in Japan, Mexico, the Philippines, Quebec, and Chile, Felipe de Jesús was the first criollo martyr in Japan. As such he made an attractive candidate as a symbol not only of martyrdom, missionary zeal, and Catholic humility—he was a criollo and not a peninsular Spaniard—he appealed to the American-born Spaniards who felt slighted by a papacy and crown that viewed them as second-class and inferior.

Felipe de Jesús was beatified in 1627. Since the middle of the seventeenth century he was substituted for Saint Francis as the horseman above an eagle in a procession. With this *beato* there was a new kind of representation. New Spain, like the entire Christian realm, had generated the necessity to have its own saints, heroes whose deeds were the beacons of glory for the land that saw them born and sheltered them.[36] But during the three centuries of its viceroyalty, Rome only recognized two beatos from New Spain, and no saints. One was martyr Felipe de Jesús. The other was Sebastián de Aparicio, a lay Franciscan beatified in 1790. He was converted subsequently in an urban emblem of the city of Puebla that celebrated his beatification with three days of festivities.

Felipe de Jesús was sworn as a patron of the capital of New Spain in 1629 and was treated as if he were a saint. His feast day of February 5 was celebrated annually by the city government with great pomp. Beginning in 1638 the cathedral also rendered homage to his veneration and his image in a chapel in its interior.[37] In 1666 the merchant Simón de Haro and his wife named him patron of the recently established church of the Capuchin nuns—a building that, according to some, occupied the site of the paternal house of the beato Felipe.

The martyr from Japan shared his privileged place with the criolla saint, Rose of Lima (Santa Rosa de Lima), canonized in 1671 after a meteoric process, being canonized quickly after her death. Known as a *beata*, Rosa de Lima was a woman who took on no specific orders or role as a nun. Rather she dedicated her life to spiritual pursuits as technically a laywoman in her native Peru. Nevertheless, her renown as a holy woman spread quickly. Rosa de Lima became so important for many cities of New Spain that images and tableaux of her multiplied from one end of the territory to the other, and she was transformed into one of the most popular figures of veneration, sometimes exceeding Felipe de Jesús. In 1670 Pedro del Castillo saw his *Estrella del Occidente* published, which told the story of the young Peruvian girl he called the "lustrous honor of New Spain."[38]

In spite of all this, New Spain, so far from Europe, was destined to occupy a kind of second-category Christianity, since it could not present a history of sanctity that tied it to apostolic times. For many criollos it was a serious problem that America could have passed a thousand and five hundred years before it could be included in the universal church by baptism. Some criollos, like the seventeenth-century savant Carlos de Sigüenza, expelled from the Jesuit order for his nighttime diversions, drew on allusions of chroniclers of the sixteenth century about the similarities between the indigenous and Christian cults. For example, he asserted that Saint Thomas, the lost apostle of the primitive church, had arrived in Mexico in the first century after Christ. His presence was endorsed by the history of a virtuous priest named Quetzalcóatl who was assimilated into the figure of the apostle. Quetzalcóatl was a Toltec deity and mythical king-priest associated with wisdom and who was incorporated into the Mexica pantheon as a principal god and patron of knowledge.

FIGURE 4. Santo Tomás en Indias
Saint Thomas the Apostle was fused with a conception of Quetzalcoatl as a
virtuous priest and apostle of the New World before the arrival of the Spanish.
Taken from Nicolás León, Bibliografía Mexicana del siglo XVIII *(Mexico:*
Instituto Mexicano Bibliográfico, 1906).

Around 1750 Mariano Fernández de Echeverría y Veytia compiled material "proofs" of the presence of Saint Thomas in Mexico: pre-Hispanic crosses, like that of Huatulco, that "demonstrated" the existence of a primitive evangelization; footprints of the apostle imprinted in rocks; indigenous traditions that spoke of a virtuous priest, white and bearded; and the presence of ancient books and traditions that supposedly contained teachings of a clear Christian tradition, like the adoration of a creator God, the Trinity, charity to the poor, monogamy, veneration of the cross, baptism, communion, confession, and priestly celibacy. The saint, who was represented with white clothing scattered with red crosses, had also ostensibly left the mark of his presence in the prophecy of the arrival by the sea in the east of white and bearded men who would appropriate the land and bring the light of the Gospel. With Saint Thomas/Quetzalcóatl the pre-Hispanic world remained thus de-demonized and a Christian salvation was inserted into its history. With this, Indians and criollos possessed a land linked to the primitive church, which ratified the presence of America in the divine mind of Christ when he sent his disciples out to preach the new faith to all nations.[39] With Saint Thomas/Quetzalcóatl, a long process of adaptation of Christianity and its saints to the necessity of New Spain longing to be recognized as one of the nations that had received special divine favor arrived at its culmination.

NOTES

1. Agustín de Vetancurt, *Crónica de la provincia del Santo Evangelio de México* en *Teatro Mexicano*, edición facsimilar (Mexico: Ed. Porrúa, 1982 [1698]), 56.

2. Juan de Grijalva, *Crónica de la Orden de Nuestro Padre San Agustín en las provincias de Nueva España en cuatro edades desde el año de 1533 hasta el de 1592*, ed. Nicolás León (Mexico: Ed. Porrúa, 1985 [1624]), 90.

3. Toribio de Motolinía, *Historia de los indios de la Nueva España*, ed. Edmundo O'Gorman (Mexico: Ed. Porrúa, 1969), 24.

4. Pierre Ragon, "Les saints et les images du Mexique Colonial" (unedited thesis, Université de Paris, 2000), 186.

5. Francisco Morales, "Santoral franciscano en los barrios indígenas de la ciudad de México," *Estudios de Cultura Náhuatl* 24 (1994).

6. Motolinía, *Historia*.

7. Jerónimo de Mendieta, *Historia eclesiástica indiana*, ed. Antonio Rubial García (Mexico: Consejo Nacional para la Cultura y las Artes, 1996), book III, ch. 59.

8. Ibid., book III, ch. 56.

9. Motolinía, *Historia*, 63.

10. Jacinto de la Serna, *Manual de ministros de indios para el conocimiento de sus idolatrías y extirpación de ellas* (Mexico: Ed. Fuentes Cultural, 1953), 65.

11. Serna, *Manual de ministros*, 64: "Y pasa tan adelante su paliación y disimulación que hacen a los santos sacrificios... sacrificando gallinas y animales, derramando pulque en su presencia, ofreciéndoles comida y bebida y atribuyéndoles cualquier enfermedad que les viene, y pidiéndoles su favor y ayuda y dándoles gracias si consiguen lo que piden, pareciendo que esto hacen con los santos a quien tienen delante."

12. Mendieta, *Historia eclesiástica*, book III, ch. 56.

13. Serge Gruzinski, *La guerra de las imágenes* (Mexico: Fondo de Cultura Económica, 1994), 61. In English as *The Conquest of Mexico: The Incorporation of Indian Societies into the Western World, 16th-18th Centuries*, trans. Eileen Corrigan (Cambridge: Cambridge University Press, 1993).

14. Pedro Carrasco, *El catolicismo popular popular de los tarascos* (Mexico: Secretaría de Educación Pública, 1976), 197.

15. *Concilio III provincial mexicano* (Mexico: Imprenta Manuel Miró y D. Marsá, 1870), 221. See also Félix Baez-Jorge, *Entre los nahuales y los santos* (Jalapa: Universidad Veracruzana, 1998), 161–99.

16. James Lockhart, *Los nahuas después de la Conquista* (Mexico: Fondo de Cultura Económica, 1999). In English as *The Nahuas After the Conquest: A Social and Cultural History of the Indians of Central Mexico, Sixteenth Through Eighteenth Centuries* (Stanford, CA: Stanford University Press, 1992).

17. Grijalva, *Crónica*, book II, ch. VI.

18. Gonzalo Aguirre Beltrán, *Zongolica: Encuentro de dioses y santos patronos* (Jalapa: Universidad Veracruzana, 1986).

19. Ragon, "Les saints," 72.

20. Lockhart, *Los Nahuas*, 340.

21. Marcelo Carmagnani, *El regreso de los dioses: El proceso de la identidad étnica en Oaxaca, Siglos XVII y XVIII* (Mexico: Fondo de Cultura Económica, 1988).

22. Solange Alberro, *El águila y la cruz: Orígenes religiosos de la conciencia criolla* (Mexico: Fondo de Cultura Económica; El Colegio de México, 1999).

23. Edmundo O'Gorman, *Guía de las actas de cabildo. Siglo XVI* (Mexico: Departamento del Distrito Federal; Fondo de Cultura Económica, 1970), acta 222.

24. Pilar Gonzalbo, "Del tercero al cuarto concilio provincial (1585–1771)," *Historia mexicana* XXXV–I (1985).

25. Jaime Cuadriello, "San José en tierra de gentiles: Ministro de Egipto y virrey de las Indias," *Memoria: Revista del Museo Nacional de Arte* 1 (1989).

26. Antonio de Robles, *Diario de sucesos notables*, 3 vols. (Mexico: Ed. Porrúa, 1972).

27. Alonso Franco y Ortega, *Segunda parte de la Historia de la Provincia de Santiago de México...año de 1645*, ed. José María de Agreda y Sánchez (Mexico: El Museo Nacional, 1900).

28. Jaime Cuadriello, coord., *Juegos de ingenio y agudeza la pintura emblemática de la Nueva España* (Mexico: Museo Nacional de Arte, INBA; Banamex, 1994), 385.

29. Francisco Pardo, *Vida y virtudes heroicas de la madre María de Jesús* (Mexico: Viuda de Bernardo Calderón, 1676).

30. Monserrat Galí, "La estampa religiosa en México," *El Alcaraván, Boletín bimestral del Instituto de Artes Gráficas de Oaxaca* II–7 (1991).

31. Ragon, "Les saints," 221.

32. Ibid.

33. Juana Gutiérrez Haces et al., *Cristóbal de Villalpando* (Mexico: Fomento Cultural Banamex; CONACULTA; Instituto de Investigaciones Estéticas de UNAM, 1997), 260.

34. Juan Bautista, *Anales de Juan Bautista*, ed. Luis Reyes García (Mexico: CIESAS; Biblioteca Lorenzo Boturini, 2002).

35. Domingo de San Antón Chimalpáhin, *Diario*, ed. Rafael Tena (Mexico: Consejo Nacional para la Cultura y las Artes, 2001), 51.

36. Antonio Rubial García, *La santidad controvertida* (Mexico: Fondo de Cultura Económica; Facultad de Filosofía y Artes de UNAM, 1999).

37. Gustavo Curiel, "San Felipe de Jesús: Figura y culto," *Actas del XI coloquio de Historia del Arte* (Mexico: UNAM; Instituto de Investigaciones Estéticas, 1988).

38. Elisa Vargas Lugo, "Proceso iconológico del culto a Santa Rosa de Lima," *Actes du XLIIem. Congrés Internartional des Americanistes* (Paris: n.p., 1976).

39. Mariano Fernández de Echeverría y Veytia, *Historia antigua de México*, 2 vols. (Mexico: Ed. Leyenda, 1944).

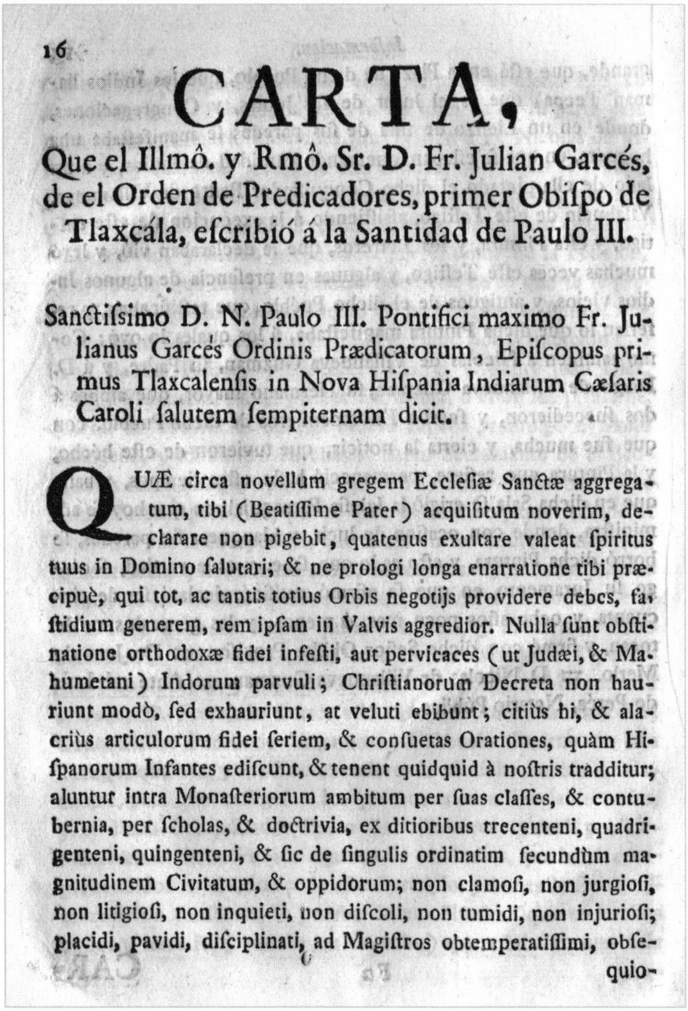

CARTA,

Que el Illmô. y Rmô. Sr. D. Fr. Julian Garcés,
de el Orden de Predicadores, primer Obiſpo de
Tlaxcála, eſcribió á la Santidad de Paulo III.

Sanctiſsimo D. N. Paulo III. Pontifici maximo Fr. Ju-
lianus Garcés Ordinis Prædicatorum, Epiſcopus pri-
mus Tlaxcalenſis in Nova Hiſpania Indiarum Cæſaris
Caroli ſalutem ſempiternam dicit.

QUÆ circa novellum gregem Ecclefiæ Sanctæ aggrega-
tum, tibi (Beatiſſime Pater) acquiſitum noverim, de-
clarare non pigebit, quatenus exultare valeat ſpiritus
tuus in Domino ſalutari; & ne prologi longa enarratione tibi præ-
cipuè, qui tot, ac tantis totius Orbis negotijs providere debcs, fa-
ſtidium generem, rem ipſam in Valvis aggredior. Nulla ſunt obſti-
natione orthodoxæ fidei infeſti, aut pervicaces (ut Judæi, & Ma-
humetani) Indorum parvuli; Chriſtianorum Decreta non hau-
riunt modò, ſed exhauriunt, at veluti ebibunt; citiùs hi, & ala-
criùs articulorum fidei ſeriem, & conſuetas Orationes, quàm Hi-
ſpanorum Infantes ediſcunt, & tenent quidquid à noſtris tradditur;
aluntur intra Monaſteriorum ambitum per ſuas claſſes, & contu-
bernia, per ſcholas, & doctrivia, ex ditioribus trecenteni, quadri-
genteni, quingenteni, & ſic de ſingulis ordinatim ſecundùm ma-
gnitudinem Civitatum, & oppidorum; non clamoſi, non jurgioſi,
non litigioſi, non inquieti, non diſcoli, non tumidi, non injurioſi;
placidi, pavidi, diſciplinati, ad Magiſtros obtemperatiſſimi, obſe-
quio-

FIGURE 5. Letter from Dominican bishop Julián Garcés to the Vatican

In 1769 the archbishop of Mexico, Antonio Lorenzana, published a new edition of the first two councils of the Mexican church, held in 1555 and 1565. Among the important issues faced by the councils was the question of Indians' roles in the church. Lorenzana included in this edition copies of the letter written by Dominican bishop of Puebla, Julián Garcés, to the Vatican, as well as the important declarations of Indian humanity and rights by Paul III. This is the first page of Garcés's letter. Taken from Concilios provincials primero y Segundo . . . dalos a luz el illmo. Sr. d. Francisco Antonio Lorenzana . . . *(Mexico: Joseph Antonio de Hogal, 1769). Courtesy of Mandeville Special Collections Library, University of California, San Diego.*

CHAPTER THREE

The "Indian Question" and the
Case of Tlatelolco

Martin Austin Nesvig

In 1543 the former confessor to Charles V, the Franciscan Alfonso de Castro, penned a vigorous defense of Indian intellect, arguing that the most talented of them should be trained to become priests in Mexico. At the time Castro was one of the two or three most influential theologians of Spain. He had published the most widely used treatises on the Inquisition of the sixteenth century, was Salamanca's favorite public preacher, and was in close contact with the theology faculty at the university in the same city, putting him in close association with Francisco Vitoria. A Dominican, Vitoria held what was called the "prime chair" in theology at the University of Salamanca, Spain's most prestigious university, placing him at the apex of academic influence and power at the time. He was famous for having made a series of lectures highly critical of the Spanish conquest of the Americas in which he defended the Dominican position that the pope had no temporal, explicitly worldly authority and that therefore the "donation" of the Americas in 1493 by Alexander VI was essentially void.[1] He had also signed Castro's treatise defending Indian education and ordination. Yet today Castro's discussion—the most vigorous defense of Indian intellect penned in the colonial era—remains unknown and ignored, falling under the long shadow cast by Vitoria and other Spanish thinkers. This essay examines not only Castro's discussion but also the much broader concern among the Spanish clergy about the nature of Indian intellect, education, and Christianization in Mexico.

Numerous crucial issues faced the Spanish priests who came to Mexico to create a new church in the Americas. Some of the questions that Spanish intellectuals, theologians, and jurists began to ask included: Were the Indians in fact human beings? Were Indians fit to receive the sacraments of the Catholic Church? Who should tend to the Indians' spiritual needs? Should Indians have access to Scripture in their native languages? Should the Indians be allowed to study theology? Should Indians be allowed to be ordained as priests? This essay examines the responses that missionaries and intellectuals had to such questions and concludes with an examination of the defense of Indian ordination and education by Castro.

The catechesis (instruction in Catholic doctrine) of the Indians formed the linchpin of debates on Indians. In 1933 the French historian of Mexico, Robert Ricard, published a book so influential that its title came to represent the very concept it set out to explain: *The Spiritual Conquest of Mexico*. Indeed, even into the twenty-first century Ricard's conceptualization of the process of Christianization of an Indian, non-Catholic population retains considerable influence. Thus "spiritual conquest" refers to that process by which the triumphalist Catholicism of the Spanish missionaries supposedly "conquered" the paganism and idolatry of the Indian pre-Hispanic religion. Yet the very term spiritual conquest, either in the sixteenth or in the twenty-first century, was never universally accepted as the proper way to speak of conversion or religion. Nor has it ever been universally accepted that the so-called spiritual conquest was successful.

In the sixteenth century many influential church intellectuals, most famously Vitoria, as professor of theology at Salamanca, argued that the military conquests of Mexico and Peru were essentially unjustified if they were undertaken with the express purpose of converting Indians or with the purpose of despoiling Indians of their natural right to self-government. In the twentieth century and into the twenty-first century historians have blanched at the term conquest as being too simple and one-sided, leaving the Indians without agency and without an intellect of their own. Recently, scholars have rethought the conceptualization of Indian-Spanish interaction on the religious front, forever placing in doubt the rubric of a "spiritual conquest" as uniform and complete. Moreover, the spiritual "conquest" was always fraught with the complexities of an ancient pre-Hispanic religio-cultural tradition that underlay the efforts of the Spanish missionaries. This meant that while many Indian communities ostensibly adopted Catholicism, many pre-Hispanic practices continued, such as the use of pulque and the clandestine worship of pre-Hispanic deities, or were integrated into Mexican society, such as the use of chocolate and the fusion of ancestor worship with All Saints' Day in the form of Day of the Dead.

One of the principal themes of this book concerns the extent to which religion as lived and practiced in colonial Mexico was a carry-over from Indian traditions, a mixture of Indian religion and Spanish Catholicism, or alternatively was a superimposition of Spanish Catholicism. But apart from the relative success or failure of a "spiritual conquest," there existed important divisions within Spanish Catholicism itself. The clergy at this time in Catholic Europe were divided between diocesan (secular) and mendicant (or regular). Diocesan clergy were associated with the diocese, or bishopric, and did not take on specific extra vows like poverty. Mendicant clergy, known as friars or monks, were clergy who took special vows of poverty and lived in monasteries. Importantly, in medieval and early modern Europe, friars in general did not administer sacraments to people outside their encloistered world. This meant that the diocesan clergy, who lived "in" the world—meaning, in cities, towns, and the countryside—and interacted with the laity on a daily basis, administered the sacraments of baptism, penance (confession), Eucharist (communion), marriage, and last rites to the populace. The sacraments of ordination and confirmation were reserved for the bishop in each diocese.

Two monastic orders have particular significance for the early development of the Mexican church: the Dominicans, founded by Saint Domingo de Guzmán in Spain and the Franciscans, founded by Saint Francis of Assisi in Italy, both in the thirteenth century. A third order, the Augustinian, also played an important role in missionary activity, importantly for our discussion here, in Michoacán. Cortés was himself a supporter of the Franciscans and for this reason asked the crown to send a group of them to begin the process of conversion in Mexico. The Franciscans arrived in 1524. The Dominicans followed shortly in 1527, and the Augustinians sent its own group of missionaries in 1532. In 1530, the first bishop of Mexico was appointed, the Franciscan Juan de Zumárraga, who later became archbishop when Mexico was raised to the level of an archdiocese. After Zumárraga's death, a Dominican, Alonso de Montúfar, was appointed archbishop of Mexico in 1551 and ruled the Mexican archdiocese for fifteen years, from 1554 until his death in 1569. The Jesuits, who arrived relatively late in the 1570s, tended to focus their energies on educating and training the Spanish and criollo population.[2]

The early dominance of the mendicant clergy in Mexico meant that the church in Mexico had special characteristics that differed from Spain. The friars viewed themselves as the shock troops of spiritual conquest. They were given wide privileges in the Indies to administer sacraments in the absence of diocesan officials—a privilege well beyond those they held in Europe. Friars had begun arriving in the Caribbean in the early years of the sixteenth century, and these privileges were formalized in two important papal bulls: *Alias felices* 1521 and *Exponi nobis fecisti* (also known as the *Omnímoda*) in 1522.[3]

The result was that instead of the diocesan clergy, Franciscans, Dominicans, and Augustinians served the Indians on a daily basis and administered the various activities normally reserved to diocesan officials—the sacraments of baptism, confession, Eucharist, and marriage, as well as the officiating of Mass. The friars also began to organize the Indians into small, community-based groups, known as *doctrinas*, to teach the Catholic faith. The power of the friars among the Indians and within the overall structure of the Mexican church did not go unquestioned. Many bishops complained vigorously that the friars wielded their authority without restraint, abused the Indians, and spent lavishly on new churches.[4]

The "Indian Question"

With the arrival of the friars and the establishment of a church structure in Mexico in the decade after the military conquest of the Valley of Mexico, a variety of consequential debates on the Indians and their relationship to the church began. The first major debate to ensue was the question over the Indians' humanity. In the early 1500s, theologians and jurists wondered whether Indians were in fact human beings, some species of animal, or, although appearing physically human, lacked basic human intellect. As was the case in all the debates on the Indians at this time, there was profound disagreement and debate over this most fundamental question.

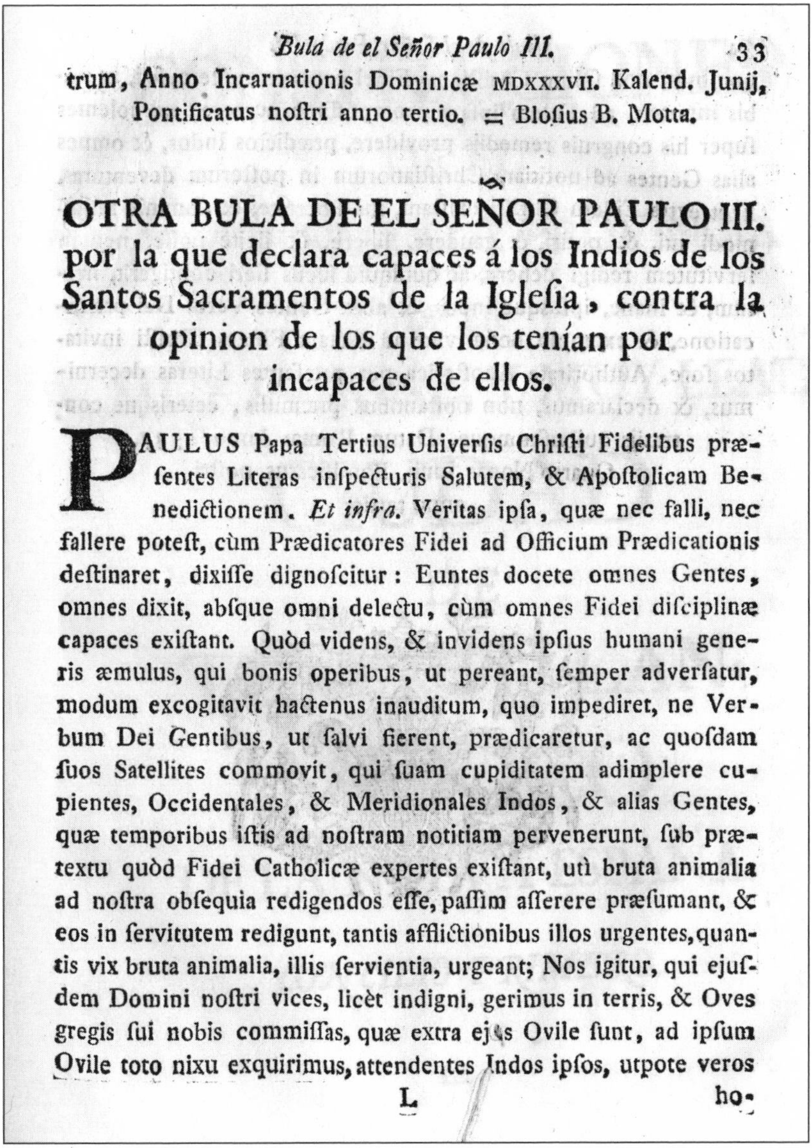

Bula de el Señor Paulo III. 33

trum, Anno Incarnationis Dominicæ MDXXXVII. Kalend. Junij, Pontificatus noftri anno tertio. = Blofius B. Motta.

OTRA BULA DE EL SEÑOR PAULO III.
por la que declara capaces á los Indios de los Santos Sacramentos de la Iglefia, contra la opinion de los que los tenían por incapaces de ellos.

PAULUS Papa Tertius Univerfis Chrifti Fidelibus præfentes Literas infpecturis Salutem, & Apoftolicam Benedictionem. *Et infra.* Veritas ipfa, quæ nec falli, nec fallere poteft, cùm Prædicatores Fidei ad Officium Prædicationis deftinaret, dixiffe dignofcitur: Euntes docete omnes Gentes, omnes dixit, abfque omni delectu, cùm omnes Fidei difciplinæ capaces exiftant. Quòd videns, & invidens ipfius humani generis æmulus, qui bonis operibus, ut pereant, femper adverfatur, modum excogitavit hactenus inauditum, quo impediret, ne Verbum Dei Gentibus, ut falvi fierent, prædicaretur, ac quofdam fuos Satellites commovit, qui fuam cupiditatem adimplere cupientes, Occidentales, & Meridionales Indos, & alias Gentes, quæ temporibus iftis ad noftram notitiam pervenerunt, fub prætextu quòd Fidei Catholicæ expertes exiftant, utì bruta animalia ad noftra obfequia redigendos effe, paffim afferere præfumant, & eos in fervitutem redigunt, tantis afflictionibus illos urgentes, quantis vix bruta animalia, illis fervientia, urgeant; Nos igitur, qui ejufdem Domini noftri vices, licèt indigni, gerimus in terris, & Oves gregis fui nobis commiffas, quæ extra ejus Ovile funt, ad ipfum Ovile toto nixu exquirimus, attendentes Indos ipfos, utpote veros

L ho-

FIGURE 6. Letter from Paul III, 1537

This is the beginning of one of Paul III's important 1537 declarations of the ability and right of Indians to receive Catholic sacraments. Taken from Concilios provincials primero y Segundo . . . dalos a luz el illmo. Sr. d. Francisco Antonio Lorenzana . . . *(Mexico: Joseph Antonio de Hogal, 1769). Courtesy of Mandeville Special Collections Library, University of California, San Diego.*

CONCILIOS PROVINCIALES

PRIMERO, Y SEGUNDO,

CELEBRADOS EN LA MUY NOBLE, Y MUY LEAL CIUDAD

DE MÉXICO,

PRESIDIENDO EL ILLMO. Y RMO,

SEÑOR D. Fr. ALONSO DE MONTÚFAR,
En los años de 1555, y 1565:

DALOS A LUZ

EL ILL.MO S.R D. FRANCISCO ANTONIO
LORENZANA,
Arzobispo de esta Santa Metropolitana Iglesia:

CON LAS LICENCIAS NECESARIAS
En México, en la Imprenta de el Superior Gobierno, de el Br. D. Joseph
Antonio de Hogal, en la Calle de Tiburcio, Año de 1769.

FIGURE 7. Concilios provincials

This is the frontispiece from Archbishop Lorenzana's eighteenth-century edition of the 1555 and 1565 Mexican church councils. Taken from Concilios provincials primero y Segundo . . . dalos a luz el illmo. Sr. d. Francisco Antonio Lorenzana . . . *(Mexico: Joseph Antonio de Hogal, 1769). Courtesy of Mandeville Special Collections Library, University of California, San Diego.*

It was at first certain Dominican friars who defended the Indians. Famously, in December 1511, in Hispaniola, the Dominican Antonio de Montesinos preached a fiery sermon condemning the brutal treatment of the Indians by Spanish conquistadors, asking: "Are they not men? Do they not have a soul and reason? Are you not obliged to love them as yourselves?" In the Church of the Trinity during this Advent sermon was a young Spanish encomendero, Bartolomé de las Casas, who was so affected, supposedly, that he joined the Dominicans and eventually became a principal critic of the encomienda system.[5] The first bishop of the diocese of Puebla (which at the time encompassed the states of Puebla, Veracruz, and Tlaxcala), the Dominican friar Julián Garcés, was an ardent defender of Indians, viewing them as innocent unspoiled children, in contrast with the Spaniards in Mexico whom he viewed as spoiled, lazy, and prone to violence and sexual deviance. Garcés, and priests like him, felt that it would be best to keep the Indians away from Spaniards, lest they corrupt the Indians with gambling, swearing, and whoring. It is possible that when in 1537 Paul III issued two bulls, *Unigenitus Deus* and *Sublimis Deus*, asserting that Indians were in fact humans and endowed with the ability to understand religion and the articles of the Catholic faith, he had been influenced by Garcés, who had written letters to his superiors in Spain on the matter.[6]

Not everyone shared Garcés's high opinion of the Indians and their moral purity. Many Spanish priests viewed the Indians as inherently lazy and corrupt. Friars found their ritual use of pulque abominable, and pre-Hispanic traditional rites like human sacrifice only added fuel to the anti-Indian bias.[7] Those who viewed the Indians as inherently immoral tended also to look askance at any efforts to recognize the Indians as intellectually or morally equal to Spaniards, arguing in terms of "civilization," meaning law, custom, and written language. For example, in Brazil it was common for the Portuguese to remark that the Indians of the coast had no F, L, or R in their language and were therefore "sem Fé, sem Lei e sem Rei," without faith, law, or king.[8] To the contrary Vitoria argued that the Indians in fact had all the important signs of civilized man: language, law, social custom, and organized religion. Vitoria did not mean to say that he thought that the Indians in the New World had developed the correct religion or laws or customs, but that by the mere presence of that development it could not be argued that the Indians were inhuman or uncivilized. Therefore, the Spaniards could not legally deprive Indians of their political dominion over themselves. According to Vitoria, one of the few just causes for military attacks on the Indians was if the Indians refused to allow the Spaniards to preach Catholicism.[9]

Others argued that their very customs and laws—the most common example used was the human sacrifice rituals practiced by the Mexica (Aztecs)—proved that the Indians were inferior and subhuman. The most notable proponent of this view was an Italian-educated Spanish jurist, Juan Ginés de Sepúlveda, who argued that Aristotle had proven that some men are slaves by nature by their intellectual inferiority. If this were the case, the Indians were clearly such slaves by nature and should rightfully be subjected to slavery by the Spanish conquerors. In a formal debate before the crown and Spain's most influential intellectuals in Valladolid, Spain, in 1550 Las Casas opposed Sepúlveda, arguing that the Indians could not legally be enslaved. Ultimately, Las Casas officially won the debate though slavery continued for some time thereafter.[10]

Besides the question of the Indians' humanity and the relative legality of the conquest, the missionaries debated the methods of evangelism. Few advocated conversion to Catholicism by force, but there was considerable debate on the proper way in which Indians were to be taught the new religion. Within this context was the all-important question of the extent to which the Indians should be instructed in the new faith and who should undertake this challenge.

The Augustinian Alonso de la Veracruz arrived in Mexico in 1536 and was one of the founders of the University of Mexico in 1553. He was a noted scholar of traditional European scholasticism, having studied theology at Salamanca under Vitoria. At this time western Mexico was relatively removed from the center of Spanish control. In fact, when the Spaniards arrived in Mexico in 1519 most of western Mexico, centered in the modern-day state of Michoacán, had never been conquered by the Mexica empire but had its own separate kingdom based in Tzintzuntzan, on the shores of Lake Pátzcuaro. In 1540 fray Alonso was sent by his order to Michoacán where he established a small college in Tiripetío.[11]

The Augustinian mission under fray Alonso's leadership differed from those early schools set up by Franciscans. Whereas most early schools in Mexico were segregated by ethnicity, fray Alonso insisted that all people, whether Indian or Spaniard, would be welcome to study at the new Augustinian college in Tiripetío, moving it later to Tacámbaro and Atotonilco. He taught theology and studied Purépecha (the principal native language of Michoacán) under the tutelage of Antonio Huitziméngari

Mendoza y Caltzontzín, son of the last king of Michoacán, while instructing the Indian noble in liberal arts, Spanish language, and theology. This interaction was innovative for the time, since in the other schools and colleges springing up in Mexico Indians were segregated in their own special schools for instruction from Spanish missionaries, as was the case in Texcoco.

Fray Alonso was one of the first humanists in Mexico to promote a wide-ranging curriculum for Indians and Spaniards alike. In addition to his central role in founding the University of Mexico, he penned treatises on humanism, physics, marriage, and the Eucharist, often specifically with an eye to the issue of Indians and their place in the new Mexican church. Fray Alonso maintained that some Indians were as capable as Spaniards in understanding the various levels of Catholicism if given the proper opportunity and education. In championing the mendicants and their various privileges, he made an enemy in the new archbishop and inquisitor, the Dominican, Montúfar, who did not appreciate humanism or its goal of making Scripture available to the laity along with more "liberal" strands of theology that called for the reform of monastic orders and the cult of the saints. Montúfar had attacked the friars on numerous occasions, saying that they spent too much money on churches, did not obey the diocesan officials, and overstepped their authority in marrying Indians.

Fray Alonso persisted in defending the same mendicant privileges, and finally Montúfar denounced the Augustinian missionary to the Inquisition in Spain for a short treatise titled *De decimis* (On Tithes). In it fray Alonso held that the Indians should not pay tithes because it would be a financial burden on them and because it would only go to support the diocesan clergy, whereas it was the mendicants who shouldered the burden of the missionary and education project throughout Mexico, including in the remote and mountainous terrain in Michoacán. Ultimately, fray Alonso was absolved by the Inquisition, but the debate was far from over. The Augustinian's run-in with the powerful archbishop was only one among a long list of encounters between two fundamentally distinct views of the Mexican church: that of the mendicants who viewed the conversion of the Indians as their special charge; and that of the diocesan authorities who viewed the power of the friars as too extensive and violating the inherent authority of the bishops. Michoacán witnessed far more dramatic encounters between the diocesan and mendicant clergy. Defenders of a centralized church, like its bishop don Vasco de Quiroga (a jurist and one-time Audiencia judge), went so far as to prohibit the Franciscans and Augustinians from building

new churches. Quiroga's supporter, the cleric Diego Pérez Gordillo Negrón
went so far as to burn down an Augustinian church in Tlazazalca, demolish
a baptismal font in the Franciscan church in Pátzcuaro, and physically attack
and threaten Franciscans if they intervened.[12]

The Eucharist was another central issue facing the missionary friars.
They asked themselves whether the Indians should be allowed to receive the
Eucharist and, if so, how often.[13] Many Dominicans held that the Eucharist,
as a sacramental manifestation of the highest mysteries of the faith, ought to
be restricted to those with extensive catechesis and that the Indians, as new
members of the church, did not merit this sacrament. An influential
Dominican, Bartolomé de Ledesma, governed the Archdiocese of Mexico
for the ailing Montúfar in the 1560s. Later he became bishop of Oaxaca and
published an influential treatise *Summa de sacramentis* (1566), which held
considerable sway among Mexican theologians in discussing questions of
administering sacraments to the Indians. Ledesma reasoned that daily communion was acceptable in absolute terms but that if someone was in a state
of mortal sin daily communion was not recommended. Others did not support any form of Indian communion. For example, the noted chronicler of
Indian culture, Dominican Diego Durán, viewed the Indians as inherently
idolatrous and therefore undeserving of the Eucharist.[14]

Others, however, supported Indian communion. Pedro de Agurto
was an Augustinian friar and student of Alonso de la Veracruz, professor
of theology at the University of Mexico, and later bishop of Cebu in the
Philippines. He argued in his 1573 *Tratado de que deven administrar los
Sacramentos de la Sancta Eucharistia y Extrema unción a los indios de Nueva
España* (Treatise That the Sacraments of the Holy Eucharist and Extreme
Unction Must be Administered to the Indians of New Spain) that it was
precisely the weak who needed the Eucharist the most; therefore, Indians
should receive communion.[15] After the Third Mexican Church Council
of 1585 it appeared that the pro-Indian communion faction had prevailed,
as the council supported the Indians' right to receive the Eucharist. Dr.
Hernando Ortiz de Hinojosa, a censor of the Mexican Inquisition and
professor of theology at the University of Mexico, wrote a memorial to
the council in his capacity as advisor, noting that many priests continued
to refuse this sacrament to Indians and that this violated church law.
Nevertheless, it appears that Ortiz de Hinojosa had a generally low opinion of Indians, stating, for example, that priests should not "demean"
themselves by accepting invitations for dinner at Indians' homes and that

Indians should be forbidden from depicting demons (as in paintings of Saint James) for fear of reverting to paganism. Here was a man "caught between two realities"—the generally bad state of the Indians (1585 was close to the nadir of the Indian population and the zenith of labor exploitation) and the recognition that Indians had innate mental capacities that equated their right to receive all sacraments.[16]

Education of the Indians and the administration of the Eucharist were only two important flashpoints in the broader debate on Indians and the missionary project in Mexico. Fierce debates and jurisdictional skirmishes broke out over other issues, such as the right or privilege of the friars to conduct Indian marriages. The mendicants would point to their privileges ceded to them in *Alias felices* and the *Omnímoda*, arguing that they were empowered to administer normally diocesan activities in the outlying regions of Mexico to the Indians. Likewise, tithes and the responsibility of the Indians to pay it or not provided constant friction between the friars and centralist bishops. The friars, however, viewed the Indians and their conversion as their special project and opposed the efforts of diocesan officials to chip away at their privileges.

Indian Language

Language was another serious issue. Mexico was home to hundreds of languages, none of which, at the time of conquest, had an alphabet. Friars and secular clergy alike had to translate not only basic Catholic concepts and words like God, Christ, cross, and Mary into Indian language but also preach in Indian languages and quote the Bible in native languages. One of the first impulses in the early decades of the missionary project in Mexico was a vigorous effort on the part of many friars to learn Indian languages and to establish schools for Indians to study Catholic doctrine, Latin, and Spanish. The Franciscans had arrived first in Mexico and as such had access to the most densely populated and strategically important Valley of Mexico, where Nahuatl (the language of the Mexica) dominated. In general, the Franciscans tended to be the leaders in Nahuatl study, but other important friar missionaries learned and promoted study of numerous other Indian languages, such as Purépecha in western Mexico, Zapotec in Oaxaca, and Maya in the Yucatán.[17]

Many missionary friars began to write short primers on the Catholic faith, called *doctrinas* (not to be confused with the physical grouping of

Indians also called *doctrinas*), in indigenous languages. These works began
to appear in numerous languages and were principally aimed at Spanish
priests. The reasoning among the authors of these works was that Spanish
priests who lived almost exclusively among Indians and whose work centered on converting Indians to Catholicism needed accurate discussions
of basic concepts in the native languages. Explaining the *Ave María* in
Spanish would have been useless to Indians who did not speak Spanish.

Major debates on Indian language works centered on the question of
translating the Bible into indigenous languages. In 1539 Zumárraga published in Spanish (and again later promoted its translation into Nahuatl) a
doctrina intended for Spanish priests and literate Spaniards. It explained
the various articles of the faith, the important prayers and the Ten Commandments, as was typical for these works. In his discussion on Scripture,
Zumárraga suggested that it was a good idea to translate the Bible into all
languages of the world to facilitate the spread of Christianity.[18] This was not
well received by conservative theologians who viewed such translation as
dangerous and offering the potential for heresy. Thus was exposed one of
the central debates between humanists and more conservative theologians
both in Spain and Mexico. Luther had translated the Bible into German,
and it was a resounding success, horrifying Inquisitional authorities and
conservative theologians in Spain, but there was no specific law banning
such translation when Zumárraga published his doctrina. In 1559 the
Spanish Inquisition banned once and for all any translation of the Bible into
vernacular (that is, non-Latin) languages, but did not specifically address the
circumstances of the New World.[19] Franciscans in particular continued to
insist that Indian language translations should be exempt from this rule,
given the unusual circumstances of Mexico and the Indies.

The central logic of the ban on vernacular-language translations of
the Bible was that the laity could not be trusted, especially in a time of
widespread heresy, to interpret the Scripture correctly. Instead, priests,
properly trained in theology, were entrusted with this task. By the 1570s
it was clear that many Franciscans defied the Spanish Index's prohibition
of vernacular (Spanish) Scriptural translations, keeping copies of them in
their monasteries and refusing to hand them over to the Inquisitional
authorities.[20] Although it is today lost, there was a popular manuscript
version of the book of Ecclesiastes in an "Indian language" (probably
Nahuatl). Eventually this translation came to the attention of the inquisitors in Mexico City, who ordered it banned in 1577. But in the process of

banning it, they convoked a panel of Indian-language missionary experts to ask the extent to which such prohibitions would hinder the missionary efforts. Unsolicited, the bishop of Yucatán, Franciscan Diego de Landa, argued against the ban in a letter to the inquisitors on January 19, 1578, stating that "until now there has been not a single thing of the Sacred Scripture translated into Indian language in this land" and that such translation was vitally important to the missionary project.[21]

The Inquisition called four theological and linguistic experts to testify on the controversy surrounding the Ecclesiastes manuscript, asking them if they knew of Indian-language translations of Scripture in circulation and what books in Indian language might be allowed for the sake of converting the Indians.[22] Two of the experts were Franciscan Nahuatl scholars: fray Alonso de Molina (himself author of a *Confessionario* in Nahuatl) and fray Bernardino de Sahagún, the intellectual leader of the Franciscan college at Tlatelolco and author of the now famous *Historia general de las cosas de Nueva España* (also called the *Florentine Codex*). Two Dominicans were also called, both experts in Zapotec: fray Juan de la Cruz, the vicar of his order in Mexico, and fray Domingo de la Anunciación, who had written a doctrina in Zapotec.

Franciscans Molina and Sahagún argued that Indian-language translations of Scripture ought to be allowed and that their prohibition would damage the efforts of the missionaries. They maintained that it would be virtually impossible for friars and missionaries to explain important concepts to the Indians in sermons without accurate translations of the Bible on which to draw. The two Dominicans did not share this view of the necessity and argued that the potential danger of heresy far outweighed the benefit.[23]

The end result was that the Bible was banned entirely in Indian languages, and no translation into any Indian language ever appeared in the colonial period. Some books, like the *Confessionario* of Molina and the *Doctrina* of de la Anunciación, were allowed to circulate but by the late sixteenth century other factors led to a radical decline in Indian-language doctrinas and primers on the faith. Plagues and widespread epidemics reduced the Indian population to less than 10 percent of its original by the early seventeenth century.[24] Amid this massive demographic disaster and the increasingly conservative view of Indian-language studies, the publication of indigenous-language material dropped sharply after the formal prohibition of the Ecclesiastes manuscript.

Tlatelolco

Tlatelolco was a semi-independent city of the Mexica empire located just to the north of the famed capital of that empire, the city of Tenochtitlan, in today's Mexico City megalopolis. In the early sixteenth century Franciscan friars established a monastery in Tlatelolco, and the church, built largely with Mexican volcanic rock, remains standing in front of what is today called the Plaza de las Tres Culturas (Plaza of the Three Cultures)—the Indian, Spanish, and Mexican-mestizo cultures.[25]

Tlatelolco became home to Mexico's most ambitious college for Indian education—the Colegio de Santa Cruz—an idealistic school of linguistic study of Nahuatl and Indian culture, where Indians, under the tutelage of such luminaries as fray Bernardino de Sahagún, studied classical Latin, Spanish grammar, and Catholic theology in preparation for the priesthood. At Tlatelolco threads of the various debates on the Indians and their inherent rights and intelligence were brought together in a focal point of discord between those who viewed the Indians as potentially fully realized members of the church and those who viewed the Indians as inherently dissolute and intellectually unqualified to grasp the higher complexities of the Catholic faith.

The debate on indigenous-language doctrinas and translations was one of the central issues of the overall Indian education project led, in general, by humanist Franciscans who viewed Mexico as a new church, a place where Lutherans and other heretics had yet to penetrate and where the Indians had lived in a state of simplicity. At the same time the debate on translating Scripture was occurring, there was a confrontation over the even more monumental Franciscan project centered in Tlatelolco that saw as its purpose the training of an Indian clergy.[26]

No school set out with such radical vision for Indian education as did the Colegio de Santa Cruz de Tlatelolco. Sebastián Ramírez de Fuenleal, the former bishop of Santo Domingo (today's Dominican Republic), began supporting an even more ambitious educational project for Indians in 1531 as president of the second Audiencia of Mexico. The Franciscans quickly supported the project and were entrusted as its custodians. The humanist Jacobo de Testera sent two Franciscans to Tlatelolco to begin instruction to Indians in 1534 or 1535 (it is unclear when they actually arrived). Around January 1536 the Colegio de Santa Cruz de Tlatelolco was inaugurated and on September 3 of the same year, the crown formally gave it a license by *real cédula* (royal decree).[27]

Inspired by Erasmian and utopian humanism, the Franciscans had three goals for the new college: (1) to form a firmly Catholic Indian laity; (2) to train a future Indian priesthood; and (3) to provide linguists and translators to help illiterate Indians obtain access to Scripture and liturgy. The methods by which this project would be achieved followed classic humanist lines. The Franciscans learned Nahuatl and in turn instructed the Indians at the college in Latin and Spanish. This was not entirely a shift from pre-Hispanic forms—the Franciscans had adopted the Mexica concept of a *calmecac*, which was a school for the Indian elite. So too would be Tlatelolco: it was to train an academic, theological Indian elite to help the missionaries in the conversion and catechesis project. But the Franciscans departed notably from Mexica education norms when they suggested that Tlatelolco was to be a training ground for priests. In pre-Hispanic educational systems, the sons of the upper classes attended the calmecac for education and moral training and the standards were rigorous even by Catholic mores. But it was understood that most of these young men would go on to marry and become laymen. The Franciscan model, however, was that of the monastery and the priesthood—a permanent state instead of the temporary state of education for the Mexica calmecac.

The Franciscans adopted the physical location of an almost exclusively Indian area and the intellectual concept of the calmecac for their own missionary efforts. This was not accidental—the Franciscans had established their principal monastery in the center of the new Mexico City, and it was there, at San Francisco, that Spaniards were educated. They chose Tlatelolco as an important site of Indian population instead of the Hispanicized center of Mexico City.

The project at Tlatelolco was not without its critics who thought the Indians were incapable of higher education and were morally corrupt. The Franciscans who promoted Tlatelolco shared to some extent this paternalistic view but with considerably less vehemence. As William Taylor explains in his essay in this collection, Franciscans did not exactly view Indians as intellectual equals but rather as innocent children (and therefore inherently immature). Nevertheless, for Franciscans the predominant metaphor of Indian religiosity was that of neophytes in Christ. Therefore, according to this logic, the Franciscans should be their guardians in their journey out of idolatry and into Christianity. The Dominicans, in general, were generally suspicious of the Tlatelolco project, both for its utopian humanism and because the Dominicans had

viewed the Franciscans in Mexico as little better than heretics and trou-
blemakers as well as being far too rich. Indeed, some Dominicans viewed
the Franciscans as a kind of fifth column striving to establish their own
unique and private church within the wider Mexican church.

Tlatelolco was guided by the principle that linguistic knowledge was
central to the success of the missionary efforts in Mexico. The Franciscan
Maturino Gilberti had promoted such a view and effort in Michoacán
with his studies of Purépecha and translations of Spanish Catholic classics
like the *Flossanctorum* (Lives of the Saints) into that Indian language.
Alonso de la Veracruz likewise had been a vigorous proponent of linguistic studies—Indians in Latin and Spanish and Spanish friar-missionaries
in Indian languages. Even the Dominicans, despite their view that
widespread translations were unnecessary and that scriptural translation
into any language besides Latin was illegal, recognized the need for basic
doctrinal and catechetical works and were the recognized experts in
Zapotec and Mixtec, the principal languages of Oaxaca.[28]

Despite the idealism of the Franciscan strain of humanism, not all
Franciscans agreed on the issues of Indian education. On the one hand, the
Franciscans tended to be idealistic about the potential of Indians to become
fully realized Christians. Simultaneously, the Franciscans were constantly
worried that they would revert to idolatry. A famous example of this tension
was the prosecution of prominent Indian nobles under the aegis of the
Mexican Inquisition when a Franciscan, Zumárraga, was both apostolic
inquisitor and archbishop of Mexico. The General Council of the Holy
Office of the Spanish Inquisition had ruled that the Indians were not subject to the Inquisition, using the exact logic of the Dominicans—namely,
that the Indians were not fully realized members of the church. Despite this
prohibition, Zumárraga prosecuted and executed on the bonfire the Indian
noble and cacique don Carlos of Texcoco for idolatry and bigamy in 1539.
As a result of this trial and execution, the General Council of the Spanish
Inquisition shortly thereafter revoked Zumárraga's authority as inquisitor
of Mexico.[29]

The other practical result of the Franciscan concerns over Indian
idolatry was the work of Sahagún at Tlatelolco, a Spanish friar who had
mastered Nahuatl and taught at Tlatelolco. For more than three decades
he taught Indians Latin and Spanish and wrote a variety of works on the
general issues of Indian evangelism and conversion. But it was his massive
historical project of pre-Hispanic Mexico that consumed most of his

energies. In the *Historia general de las cosas de Nueva España*, Sahagún engaged in what some scholars have called the first full-scale anthropological fieldwork. His *Historia* was a wide-ranging study of the culture, religion, society, and history of Mexico before the Spanish conquest. One of the basic ideas was to provide a guide to that culture and religion for missionaries. Since he was a master of Nahuatl, he began to conduct widespread interviews with Indians from the Valley of Mexico. He employed Indians fluent in Spanish and Latin as scribes to write down the information gathered in these interviews.[30]

The result of several decades of intense work, Sahagún intended to publish his monumental work, but he encountered opposition from within his own order. Many began to worry that in his history the Indians would rediscover information that they might have forgotten and therefore relapse into idolatry. Indeed, within the Franciscan order in Mexico there was a wide range of thought concerning the Indians and their culture. They learned Indian languages to understand their culture but were horrified by things like pulque and bigamy. Sahagún, like others in his order, viewed pre-Hispanic religion as satanic and idolatrous yet considered its historical preservation as an important piece of the evangelization project. In other words Sahagún's work was to act as a guide or encyclopedia for the young and inexperienced missionary. Other Franciscans, however, viewed Indian culture with such horror that they felt it best to demolish rather than preserve it. Zumárraga, for one, promoted the view that it was best to destroy Indian representations of pre-Hispanic religion and deities. In a 1532 letter to the general chapter of the Franciscan order, Zumárraga reported that in Mexico "more than 250,000 men have been baptized, 500 temples have been destroyed and more than 26,000 figures of demons, which the Indians worshipped, have been demolished and burned."[31] De Landa destroyed countless Mayan books on astrology, history, and religion. The same impulse to eradicate Indian religious representations led also to the confiscation of Sahagún's work four decades later. Sahagún was ordered to send his manuscripts to Spain in the 1570s, where Philip II had them banned, and they remained unpublished for more than two centuries. In its own day, the *Historia general* was viewed with skepticism and fear, but today it is recognized as one of the great achievements of both Tlatelolco and the Franciscan missionary effort and Nahuatl studies.

Although Sahagún is today remembered as the linguistic genius of Tlatelolco, it was a Spanish Franciscan in Salamanca who was its greatest philosophical defender. Alfonso de Castro, a theologian and legal scholar in Spain, was second only to Vitoria in influence among sixteenth-century Spanish intellectuals, yet he is forgotten today among North Americans. He wrote an unpublished *parecer* (or, minitreatise) in 1543, asking the fundamental question: Should Indians be trained in liberal arts and theology and thus trained for the priesthood? Castro specifically had Tlatelolco in mind as an example of the effort to train Indians in theology. The content of this parecer and Castro's argument form an important part of the Franciscan defense of the Indians and their inherent intellectual capabilities.[32]

Born in Zamora in 1495, Castro began his university studies around 1507, probably at Alcalá de Henares. In 1510, Castro took the Franciscan habit in Salamanca. By 1515 he held a chair of theology at Alcalá and subsequently taught theology in the Franciscan house at Salamanca. Charles V made him his confessor as well as royal advisor.[33] By 1535 he had made Salamanca his permanent home in the Franciscan monastery where he taught and preached what were considered the most popular sermons of his day. In 1545 and 1547 he went to the Council of Trent as Philip II's personal theologian. He was nominated bishop of Compostela in 1557 but fell ill and died on February 4, 1558, before taking possession of the diocese.[34]

Castro was a prolific and wide-ranging writer. As a trusted servant of the Charles V, he was charged with defending the marriage of Catherine of Aragon to Henry VIII of England in his lost *Memoria sobre la validez del matrimonio de Catalina de Aragón con Enrique VIII*. His *Adversus omnes haereses* (Against All Heresies), published first in 1534 in Paris, represented his debut as a serious theorist of law and theology; this work went through twenty editions between 1534 and 1568. His *De justa haereticorum punitione* (On the Just Punishment of Heretics) of 1547 solidified his reputation as a formidable theorist.[35]

Besides these influential treatises, Castro wrote a discussion of Indian ordination and Tlatelolco, "Utrum indigenae novi orbis instruendi sint in mysteriis theologicis et artibus liberalibus" ("Whether Indians of the New World Should be Instructed in Theological Mysteries and Liberal Arts") in Salamanca in 1543. It was directed to the Council of the Indies in an effort to defend the Franciscan project of training an Indian priesthood at Tlatelolco.[36] In this treatise Castro emerged as the most vigorous defender of Indian intellectual ability and Indian ordination as priests of the sixteenth-century Spanish empire—something that even the so-called defenders of the Indians, Las Casas and Vitoria, did not advocate.

Castro wrote his argument when Tlatelolco was at its height, producing brilliant trilingual Indian scholars fluent in Nahuatl, Latin, and Spanish. Vitoria himself signed the manuscript with his approval, noting that he could not fathom the ignorance of those who rejected the goals of educating Indians—strong words for a man whose own order militated against the Tlatelolco project. Although Castro was clearly at the center of this major debate, his *parecer* has remained unknown and overshadowed by the considerably more extensive efforts of Sahagún. Nevertheless, Castro fully understood the central issues surrounding the project at Tlatelolco and condensed them into a forceful defense of Indian education.

Castro outlined three objections to Indian education in theology: (1) Indians are inconstant in the faith, easily revert to idolatry and paganism, and can thus use the doctrine against the faith; (2) the biblical warning applies that one ought not cast pearls before swine lest they trample them underfoot; since the mysteries of the faith are indeed pearls of wisdom and since the Indians are irreparably united to polygamy and sodomy, they should not be allowed to denigrate the pearls of wisdom; (3) just as Scripture contains, as a tabernacle, the mysteries of the faith, and even the populace of the Old Testament did not see those mysteries, so too the Indians should be denied access to those mysteries.

Before Castro rejected each of these objections in turn, he offered a more general defense of Indian higher education and ordination. He looked to the primitive church of the first three centuries as evidence that not only should neophytes be given the opportunity to study the faith, but that the primitive church itself trained an indigenous clergy to continue its missionary efforts. Castro first asserted some basic early modern conceptions about theology and the laity. It was long standard to argue that the laity did not need to study the more complex mysteries of the faith. Castro also relied on Corinthians (I Cor. 3:1) in which Paul says that infants in Christ were fed with milk in place of solid food until they were ready to digest more substantive matter and held that the newly converted should not study higher mysteries of the faith. But, rejecting the argument that the Indians as an entire race were inconstant, Castro asserted that the question had nothing to do with ethnicity or nationality, but with faith. Indeed, just as among old believers, as in the case of Spaniards, only some men were properly endowed to study theology. So too was the case with the Indians.

For Castro, it was a question of individual intelligence and faith, not skin color or national origin. In 1543 this was a radical and innovative claim. Even Las Casas viewed Indians as mentally inferior and wholly supported the view that black Africans deserved slavery. When Castro asserted that Indians were much like Spaniards—some stupid, some mediocre, and some inherently brilliant—he promoted a view even more radical than many of the idealistic Franciscans who were working in Tlatelolco. He held that as new converts grew in the faith, some would be recognized for their abilities and those should be instructed in theology and trained as priests in order to spread Catholicism among the lay Indians. Castro concluded that, "there are men who think that Holy Scripture and true theology should not be revealed to the Indians nor that the degree of doctor be committed to them, because in their supercilious arrogance they want to claim this position only for themselves."[37] Although Castro did not refer specifically to the Dominicans, he almost certainly had them in mind (in particular, the founder of the Dominican mission in Mexico, Domingo de Betanzos, a noted enemy of Indian education). He viewed the Dominicans as arrogant and criticized them extensively in his work on law. In one of his treatises on heresy, for example, he rejected the view that simply by virtue of being a Dominican one was exempt from suspicion of heresy—a view, he said, that he "could not stomach."[38]

Castro made a further, practical, point for the ordination of Indians. If the missionary project ostensibly had as its goal the salvation of souls, then were Spain to lose the Indies and the Indians were left without Spanish priests, who would continue the work of evangelization, preaching, and interpretation of Scripture? To his mind this was a far worse potential conclusion than the possibility (which, in any case, he rejected) that Indians would misinterpret theology. For Castro the danger that millions of souls would be lost to the devil was much worse than the danger that some Indians would become bad priests. He suggested that the Mexican church was just like the early church of the Middle East, pointing out that the original Christian Church would never have grown if converts were prohibited from becoming priests.

Drawing on the Socratic/Platonic view that learning is about coming to correct conclusions rather than thinking individually, Castro pointed out that education produces not only faith but also obedience. Thus training an Indian clergy would allow the Indians to learn obedience to the Holy Mother Church as well as faith in Christ. Besides these practical concerns, there were theological ones. Augustine had taught that those who have a true desire to learn the mysteries of the faith ought to be allowed to do so in ascending order of complexity. Furthermore, a staple of Augustinian thought was that the church was the congregation of the faithful. Were not the Indians among those faithful, having been baptized, asked Castro? Surely that was the case. Therefore, he argued that one could not correctly draw a distinction between Spain and Mexico, since in both cases baptism and the Gospel produced faithful Christians.

Castro concluded by constructing specific rejections of the three objections to Indian theological education at the beginning of his text. As for Indian inconstancy, Castro used an argument common to many Franciscan missionaries: by nature the Indians were highly religious, pious, and faithful. Moreover, Castro noted that the question of innate nature failed to appreciate the soteriological (meaning, the potential for salvation) value of baptism and faith. He accepted that Indians may have been idolaters, fornicators, or sodomites before baptism, but concluded that such cultural evidence was a moot point since the important question was their faith and constancy after baptism. On this score Castro found the objection stupid and ignorant (using precisely such language). He made the same argument for pearls before swine. If, before baptism, Indians were given over to "obscene vices" this was unimportant—so long as they were baptized and held faith they could not properly be called swine undeserving the pearls of the faith. Third, he rejected the prohibition on lay interaction in mysteries of the faith on a basic level as uncharitable and un-Christian. For Castro, "by his passion [crucifixion] God withdrew the veil from us so that we might see the mysteries clearly."[39]

All in all, Castro offered a forceful argument in favor of Indian education and ordination. This argument has been forgotten in the modern investigation of Tlatelolco, linguistics, and Sahagún as the supposed first anthropologist of the Americas. Yet Vitoria signed the parecer of Castro offering his support, demonstrating that Castro's short treatise was received in the same circles of debate known as the School of Salamanca—where professors and jurists disputed the humanity of the Indians and affected royal policy. My suggestion is that given the heavily theological content of Castro's discussion it has been largely ignored. Why have Vitoria and Las Casas endured as subjects of historical inquiry, where Castro has largely faded from view? Las Casas has endured because he is seen today as a champion of modern concepts like political rights despite his constant support for black slavery, whereas Castro argued for educational opportunities and religious training. In the case of Vitoria, his popularity is more complex. Although he was a theologian like Castro, he was a political theorist, a wholly "modern" occupation. But if one looks to the evidence in terms of editions published, book sales, library purchases, citation by contemporaries, availability in bookstores in the sixteenth and seventeenth centuries, Castro dwarfs Las Casas and Vitoria as an author. Indeed, few theologians of the early modern period viewed Las Casas as a serious intellectual. In Mexico, before the mid-1600s editions of Las Casas were virtually nonexistent whereas Castro's influence was widespread among the high-ranking clergy and jurists.[40]

Again, the question: Why has Castro become a forgotten historical actor? The reason appears to be linguistic. Castro's works have not been translated. Although his discussion of Indian ordination has been translated into a brief and incomplete edition in Spanish, it has attracted little attention, and his major theological and legal works have never been translated out of Latin. The project of Tlatelolco was the training in multiple languages and the goal the linguistic and cultural interaction between three cultures: Indian, Spanish, and Latin/theological. The most effective defender of Tlatelolco is now forgotten as the direct result of linguistic barriers.

Just as Castro's parecer was forgotten and Sahagún's massive *Historia general* went unpublished for two centuries, so did Tlatelolco fall into disrepair and decline. Royal funding for the humanist project was cut. In 1559 the Index of Prohibited Books condemned vernacular scriptural translations and in 1577 the Inquisition prohibited the Indian-language Ecclesiastes manuscript. Plagues and epidemics reduced the Indian population of Mexico dramatically. The first two Provincial Councils of the Mexican church in 1555 and 1565, dominated by the Dominicans and their champion, Archbishop Montúfar, prohibited the ordination of Indians as priests. As a result, the idealistic fervor of men like Castro was defeated in very real terms. By 1570 Tlatelolco ceased to function as a formal theological school for Indians, and while it continued on a much smaller scale as a monastery, it was a shadow of its former glory.

NOTES

1. For a standard discussion of this, see Anthony Pagden, *The Fall of Natural Man: The American Indian and the Origins of Comparative Ethnology* (Cambridge: Cambridge University Press, 1986).

2. Pilar Gonzalbo Aizpuru, *Historia de la educación en la época colonial: La educación de los criollos y la vida urbana* (Mexico: El Colegio de México, 1999); Robert Ricard, *The Spiritual Conquest of Mexico*, trans. Leslie Byrd Simpson (Berkeley: University of California Press, 1982). For a comprehensive overview, see Mariano Cuevas, *Historia de la Iglesia en México*, 5 vols. (Mexico: Ed. Patria, 1946–47). For further discussion of issues of jurisdiction and church development in colonial Mexico, also see John Frederick Schwaller, ed., *The Church in Colonial Latin America*, Jaguar books on Latin America, no. 21 (Wilmington, DE: Scholarly Resources, 2000).

3. Jesús García Gutiérrez, ed., *Bulario de la Iglesia mejicana: Documentos relativos a erecciones desmembraciones, etc. de Diócesis mejicanas* (Mexico: Ed. "Buena Prensa," 1951). For more general discussions of the development of the clergy in sixteenth century Mexico, see John Frederick Schwaller, *The Church and Clergy in Sixteenth-Century Mexico* (Albuquerque: University of New Mexico Press, 1987).

4. As was the case with Archbishop Montúfar and his attempts to impose a centralized, Tridentine order on the Mexican church in the 1560s. See Cuevas, *Historia de la Iglesia en México*. Transcriptions of many of Montúfar's attacks on the mendicants can be found in Robert Ricard, *Etudes et documents pour l'histoire missionnaire de l'Espagne et du Portugal* (Louvain, Belgium: AUCAM, 1930).

5. See Marcel Bataillon and André Saint-Lu, *Las Casas et la défense des Indiens* (Paris: Julliard, 1971).

6. See Julián Garcés, "Carta a la Santidad de Paulo III," in *Bulario de la Iglesia mejicana*.

7. For an intriguing recent study of missionaries and attitudes toward Indians and cultural morals, especially concerning pulque and drunkenness, see Sonia Corcuera de Mancera, *El fraile, el indio, y el pulque: Evangelización y embriaguez en la Nueva España (1523–1548)* (Mexico: Fondo de Cultura Económica, 1991). For discussions of the use of alcohol by Indians on a local level, see William B. Taylor, *Drinking, Homicide, and Rebellion in Colonial Mexican Villages* (Stanford, CA: Stanford University Press, 1979).

8. See João Adolfo Hansen, "A servidão natural do selvagem e a guerra justa contra o bárbaro," in *A descoberta do homen e do mundo*, ed. Adauto Novaes (São Paulo: Companhia das Letras, 1998).

9. Francisco de Vitoria, *Political Writings*, ed. Anthony Pagden and Jeremy Lawrance (Cambridge: Cambridge University Press, 1991).

10. The best overview of the debate in English is found in Pagden, *Fall of Natural Man*. Also see Venancio P. Carro, *La teología y los teólogos-juristas españoles ante la conquista de América*, 2 vols. (Madrid: Marsiega, 1944), Demetrio Ramos, ed., *Francisco de Vitoria y la escuela de Salamanca: La ética en la conquista de América* (Madrid: Consejo Superior de Investigaciones Científicas, 1984) for more detailed discussions of Spanish theology and jurisprudence and their relationship to questions of natural law, dominion, and papal power.

11. For a good intellectual biography of the Augustinian, see Arthur Ennis, *Fray Alsono de la Vera Cruz, O.S.A. (1507–1584): A Study of His Life and His Contributions to the Religious and Intellectual Affairs of Early Mexico* (Louvain, Belgium: E. Warny, 1957). For more comprehensive discussion of his intellectual achievements in the context of colonial Mexican philosophy and theology, see José Manuel Gallegos Rocafull, *El pensamiento mexicano en los siglos XVI y XVII* ([Mexico]: Centro de Estudios Filosóficos, 1951).

12. For discussion of these events, see Ricardo León Alanís, *Los orígines del clero y la iglesia en Michoacán, 1525–1640* (Morelia: Universidad Michoacana de San Nicolás de Hidalgo; Instituto de Investigaciones Históricas, 1997).

13. An excellent overview of the issue is found in Luis Martínez Ferrer, *La penitencia en la primera evangelización de México (1523–1585)* (Mexico: Universidad Pontificia de México, 1998).

14. Josep Ignasi Saranyana, "La eucaristía en la teología sacramentaria Americana del siglo XVI," in *Eucaristía y nueva evangelización. Actas del IV Simposio la Iglesia en España y América: Siglos XVI-XX* (Córdoba: Caja Sur, 1994).

15. Saranyana, "La eucaristía." For details of Agurto's career, see Archivo General de la Nación (México) (AGN), Inquisición, vol. 66, exp. 5, fs. 45–82; and Albero María Carreño, ed., *Efemérides de la real y pontificia universidad de México según sus libros de claustros*, vol. 1 of 2 (Mexico: UNAM, 1963).

16. Saranyana, "La eucaristía." For his role as theological advisor at the Council, see Martínez Ferrer, *Penitencia en la primera evangelización;* and Stafford Poole, *Pedro Moya de Contreras: Catholic Reform and Royal Power in New Spain, 1571–1591* (Berkeley: University of California Press, 1987).

17. For a recent overview of Indian language studies, see Bárbara Cifuentes con la colaboración de Lucina García, *Letras sobre voces: Multilingüismo a través de la historia* (Mexico: Centro de Investigaciones y Estudios Superiores en Antropología Social; Instituto Nacional Indigenista, 1998).

18. Juan de Zumárraga, *La doctrina breue muy prouechosa* (Mexico: Cromberger, 1543).

19. J. M. de Bujanda, *Index de l'inquisition espagnole, 1551, 1554, 1559,* directeur J. M. de Bujanda, vol. V of XI, Index des livres interdits (Sherbrooke, Quebec; Geneva: Centre d'études de la Renaissance, Université de Sherbrooke; Librairie Droz, 1984).

20. As manifested in the inventory of books pulled out of circulation in the early 1570s found in AGN, Jesuitas, III–26, exp. 2.

21. AGN, Inquisición, vol. 90, exp. 42.

22. AGN, Inquisición, vol. 43, exp. 4.

23. AGN, Inquisición, vol. 43, exp. 4.

24. For overviews of the epidemics, see Noble David Cook, *Born to Die: Disease and New World Conquest, 1492–1650* (Cambridge: Cambridge University Press, 1998); and Alfred W. Crosby, *The Columbian Exchange: Biological and Cultural Consequences of 1492*, forward by Otto von Mering (Westport, CT: Greenwood, 1973).

25. To contemporary minds Tlatelolco is a reminder of the seventy-year protodictatorship of the PRI and its secret state police active in itscampaign of intimidation of the 1960s and 1970s, in which many were imprisoned, tortured, or disappeared for political reasons. On October 2, 1968, hundreds of students protesting the policies of the PRI were gunned down in a government-sponsored massacre in the plaza.

26. A great deal has been written about Tlatelolco's most famous proponent, Sahagún. The literature is extensive. See, for example, Luis Nicolau D'Olwer, *Fray Bernardino de Sahagún (1499–1590)*, forward by Miguel León-Portilla, trans. Mauricio J. Mixco (Santa Fe, NM, and Salt Lake City: School of American Research; University of Utah, 1987); Miguel León-Portilla, *Bernardino de Sahagún: Pionero de la antropología* (Mexico: UNAM; El Colegio Nacional, 1999); Michael Mathes, *Santa Cruz de Tlatelolco: La primera biblioteca académica de las américas* (Mexico: Archivo Histórico Diplomático, 1982).

27. José María Kobayashi, *La educación como conquista (empresa franciscana en México)* (Mexico: Fondo de Cultura Económica, 1974).

28. Cifuentes and García, *Letras sobre voces*; Joaquín García Icazbalceta, "La orden de predicadores en México," in vol. 2 of 10, *Obras* (Mexico: Imp. de V. Agüeros, 1896–99).

29. Richard Greenleaf, *Mexican Inquisition in the Sixteenth Century* (Albuquerque: University of New Mexico Press, 1969); *Historia de la Inquisición en España y América*, general ed. Joaquín Pérez Villanueva and Bartolomé Escandell Bonet, 3 vols. (Madrid: Biblioteca de Autores Cristianos; Centro de Estudios Inquisitoriales, 1984–2000).

30. See Sahagún, *Florentine Codex*.

31. Quoted in Joaquín García Icazbalceta, "La destrucción de antigüedades," in vol. 2 of 10, *Obras*: "baptizata sunt plusquam ducenta quinquaginta millia hominum; quingenta deorum templa destructa sunt, et plusquam vicesies mille figurae daemonum, quas adorabant, fractae et combustae."

32. The original manuscript is today in the Archivo General de Indias in Seville. I have relied on a transcription: Alfonso de Castro, "Utrum indigenae novi orbis instruendi sint in mysteriis theologicis et artibus liberalibus [ms., Salamanca, 1543]. Edición, transcripción y notas por Juan B. Olaechea Labayen," *Anuario de estudios americanos* 15 (1958).

33. Charles was King Charles I of Spain and Emperor Charles V of the Holy Roman Empire, though he was generally referred to as Charles V by contemporaries, referring to his pedigree as heir to the Hapsburg line.

34. Teodoro Olarte, *Alfonso de Castro (1495–1558): Su vida, su tiempo y sus ideas filosóficas-jurídicas* (San José: Universidad Nacional de Costa Rica, 1946).

35. For print editions of Castro, see Emil van der Vekene, *Biblioteca bibliographica historiae sanctae inquisitionis*, 2 vols. (Vaduz, Luxembourg: Topos, 1982).

36. Juan B. Olaechea Labayen, "Opinión de los teólogos españoles sobre dar estudios mayores a los Indios," *Anuario de estudios americanos* 15 (1958). A Spanish translation of Castro's treatise can be found in Ignacio Osorio Romero, *La enseñanza del latín a los indios* (Mexico: UNAM, 1990).

37. Castro, "Utrum indigenae": "Hi autem qui sentient Sacram Scripturam et veram Theologiam non esse indis revelandam nec illis doctoris officium committendum, forte quia superciliose nimis et arroganti sibi solis hoc munus vendicare volunt."

38. Alfonso de Castro, *Adversus omnes haereses* (Cologne: ex officina Melchioris Nouesiani, 1549), 20: "non possum stomachari in eso qui ut suum institutum laudent, non verentur coram populo iactare et dicere, eum qui semel habitum illius ordinis susceperet, non posse in fide errare eut deficere."

39. Castro, "Utrum indigenae": "Deus per passionem suam abstulit a nobis velamen ut clarius mysteria videre possimus."

40. For data on book editions, see Martin Austin Nesvig, "Pearls Before Swine: Theory and Practice of Censorship in New Spain, 1525–1640" (Ph.D. dissertation, Yale University, 2004), esp. appendices 4 and 5.

FIGURE 8. Monaquía Indiana

Juan de Torquemada was one of the early Franciscan missionaries in Mexico and composed an important synthesis of Franciscan chronicles of its order's activities in sixteenth-century Mexico. This is the frontispiece from the 1723 edition, depicting a Franciscan preacher teaching Indians the Catholic doctrine. Taken from Juan de Torquemada, Primera parte de los veinte i vn libros, rituals I Monarchía Indiana *(Madrid: Nicolás Rodríguez Franco, 1723). Courtesy of Mandeville Special Collections Library, University of California, San Diego.*

CHAPTER FOUR

Between Nativitas and Mexico City

An Eighteenth-Century Pastor's Local Religion

WILLIAM B. TAYLOR

When it first appeared in 1986, readers of the "Folk Religion" entry for *The Encyclopedia of Religion* were in for a surprise.[1] Rather than a standard treatment of rural "folk" or "popular" religion as something free-standing and self-generated—its authenticity established by the ways it stood apart from "high," official religion, and a universal church—author William Christian offered a more synoptic and processual conception of traditional religious practices in small places. Combining "the local natural and social world, as well as the wider social, economic, and political network of which they are a part," he called the subject "local religion" rather than folk religion. Christian emphasized that "the practical impingement of the institutions of a central religion on the religious life of peasants" could be as much a part of the history of popular faith as "the ways in which local practices may have departed from and challenged doctrine."

Christian's rethinking of the categories of high and low religion—without dissolving the distinction—complemented the ways I had begun to understand priests in their parishes in colonial Mexico and Indian peasants with parish priests.[2] I read his *Local Religion in Sixteenth-Century*

Spain (1981) and *Apparitions in Late Medieval and Renaissance Spain* (1981), and looked forward to the books and essays that followed. His Spanish studies interested me both as efforts to describe local religion in particular places and times, and for the connected and comparative possibilities they open to Latin Americanists. By "connected" I mean the ways Iberian practices and habits of thought became American.[3] And I mean "comparative" in the sense that differences between Spanish and American practices call for close examination and explanation, too.[4]

Christian's idea of local religion is best viewed as a challenge to fixed dichotomies in the study of religions (even when actors seem to express the dichotomies) that invites historical study, paradox, and wide-ranging contextualization. His local religion is not a magic wand of prescriptions about local practices, power, and principles of faith, but his Spanish studies provide suggestive leads for connected and comparative study of Mexico in the colonial period and beyond. Some of his leads invite comparisons about process: Did Marian and Christocentric devotions follow a similar course in Spain and Mexico? Were the origin stories for miracle shrines the same? Did sacred journeys differ? If so, why? Other leads invite more structural and functional comparisons: Were devotees' motives for visiting shrines and approaching the divine mainly instrumental, seeking personal favors in this life more than honoring the divine and acting on convictions and anxieties about salvation?[5]

This essay takes up one of Christian's structural leads: the idea that priests carried their own accumulated local religion and networks of authority, power, and knowledge with them into pastoral service. Parish priests were not just disembodied voices of official doctrine, orthodoxy, and institutional order. A seminary education, ordination, liturgical duties, and an institutional career did not wash away all the habits of faith they brought to the priesthood. The devotional practices they knew from childhood; their preference for particular saints and Marian advocations, holidays, scriptural passages, prayers, places, and miracle stories; their talents and inclinations as public figures and practitioners of the faith; and their personal sense of calling to the priesthood all may come into play.

This is largely the story of Francisco Antonio de la Rosa Figueroa, an eighteenth-century Franciscan friar of the Province of the Holy Gospel headquartered in Mexico City. The place and time are his period of service as pastor of the doctrina (protoparish) of Nativitas Tepetlatcingo, an Indian pueblo some eight miles south of downtown Mexico City, during

1739–40 and 1743–45. Father de la Rosa's extensive account of his time in Nativitas and miracles worked through an image of the Virgin Mary he found there determines this focus. Composed in 1775 and 1776, near the end of his life, it fills both sides of twenty-two folio sheets with closely spaced lines of his labored script.

There is more to his account than can be presented in this essay.[6] I concentrate here on two of its features that bear on his local religion and the people of Nativitas. One is the bifocal vision of place and time in his presentation of the miracles: Nativitas and Mexico City; and the 1740s events and the 1775–76 composition of the text. The other is his view of Nativitas's Indian parishioners as impediments or, at best, incidental witnesses rather than protagonists in the story of divine favor he tells. Father de la Rosa's personality, opinions, and enthusiasms come through strongly in his text, but his Indian parishioners are heard in it, too. I have given the parishioners a larger and different place in the story of local religion than he does by considering his treatment of them in light of other documentation about the community in the eighteenth century and other ways of reckoning with their activities. In discussing de la Rosa himself I have also reached beyond his self-conscious narrative to the record of his career that he would not have thought important to the story at hand or how he remembered his life.

The Pastor and His Text

Francisco de la Rosa's background and career take shape in scattered administrative records and passing remarks in his text. Mexico City was the pivotal place in his life, even during his residence elsewhere in central Mexico. He was born there in 1698, the only child of criollo Spanish parents. His father and several other members of the extended family were traders and shopkeepers. His father eventually served as *alcalde mayor* in two marginal districts, but was removed for some mismanagement of funds and died in penury, in the care of his son. De la Rosa began his religious vocation comparatively late and with two false starts, first as a Dominican novice in Mexico City in 1722 or 1723. He requested release from his vows soon thereafter, became a Franciscan novice in the Convento Recoleto de San Cosme in August 1723, again asked to leave after four months, and spent the following year in Chalcatzingo (Morelos) studying Nahuatl with the parish priest. He was readmitted to the Franciscan novitiate in May 1725 with the understanding that his earlier false starts had been "without blemish of any kind." He was ordained in the Province of the Holy Gospel and approved for pastoral duty by 1733.[7] At some point in the 1730s he was also licensed to do notarial work for the Inquisition. He was particularly proud of this association, and continued to correspond with Inquisition judges on matters of faith long after he left pastoral service.

De la Rosa opened his account of Nativitas's miraculous image of Mary with his own history of unhappy pastoral assignments, first in 1734 as assistant pastor in Tepepan, an Indian community in the Valley of Mexico near Xochimilco with a small shrine to Our Lady of los Remedios. After unspecified troubles with parishioners there, he was in Cuernavaca the next year when a group of zealous Spanish Franciscans from the newly established Colegio de San Fernando in Mexico City arrived to preach and hear confessions.[8] "This mission so startled my spirit and so moved my inclination to the missionary's life that I immediately decided to seek a way to leave the ministry among Indians and enter the Colegio de San Fernando," he wrote. Anxious to become part of their exalted enterprise of spiritual revival and leave behind the aggravations and tedium of a ministry among Indians, he applied for membership. But after a month's residence at the college he was denied a permanent place among the missionary preachers—denied, he thought, because just one member opposed him—and returned to the home monastery of his province in Mexico City.

After brief and equally unhappy appointments in several other Indian communities of central Mexico, he was assigned in 1739 to Nativitas Tepetlatcingo, south of Mexico City on the road to Coyoacán.[9] There he found a small, rundown establishment and few signs of spiritual life. "The little cloister," he wrote,

> seemed suspended in air; the church and sacristy crumbling; the
> walls riddled with harmful salt deposits; the paraphernalia of
> the liturgy absolutely indecent because of the Indians' filthiness;
> the store of possessions did not correspond to the written
> inventory; the account book was as full of crossouts and era-
> sures as the inventory. Considering all this, my blood froze.

On the advice of his friend Antonio Ramírez del Castillo, vicar general of the Archdiocese of Mexico, Father de la Rosa had Nativitas's rough wooden statue of the Virgin Mary reshaped by an Indian sculptor in

Tlatelolco. (One of the two major Indian districts of Mexico City. The other, San Juan, has an even more important place in this story that de la Rosa passes over.) To his astonishment the statue was transformed into an object of exquisite beauty. He moved quickly to have it richly attired with gold jewelry, pearls, and its own splendid wig. A "sacred magnet of hearts," he called it at one point, "celestial pearl" at another. He and the vicar general came up with the idea of displaying the image in Mexico City in order to increase its fame, raise funds for rebuilding the convent and church at Nativitas, and cover other costs of serving Our Lady. According to de la Rosa's account, the spirituality of the Indian parishioners was rekindled by their beautified statue, and they encouraged their priest in his plans to dignify the devotion with building projects and promote it beyond the pueblo. He noted in passing that elders from the pueblo always guarded the statue on its visits to the city.

Father de la Rosa started to promote the devotion to this image of Our Lady and rebuild the church and convent, but within a year he was transferred, first to Xochitepec, Morelos, and then to Santa María la Redonda, an Indian doctrina in Mexico City. Reluctantly he complied. (Indeed, these transfers may have been intended to teach an overactive spirit a lesson in obedience. He was quick to assure his Franciscan readers in 1775 that he always obeyed superior orders, as if there might be some lingering doubt.) Dispirited by the indifference and disobedience of his parishioners in Santa María la Redonda and broken in health, he tried to resign after less than two years there.[10]

To his surprise and delight, he was reassigned to Nativitas in 1743. Warming to the challenge, he set to work collecting money, materials, expert advice, and labor to rebuild the church and convent. He added a secure little roadside chapel for prayers and donations by passersby, furnishing it with a fine painting of his beloved statue of Our Lady, which he called Nuestra Señora del Patrocinio (Our Lady of Intercession). As his trips with the statue to the homes of wealthy residents of the capital became more frequent, the fame of the statue in the city grew. His ambitious plans and popular devotion in the city culminated in a great rosary procession of the statue through the center of the city during the Feast of the Immaculate Conception in early December 1743. According to de la Rosa's account, it was a lavish and joyful, yet decorous affair, with crowds of people following the statue into the cathedral and on to a special service he conducted at the Church of Regina Coeli (Queen of Heaven).

Now, with popular devotion at a glorious peak and a succession of miracles about to begin, Father de la Rosa was leading the spiritual revival he had dreamed of among the friars of the Colegio de San Fernando in 1735.

But the story of public devotion to Nuestra Señora del Patrocinio soon took an abrupt turn, largely unexplained in de la Rosa's telling. By the fall of 1744 his superiors denied him permission to take the statue to Mexico City, and before another year passed he was removed from Nativitas and assigned to the archive and library of his home monastery in Mexico City, remaining there until his death in 1777.[11] The excitement about Nativitas's image of Nuestra Señora del Patrocinio, at least in Mexico City, seems to have cooled about as fast as it warmed in the early 1740s. The only hint I have found of a subsequent history for the statue in Mexico City is a brief news item in the *Gazeta de México* for February 25, 1784, that it was among the images honored with a procession and novena of prayers during the epidemic that winter.[12]

Unlike devotional histories of miraculous images published at the time, much of de la Rosa's account is written in the first person and offers an unusually direct glimpse of the author's devotion to this image of the Virgin Mary and the enthusiasm and trouble his activities caused. It is distinctive also in being more than the vague reminiscence of an elderly priest hurrying to memorialize a defining time of his life and testify to the Virgin Mary's grace before the story was silenced by his death. The level of detail about putative miracles and his own contributions to the image's former popularity—sometimes detailed in ways that make a modern reader wince—is unusual. Attention to detail was second nature to him (his first impulse at Nativitas in 1739 was to size up an armoire in the sacristy for the administrative archive he planned to assemble), but it was also a rhetorical device to establish the text's authority and his own importance. In this it bears comparison to Bernal Díaz del Castillo's account of the Conquest of Mexico, his "True History of the Conquest of New Spain." Both Bernal Díaz and de la Rosa took care to prove themselves trustworthy, almost omniscient eyewitnesses with their wealth of firsthand information. De la Rosa wrote that his account of events and the collections and expenditures on behalf of Nuestra Señora del Patrocinio were based on copious notes he took at the time. He assured the reader that those notes and his personal participation in the events enabled him to be thorough and accurate: "Over the course of nearly three years I saw and experienced the mercies of this sovereign Queen in the way I recount here, without excessive praise or hyperbolic exaggerations." Both he and Bernal Díaz spent some of their twilight years looking back—actively looking, to be sure—on a career in the New World with an epic thread, but less glory and reward than they had hoped for.

Like Bernal Díaz's text, de la Rosa's is a historical account with two perspectives—one near to the events of 1739–45, the other more retrospective. For the most part it is a straightforward chronological presentation that retains some of the freshness of his experience and observations from the 1730s and 1740s, but with a shift in tone toward the end that underscores the preoccupations driving him to compose it in 1775–76. De la Rosa included his last copy of the printed image made for the grand celebration and procession of December 1743, placing it in the middle of the manuscript at the point chronologically when it was made and distributed. But it was there as more than documentation or a souvenir. He had commissioned one of the city's finest engravers, Manuel Troncoso, to create the image, and the result was gratifying. As de la Rosa explained, prints from Troncoso's beautiful engraving could themselves be a sacred medium if the devotion to Mary was fervent and sincere, including this one. He assured readers that a young woman recently recovered from a life-threatening seizure when she prayed to Nuestra Señora del Patrocinio and placed this print on her stomach. And a garbanzo bean that a small boy had stuffed way up his nose popped out when the print was placed on his head just a few days before de la Rosa finished writing his account.

"My Lady has covered the cost of the construction, confirming her sponsorship with frequent miracles"

Father de la Rosa's narrative is sprinkled with a bookkeeper's lists of the money, jewels, and building materials collected, and the outlays for construction and promotion of the cult of the Virgin during his service in Nativitas. It also contains more autobiography than one would expect to find in a published devotional history of a shrine or prodigious image. But it has in common with published devotional histories a keen interest in providential signs of the Virgin Mary's presence and special favors granted to faithful followers of Nuestra Señora del Patrocinio during those heady days of ardent devotion in the early 1740s. In his enthusiasm de la Rosa was quick to call them miracles—the term reserved for events that the church hierarchy had certified supernatural.[13] Building materials mysteriously became available; workers narrowly escaped harm at the construction site, and generous donors and other devotees recovered from illness.[14] He shaped his narrative around these "miracles," much like the official *informaciones jurídicas* compiled in the late sixteenth and seventeenth centuries to establish the authenticity of putative miracles.[15]

The account presents a master list of thirty-five miracles that express the author's bifocal vision of Nativitas and Mexico City. Most—twenty-six of thirty-five events—took place in Mexico City or for the benefit of *capitalinos* (capital residents). Individuals recovered their health or were protected from harm in nineteen of the twenty-six Mexico City miracles. Two of the other seven were gifts of building materials. The rest included the recovery of a lost animal, fulfillment of a prediction by a pious nun, an answered prayer for closing a gambling house, and two unspecified favors. One-third of the miracles were associated with Troncoso's prints rather than the statue. These miracles extended the reach of the Virgin Mary's mercy to the public places and homes of the weak and poor. Two-thirds of the individual beneficiaries of her grace were poor people, and most of the remaining third who enjoyed higher social standing and wealth were married women. Altogether, women account for fifteen of the twenty-five miracles for individuals. Were the poor and nominally powerless of Mexico City the most avid believers in the Virgin's mediation and this particular advocation? De la Rosa evinces no interest in the question, but perhaps the printed image of the statue is rare—even though four thousand copies were made and distributed at the time of the rosary procession—because they were used up as devotional objects by the urban poor.[16]

In the presentation of miracles, de la Rosa's gaze turned especially to Mexico City—America's Rome and Jerusalem—home to dozens of shrines and his own hometown; a place replete with distinguished people, patrons, friends, rivals, fellow Franciscans, and divine presence. People of the city were especially deserving and especially favored, he seemed to say. Repeatedly in his account, important criollo and peninsular Spanish merchants, governors, priests, architects, and other professionals in the capital—or more often their devout wives, sisters, or daughters—asked to have the image brought to them for a day or two. And when they did, good things often followed. They or a relative or servant recovered from serious illness or were saved from harm, and they reciprocated with a generous donation or helped him and his cause in some other way. De la Rosa proved himself a criollo patriot in other writings, and criollo Spaniards and their minions were especially favored in the miracles, but his strong sense of social and racial hierarchy did not simply determine his understanding of who might be worthy of the Virgin's favor.[17]

The two overarching patterns in his presentation of the thirty-five miracles then are (1) Mexico City's favored place in the story and (2) the Virgin Mary's benevolence to her most ardent and self-sacrificing devotees, whatever their race or means.[18] The two patterns converge in his discussion of an explosion at a fireworks factory in the city that touched off a raging fire in 1744. The fire was suddenly extinguished when pious onlookers made way for the statue to be brought forward. He went on to tell of the recovery of a mulato (a person of mixed African and Spanish heritage), badly injured in the explosion, who was admitted to a hospital reserved for Spaniards thanks to the Virgin's protection. In his estimation, the man's racial inferiority was overcome by his selfless devotion to Nuestra Señora del Patrocinio and his good reputation in the city, as well as the Virgin's grace. Beyond the idea that America's Rome/Jerusalem and the special protection of the Virgin Mary invited a communion of believers eclipsing social divisions, this incident gave de la Rosa an opportunity to shape his main themes around a pious admonition:

> The most Holy Queen continued to make her presence felt
> for, once the fire was extinguished and the danger had passed,
> as I was taking her to the hospital she brought with her a
> *mulato* who was wounded all over his body and being carried
> on a plank. I say that She brought him with her to the hospital,
> under her protection, because only Spaniards were admitted
> there, yet his being a *mulato* was no obstacle in this case
> because of the respect owed to Most Holy Mary who had just
> performed a miracle by extinguishing the fire. How could the
> Sovereign Queen fail to help this *mulato* who every week gave
> half a *real* to fray Agustín Zuleta for the convent building fund?
> In all this the friar marveled at the profound judgments of God,
> as did I. He reported to me that three days before, when he had
> gone to the fireworks factory to ask for donations for Our Lady,
> one of the workers rudely responded, "I'll make no donation,
> father," and this *mulato* responded, "but I will do it, Father,"
> and took out his half *real*. Fray Agustín marveled at how Our

Lady protected the *mulato* but not the other man, whose head
was smashed by a plank in the devastation done by the fire.[19]

De la Rosa himself seems to have been the most favored of the faithful. A chain of "miracles" kept him safe and well during his mission for
Our Lady. He was saved from a kicking mule in the city, from falling
debris, from a falling flower pot, and from a collapsed ladder in Nativitas;
he was restored to health from chronic illness; and he found building
materials and expert advice when all seemed lost. Perhaps he meant to
say that he was just the humble instrument of God's grace and of a
groundswell of public devotion to Our Lady who was protected and
favored in order to carry out the work. But a more self-justifying message
rises from his text: he was most favored because he was most worthy. We
hear repeatedly that thanks to him three thousand pesos in money and
materials were collected for Our Lady.[20] In effect, he and the Virgin Mary
are the protagonists of the story. His text shows no curiosity about
Nativitas's experience of the Virgin and the statue before his arrival, or
whether his parishioners had their own providential origin story to tell.
Rather, the story of the statue begins and ends with him and the miracles
he witnessed. It begins with his discovery of a neglected, unattractive
image, brought to light, life, and beauty by his efforts, directed by some
secret impulse.

"In a highly indecent state thanks to the Indians' neglect"

Father de la Rosa certainly did not think the impulse propelling these
events was coming from his parishioners.[21] On the contrary, he found the
Indians of Nativitas ignorant, lazy, truculent, and superstitious. Perhaps
in principle they were capable of authentic piety and good works, but not,
apparently, without his lead, and they were disinclined to follow.

Indians were little favored by the Virgin in his account of miracles.
Most of the nine favors of the Virgin at Nativitas were impersonal and
imperfect, not the robust cures and transformations that awaited deserving individuals in Mexico City. It was as if faith in Nativitas was not deep
enough to merit more than half-miracles: building materials sometimes
became available under mysterious circumstances; a leaning wall did not
collapse; no one was seriously injured when a ladder broke; twenty sick
Indians survived a typhus epidemic, but some of their children died; a

man escaped death in a fall, but suffered lasting injuries; another man lived to tell of being run over by a coach, but he was badly injured; and a pregnant woman survived an especially dangerous birthing with the aid of Our Lady's printed image, but died shortly thereafter at the hands of ignorant Indian midwives.

These dangerous situations often were the Indians' own doing, as when a flowerpot carelessly placed on a ledge by Indian sacristans nearly brained Father de la Rosa, or when two men tumbled off a broken ladder:

> Having made a hole in the face of the wall to hold the head of a supporting beam . . . a mason was standing on a stepladder, holding one end of the supporting member. At the same time, another mason was on a flimsier ladder with a crowbar, digging out the wall where it was to receive the breastwork. The ladder was shaking as he struck with the tool. Another Indian was on the top rung of another ladder, supporting the head of the breastwork, while another one was on the ground raising it with a pole, and another one was helping with a stout stick. The rest of the Indian laborers were watching stupidly without offering to help support the base of the ladder so it would not slip when the mason struck with the crow bar, so I scolded them and went under the ladder myself. With both hands, I drew it to my chest. Seeing me do this, a boy began to climb the ladder instead of staying below. As I called out to him not to climb up, the ladder I was holding in place broke apart and the Indian who was using the crowbar, the one who was supporting the beam, and the breastwork itself all fell straight toward me. I invoked the Most Holy Virgin as my head, brain, and spine were about to be struck by the force and weight of the breast- work. Somehow my body fell outside the wreckage. . . . Only the blow from falling to the ground hurt me a little on one side. Neither of those who fell from above landed on top of me, as would have been natural; nor were they injured.

One exception to the tepid faith and imperfect miracles de la Rosa associates with Indians is don Mathías de la Cruz, the Indian sculptor who restored the Nativitas statue. Mathías was a don—an Indian of high status and distinguished lineage—and he was from Tlatelolco, the famed

Indian seat of government within greater Mexico City where the Franciscans had trained talented Indians for the priesthood in the sixteenth
century. He was "a very good Christian who had a very good command
of the Spanish language." "More than being a very good Christian
(because he did not get drunk), he was very priestly."[22] And he followed
instructions:

> The Vicar General contentedly hired him to do the work,
> giving him many instructions that every time he took up the
> carving he was to invoke the Most Holy Virgin, and when he
> would work on the face and hands he had to confess and take
> communion in honor of the Most Holy Queen, entrusting
> his actions to her sponsorship so that an image would come
> from his hands as if it had been created by an angel. The
> Vicar General's inspired severity made his words so persuasive
> that the Indian was greatly moved, promising to confess and
> take communion before working on the face and hands of
> the holy image.

Model Christian that he was, don Mathías "took refuge in the Most
Holy Virgin" with a heartfelt prayer when his two-year-old son suddenly
began to suffocate from a tremendous attack of croup:

> He held a lighted candle in his hand, knelt, and, full of faith
> said to her, "My Lady, you have chosen to emerge so beautifully
> from my unworthy hands. Please do not let my son die. I have
> faith that this candle will not go out and that you will return
> him to me safe and healthy." Great marvel! The Sovereign
> Queen chose, on one hand, to reward the faith and confidence
> of the Indian, and on the other to reward the devotion with
> which he restored her Holy Image. Before the candle went
> out the child was so free of the dangerous attack that he was
> safe and healthy again.

Don Mathías is Father de la Rosa's exception that underlines the rule.
He is different from every other Indian de la Rosa mentioned during his
short and troubled career beyond the archive and library. Whether in
Nativitas, Santa María la Redonda, or other pueblos, he was disheartened

by what he considered Indians' feeble Christianity and superstitions (which he was inclined to regard as idolatry), and he was often at odds with those he served. Judging by his writings and court appearances, none of the uplifting times in his career had to do with serving Indians. Yet he also wrote of "My poor little ones" and "my zeal to educate Indians in the faith," and he had dedicated himself to learning Nahuatl, the native language of his parishioners.

Perhaps this paradox of zeal to educate and disdain for the student has as much to do with the Franciscans' view of Indians in the sixteenth century and de la Rosa's sense of a Franciscan tradition in Mexico as it does with the vehemence of his own paternalistic zeal. The proudest time of the Franciscans in Mexico was "the spiritual conquest"—their evangelizing campaign as preachers, teachers, and protectors among Indians in central Mexico during the first decades of Spanish colonization. Millions of Indians came to know Christianity under the guidance of the great heroes of de la Rosa's province—the famous "Apostolic Twelve" missionaries who arrived in 1524, the indefatigable teacher and defender of Indians, Pedro de Gante, and the first bishop of Mexico, Juan de Zumárraga.[23] In the early debates over the nature of American natives, the Franciscans in Mexico staked out what became the mainstream colonial conception of Indians as children. Early Franciscans rejected both Ginés de Sepúlveda's view of American natives as natural slaves and barely human, and Las Casas's view that they were fully realized humans who lacked only the true religion. Instead, they considered Indians to be young in their humanity and in need of tutelage if they were to reach their human potential. A key difference between de la Rosa and early evangelizers like Gante and the famously impoverished Motolinía (the word is Nahuatl in origin, meaning impoverished, and was given him by his Indian parishioners impressed by his vows of poverty and humility) was that they understood Indians-as-children to mean childlike, innocent. Their potential to become cultured Christians was great. Two centuries later, de la Rosa could not shake off his conviction that Indians were childish rather than childlike—disobedient mischief-makers, if not devious idolaters in the devil's clutches. He wanted to inspire the multitude; he had too little of the steadying patience and forgiveness to teach to the few. In his way, de la Rosa understood that he hoped for a grander mission than that of a family doctor of Indian souls.

Would the people of Nativitas have agreed with these stories of miracles, troublesome Indians, and service to the Virgin Mary? Not likely, but there is no record of the providential stories they told then. That they were more devoted to the Virgin, the liturgy, and the religious life of their community than he acknowledged is more certain, and their devotional practices and store of sacred things were more numerous and varied than he described in his narrative about this one image. He knew this well enough judging by the detailed lists of the church's possessions he compiled at Nativitas and the earlier inventories he found among the church papers. The inventories of the sacristy and church from 1718 to 1738 document that Nativitas had a full supply of vestments, silver chalices, candleholders, altarcloths, and other liturgical items. In addition to the main altar dedicated to the Virgin Mary, the church boasted altars to Christ, Joseph, the Virgin of Guadalupe, Souls in Purgatory, San Diego, Our Lady of the Rosary, Our Lady of Sorrows and the Holy Sepulchre, and Our Lady of the Rosary.[24]

The report on moveable property in the Nativitas church written shortly before Father de la Rosa first went there noted that some of the liturgical items were old and needed repair. It also warned the Indian sacristans not to lend anything to the subject village of San Simón for their Palm Sunday festivities and not to pawn precious things from the sacristy in the local taverns. Even so, the church of Nativitas was better furnished than he acknowledged in his text, both before his arrival and after his departure, and the Virgin Mary in several representations had long been the central devotional figure in this doctrina named in honor of the Nativity of the Virgin.[25] Although the image of the Virgin Mary was not beautiful to his eye before it was restored, this opinion was not universal and the people of Nativitas had not neglected it. It was there on the main altar in 1690, described by the Franciscan pastor as "exceedingly beautiful" (de peregrina hermosura), nearly fifty years before Father de la Rosa's time.[26] His own inventory of jewels and other precious belongings of Our Lady in 1739 included a gold-plated silver "imperial crown" and a chain of fifty-nine French coins that were placed over the shoulders and hands of the statue "when they took it out on procession and showered it with confetti."[27]

Even in de la Rosa's text the people of Nativitas honored the Virgin more than one would expect from his statements about their indifference and dirty hands. They contributed thirty pesos for the restoration of the statue and received the beautified image with great rejoicing. Leaders of the community stood guard whenever the image traveled to Mexico City at their pastor's frequent urging, and they moved the lumber and stone for the construction projects and did most of the work on site.[28] He thought they were careless stewards of the coveted statue and little church, but both the statue and the church were there long after he left. In 1807, with the backing of the Indian governor of Mexico City's Parcialidad de San Juan, the parish priest, and the *provisor de indios* (the archbishop's administrator for Indian affairs), leaders of Nativitas gained permission to collect alms in order to rebuild the church from its foundations. The old structure was, again, much deteriorated and they wanted it to be "decente" (proper).[29] The community alms collector at the time referred to the wonder-working image as Nuestra Señora de Nativitas, not the Nuestra Señora del Patrocinio of de la Rosa's text.[30]

Nativitas in the eighteenth century is less accessible to historians than Father de la Rosa's views and activities thanks to his long paper trail, but it was not as fixed and featureless a place as he seemed to suggest. Both de la Rosa and people of Nativitas may have regarded the pueblo and the capital as separate worlds, but Nativitas were almost as much a part of Mexico City as de la Rosa himself was. People of Nativitas had taken up residence in the city, without losing their ties to their pueblo a three-hour walk away. Their economic activities—brickmaking, haymaking, salt and saltpeter processing—were directed to the urban market and routinely took local people there on business.[31]

De la Rosa would pay a price for thinking of Nativitas as a timeless place apart and underestimating his parishioners' political connections in the city and their appetite for litigation. There was, for example, more to the pueblo's invitation to the governor and other dignitaries of the Indian Parcialidad de San Juan to celebrate the return of the refurbished statue than the angelic voices of the cantors they brought along.[32] As Joseph Vásquez, the newly appointed royal lieutenant for the Nativitas area would learn in late 1739, the elders of Nativitas looked to the governor of San Juan and the chief judge of the Audiencia of Mexico as their political patrons and authorities and would resist direction from other officials. The dispute over their resistance to Vásquez's authority and what he called "the violent deaths and other grave excesses committed outside the city," dragged on through most of de la Rosa's time in Nativitas, yet he seems to have missed its implications for his own contingent authority.[33] He would recognize too late that he could not simply have his way in Nativitas.

Conclusion

At one level, Father de la Rosa's ambitions and career retrace the sixteenth-century history of Franciscans in Mexico—from an expansive, evangelizing zeal and some freedom to act on it; to intervention by superiors; to conflict, withdrawal, and disappointment over the interference and incomplete results; to a longing for renewal. But these were not neat sequential stages in de la Rosa's life, and there are other differences that have much to do with this friar and his time.

Like the founding generation, he was a doer more than a thinker, a self-described man of "ardent zeal" focused on the idea of spiritual revival and conquest. But he was a less independent, less-imposing figure than such famous predecessors as Pedro de Gante, Motolinía, and Martín de Valencia. He was a weaker character ensnared in the institutional life of the order and the politics of a different time, a city man much attached to his role as an occasional notary and inspector of books for the Inquisition.[34] He could care more about his personal dignity and reputation than was fitting for a mendicant (memorably here when he abandoned a "ridiculous mule" at the entrance to the city rather than be seen collecting alms in such an "indecent" manner).[35] Above all, his idea of evangelizing mission was clouded by his Mexico City preoccupations and his low opinion of Indians as fellow Christians. He seems to have been happiest and most effective amid stacks of documents, conducting the business of the archive and library. There, his punctiliousness, energy, and talent for managing records and ordering facts made him invaluable to the Franciscans in the years of litigation for the order that followed his removal from Nativitas.[36]

The years spanned by de la Rosa's association with the image of Nuestra Señora del Patrocinio (1739–75) were momentous for the institutional church and local religion in the viceroyalty, and it was an especially trying period for the Franciscans. Royal officials and regalist bishops were moving to curb "excessive" popular devotions and the influence of friar-pastors. They decreed fewer and less elaborate feast-day celebrations, challenged the use of Indian languages in the liturgy, virtually removed the mendicant orders from their traditional pastoral responsibilities in central and southern Mexico, and limited the authority of parish priests in other ways.[37] Between 1749 and the time he composed his account of Nuestra Señora del Patrocinio, the Franciscans lost nearly all their doctrinas (including Nativitas), and other reforms to further professionalize and subordinate the clergy were well under way.

De la Rosa was alert to these changes, especially during his years in charge of the archive and library, and he was an avid student of early Franciscan history in Mexico.[38] But he was blind to patterns of a less-remote past and how his own troubles folded into the higher politics of church and state that swirled around him. He was convinced that his troubles at Nativitas and elsewhere—including his failure to win a place among the friars of the Colegio de San Fernando, the string of reassignments, and his eventual removal from pastoral service—had to do with fickle Indians and the vagaries of personal patronage and opinion. He was certain that a lone dissenting member of the Colegio de San Fernando, a new Franciscan provincial who arbitrarily took the Indians' side, and the retirement of his friend and patron Antonio Ramírez del Castillo as vicar general of the Archdiocese of Mexico caused his professional misfortunes. His account gives no inkling that aggressive promotion of Nuestra Señora del Patrocinio, loose talk of miracles, impolitic criticism of colonial authorities, impatience with parishioners, and thirst for the glory of a distant past might be considered excessive, even dangerous, by archbishops, Audiencias, viceroys, and Franciscan superiors of his time. He was surprisingly unconcerned by (if he was aware of) the many times a pastor's "improving," replacing, or merely moving a religious image to a different place in the church led to angry commotions, bloodshed, and litigation with Indian parishioners in central Mexico during the seventeenth and eighteenth centuries. Whereas de la Rosa's idea of a fitting devotion kept drawing him and the statue back to the city, it is not surprising that people of Nativitas wanted the Virgin Mary to work her wonders at home as the fame of their image spread.[39]

De la Rosa had been careful to obtain Archbishop Vizarrón's permission to organize the rosary procession in the city and gain an indulgence from him for the participants. Nevertheless, this longtime archbishop (1731–47), who also served as viceroy from 1734–40, was, in the long run, bound to take a dim view of this kind of popular euphoria. Was it just whim on the part of de la Rosa's provincial and the Indians of Nativitas that ended the statue's visits to the city? Was it mere coincidence that a month after he was removed from Nativitas in 1745 the archbishop closed the shrine of Nuestra Señora de los Angeles at Tlatelolco because it attracted disorderly crowds? These were not de la Rosa's questions, but Archbishop Vizarrón had good reasons to cool off an overheated pastor and tranquilize many of the Marian devotions that had gained popularity in the Valley of Mexico in the wake of the great epidemic of 1737. Vizarrón's personal devotion to Our Lady of

Guadalupe and his conviction that the Blessed Mary in this guise had saved Mexico City in 1737 led him to promote her as patroness of the city and viceroyalty and to pursue a campaign in Rome for official papal recognition (which came in 1754, after Vizarrón's death). Promoting one image as the dominant symbol of identity and protection for New Spain and its capital city was in line with the regalist program of centralizing and standardizing devotional practices, and de la Rosa's Franciscan superiors had more pressing battles to fight than the cult of Nuestra Señora del Patrocinio. They must have been concerned by de la Rosa's persistent problems in Nativitas and his dreamy vision of a return to the sixteenth century as they struggled to convince eighteenth-century royal governors and archbishops of their order's importance to the future of crown and church in New Spain.

Father de la Rosa's vivid account of the wonders of Nuestra Señora del Patrocinio stood out from the run of routine administrative papers I had been reading in the archive of the Province of the Holy Gospel. Only later did I recognize that his mark was everywhere in this colonial archive. He had been through all these documents before me, poring over their contents, putting them in order, filling in gaps, and writing explanatory notes here and there. How this archive became his—how it was an extension of his longtime aspirations as a Franciscan—took me by surprise when I began to find his tracks in other archives and libraries in Mexico City, Austin, Berkeley, and Chicago. Some of the records that surfaced were pieces of an ambitious project he undertook single-handedly late in life to identify and catalog all the Franciscans of his province beginning with the first group of twelve in 1523. Compiled between 1760 and 1770, the principal item is a 483-page "Bezerro general menológico y chronológico de todos los religiosos que ha avido en la Provincia." The term "*menológico*," meaning a register of saints with brief biographies of each one, suggests his commemorative purpose and the epic terms in which he saw the history of his province, especially in its early years. At the time he made his last entry, more than fifty-two hundred deceased members had been entered. Each is classified alphabetically under the first letter of his surname, then chronologically by date of profession. Work on this elaborately cross-indexed catalog of the membership and related inquiries into the accomplishments of his predecessors, "cost me a tremendous effort... which consumed many years of work," he wrote in his sometimes over-the-top way.[40]

He had been removed from his post at Nativitas, prevented from actively continuing his Marian mission, and left with less exalted (if not unimportant) duties that kept him out of circulation. But he was not broken by the experience or left in a state of suspended animation, nor, to all appearances, was he embittered. Here in the various indexes he compiled and the archive of the Province of the Holy Gospel, as well as in his many unpublished writings, was evidence of a busy, purposeful life within cloistered walls.[41] His consuming passion for lists and good order, his new, more restricted circumstances, the troubling political changes then facing the Franciscans in Mexico, and his hankering after transcendent service turned him toward the history of his province's work in Mexico. It was a history he found liberally sprinkled with miracles and exemplary evangelizers. This work of preserving and in some sense reliving the collective history of his province led him back to his own exalted time at Nativitas and forward to the composition of his account of the miracles of Nuestra Señora del Patrocinio and thoughts of revival.

The little church with one bell tower is still there in the parish of Nativitas, facing a noisy eight-lane thoroughfare between the Viaducto de la Piedad and Eje 5, no longer beyond the city limits. A rectangular stone high on the front wall is dated 1563, but there has been extensive reconstruction, and not only under Father de la Rosa's busy direction.[42] The statue of Our Lady displayed at the altar could well be the one restored, revered, and promoted by Father de la Rosa. It is draped in a fresh cloak, its new hair restyled, its painted surfaces in fine condition. His title for the statue—Nuestra Señora del Patrocinio, Our Lady of Intercession—has been forgotten. It is known only as Nuestra Señora de Nativitas. The origin story parishioners tell underscores the statue's providential attachment to this place, without a hint of its travels and fame in the city during the eighteenth century. As the story goes, when the image was being taken from the hospital village of Santa Fe long ago in the sixteenth century, it became irresistibly heavy there at Nativitas and could not be moved further. Local people heeded this sign from Our Lady and built a chapel on the site to house the image. Once a year, during the *fiesta patronal* in September, the image is carried through the streets that trace the parish limits. The privilege of sponsoring the fiesta is reserved for the old families of the neighborhood that have not moved away.[43]

NOTES

1. New York: Macmillan, 16 vols., 5:370–74.

2. Begun in 1979, my work on the subject eventually became *Magistrates of the Sacred: Priests and Parishioners in Eighteenth-Century Mexico* (Stanford, CA: Stanford University Press, 1996). Colonial Latin Americanists might also find Aron Gurevich's *Historical Anthropology of the Middle Ages* (ed. Jane Howlett [Chicago: University of Chicago Press, 1992]) helpful in reckoning with standard categories in religious studies. By religion, I am thinking mainly of faith in practice—lived allegiance to a cosmic order that transcends human power.

3. This is a line of inquiry pursued rather single-mindedly by George Foster in *Culture and Conquest: America's Spanish Heritage* (New York: Viking Fund, 1960), which posited that "Indian" peasant culture in Mesoamerica is essentially the product of transfers from Spain rather than the persistence of indigenous traditions.

4. Of course, similarities could also be fortuitous and anterior more than connected, and differences could stem from connected histories in various ways.

5. This is not the place for an extended discussion of Christian's approach to local religion. Ironically, the sharpest criticism seems to have settled on the ways his studies reinforce the distinction between high and low religion—by (1) overplaying the power of the state in local affairs during the early modern period; (2) emphasizing the instrumental and mundane in his treatment of popular interest in shrines, images, and devotions; and (3) gliding over the importance of the liturgy in the lives of practicing Catholics, as Brian Larkin's essay in this volume suggests.

6. In an earlier article I emphasized this sculpted image of the Virgin Mary and the "biography" and charismatic properties of the printed likeness de la Rosa commissioned: "Nuestra Señora del Patrocinio y Fray Francisco de la Rosa: Una intersección de religión, política, y arte en el México del siglo XVIII," *Relaciones* 73 (1998). De la Rosa's personal network of patronage, affiliation, friendship, and rivalry in Mexico City; his historical perspectives; and his labors after 1745 in the context of Franciscan history and Bourbon politics deserve attention, too, as do his other extant writings, all of them unpublished. I hope to edit an English translation of his manuscript about Nuestra Señora del Patrocinio with a fuller introduction to the author and his work.

7. His checkered history as a novice is documented in the library of the Instituto Nacional de Antropología e Historia (Mexico City), Fondo Franciscano, libro de informaciones de los novicios del Convento Recoleto de San Cosme, 1704–1728, vol. 7, fols. 597–612.

8. The gist of de la Rosa's formal complaint to the Audiencia about his Indian parishioners on May 22, 1734, would be repeated often during his eleven years of pastoral service. He expressed his frustration over their superstitions, heavy drinking, adultery, indifference to the faith, disobedience, and other signs of what he took to be the devil's work. Biblioteca Nacional, Archivo Franciscano (hereafter BN AF) caja 109, doc. 1505.

9. These assignments were in Calimaya (Valley of Toluca) in 1737 and Mazatepec (Morelos) in 1738. At Mazatepec he was at the center of a new controversy over idolatrous practices, denouncing the pueblo of Coatlan for "calling on witches to divine stolen items by ingesting peyote, pipizintles, and other herbs," which he judged to be pacts with the devil. He directed some of his criticism toward the alcalde mayor, intimating that his failure to monitor these superstitions was motivated by personal greed (Archivo General de la Nación [hereafter AGN] Inquisición, vol. 820, exp. 5, fol. 135). An appointment in modern Morelos during the eighteenth century could be a rude introduction to the ministry. See Taylor, *Magistrates of the Sacred*, app. 3.

10. His service in Xochitepec and Santa María la Redonda from July 1740 to January 1743 was especially unhappy. He clashed with Indians and mestizos of Xochitepec over alleged witchcraft and denounced "the ignorance and idiocy of these people." He seems to have suffered emotionally from these conflicts. "I say that the wailings of my conscience are so profound and unceasing because the Catholic zeal of the Christian religion in the house of the Lord, which is the Holy Church, eats my heart out. I cannot rest until I put these great and stupendous abominations against Our Most Holy Faith before the exalted comprehension of this Saintly Apostolic Tribunal," he wrote to the Inquisition from Xochitepec on May 23, 1741 (AGN, Inquisición, vol. 820, exp. 5, fols. 134–37).

Within weeks of his letter to the Inquisition, he was transferred to Santa María la Redonda, and bad turned to worse. By spring 1742 he had launched a series of judicial actions in which he complained of his new communicants' insolence, disobedience, lawlessness, and sacrilegious ways. He was ill and afraid, as well as angry over their failure to fulfill their spiritual duties or support the work of the parish. He suspected that several parishioners he had punished were plotting to kill him, and he added that the district governor paid no heed (BN AF, caja 141, doc. 1732, and Bancroft Library, University of California, Berkeley, M-M 135, exps. 14 and 19). De la Rosa's troubles in Santa María la Redonda were not all of his own making. His predecessor there in the 1690s also reported "graves desórdenes" and other provocations (Bancroft Library M-M 135, exp. 15, 1696).

11. He was back in court with the people of Nativitas, bringing a suit against them to the archbishop's vicar general on October 16, 1744, in response to an earlier complaint they had made against him. An apparently amicable agreement was reached on May 24, 1745, four months before he was removed from Nativitas (Bancroft Library M-M 135, exp. 28).

12. Quick to identify shrines and miraculous images when he found them, José Antonio de Villaseñor y Sánchez did not mention this image in his paragraph about the pueblo of Nuestra Señora de Nativitas (*Suplemento al Theatro Americano: La ciudad de México en 1755* [Seville: Escuela de Estudios Hispanoamericanos and Mexico: UNAM, 1980], 116).

13. The Council of Trent decreed in its 25th session, Dec. 3–4, 1563, that "no new miracles be accepted or new relics recognized without the bishop's examination and approval." There is no sign that de la Rosa s ought Episcopal certification of the events he calls miracles in his text. More circumspect colonial reporters of uncertified supernatural events wroteof "marvels" and "prodigious events" (*maravillas* and *prodigios*) rather than miracles.

14. Miracles or magnanimity and self-interest? It was all the same to Father de la Rosa, who was inclined to find the hand of God behind everything positive that related to the promotion of Nuestra Señora del Patrocinio. The donor who served as "godfather" of the ceremonial blessing of the restored statue when it was returned to Nativitas was a gunpowder supplier who presumably saw a business opportunity as well as a chance to demonstrate his devotion to the Virgin (BN AF caja 109, doc. 1494, parag. 6; de la Rosa numbered the paragraphs of his text, not the pages). The Virgin Mary as benefactress of building materials and protectress of workers on the construction site were uncommon claims for the supernatural in official sources from colonial Mexico, but they were not unknown in Iberian tradition. Several cases are included in the thirteen-century *Cántigas de Santa María*. See *Songs of Holy Mary of Alfonso X, The Wise*, trans. Kathleen Kulp Hill (Tempe: Arizona Center for Medieval and Renaissance Studies), cántigas #356, 358, 364.

De la Rosa neglects to say how often his frequent appeals for supplies failed to bear fruit. One of his failures is recorded in the minutes of Mexico

City's municipal council on July 7, 1743. In that session of the council
his petition for "some lumber, even if it is old, a little lime, and the large
quantity of stone left along the Calzada de San Antón, which the Indians
can collect" was read. All but one of the eight councilors in attendance
that day rejected the petition. The councilor who did not vote against
the petition abstained because he served as the principal lay adviser to
Franciscan convents in the city (Archivo Histórico de la Ciudad de
México [hereafter AHCM], número de inventario 68A, fol. 75v).

15. De la Rosa's text can be read as the belated *información jurídica* that had
not been compiled in the 1740s. He wrote in the text, "The authentication
never took place because I was removed from the convent." It is more in
the form of an información jurídica than a standard devotional history.
The difference is illustrated by the two texts for the Cristo Renovado de
Santa Teresa composed by Alonso Alberto de Velasco and published in the
late seventeenth century, (*Renovación por sí misma de la soberana imagen de
Christo Señor, que llaman de Ytzimiquilpan* ... [Mexico: Viuda de Francisco
Rodríguez Lupercio, 1688] [an información jurídica] and *Exaltación de la
divina misericordia en la milagrosa renovación de la soberana imagen de
Christo* ... [Mexico: Viuda de Juan de Ribera, 1699] [a devotional history]).

16. Or perhaps most were thrown away as worthless scrap paper? I suppose
the print and paper are too fine, and the artist too famous, to be treated
as trash.

17. Especially in his long treatise against Archbishop Lorenzana's native
languages policy (Bancroft Library M-M 101 "Vindicias de la verdad"
[Vindications of truth]).

18. The twenty-one beneficiaries of the Virgin's miracles in the capital
included three criolla *doñas* (women of high status), the mother of a
master architect, the daughter of a don, a bishop's page, the son of
a Spanish military man, a nun, a pharmacist, two criolla builders,
a castizo carder, two Indians, a mulato laborer, a mulata maid, the wife
of a coachman, a non-Indian woman living in a tenement, two criollos
of modest means, and a guard's daughter.

19. BN AF, caja 109, doc. 1494, parag. 32.

20. First in parag. 3 ("You will be astonished to find in the folio inventory book
that I fashioned, in file 58 of this archive, that my collections for the sacred
paraphernalia and repairs to the monastery exceeded 3,000 pesos"); then in
parag. 8 ("the funds totaling more than 3,000 pesos free and clear added by
me to the poor little monastery of Nativitas") and his list of collections and
expenses at the end of the text.

21. This certainly was de la Rosa's opinion in 1775. Was it just a retrospective view, colored by his departure from Nativitas under duress in 1745 after his parishioners lodged complaints against him? I don't think so. Judging by his letters to the Inquisition and the Audiencia of Mexico in the 1730s and 1740s—before and during his tenure at Nativitas—his opinion of Indians in general and the people of Nativitas in particular were no different in 1740 than they were in 1775. Furthermore, the explanation in the text of why he was removed did not center on his troubles with the people of Nativitas.

22. BN AF, caja 109, doc. 1494, parags. 4 and 7.

23. Bernardino de Sahagún, the great Franciscan student of Nahuatl and native traditions in the mid-sixteenth century, would not have made de la Rosa's roster of heroes. According to Luis Nicolau D'Olwer, de la Rosa denounced at least one of Sahagún's Nahuatl texts (the *Psalmodia*) to the Inquisition "with such success that only 3–4 copies survive" (*Bernardino de Sahagún [1499–1590]* [Salt Lake City: University of Utah Press, 1987], 75).

24. Not to mention paintings of the Christ of Chalma and Our Lady of La Piedad, among others.

25. In the 1690s, Agustín de Vetancurt, *Teatro mexicano* (Mexico: Viuda de Juan de Ribera, 1697), quarta parte, tratado segundo, capítulo 1, 87–88, described Nativitas as a small pueblo dedicated to the Nativity of the Virgin, with three subordinate villages and an adult population of about 230 Indians and eight Spaniards. Its convent housed three Franciscans who ministered to the spiritual needs of the Indians under the jurisdiction of the provincial headquarters in Mexico City.

26. BN AF, doc. 1281, memorias, inventarios y directorios de conventos, 1644–1761.

27. BN AF, caja 123, doc. 1025, libro de inventarios, autos de visita, 1739–1753. A 1726 record of endowed masses at the church of Nativitas attests to enthusiastic devotion there to the Nativity and Assumption of the Virgin Mary before de la Rosa arrived (BN AF, caja 92, exp. 1397).

28. BN AF, caja 109, doc. 1494, parags. 4, 5, and 22.

29. This initiative is recorded in a petition by the alms collector of Nativitas for an official copy of his license after he was robbed of his papers and money (AGN, Clero Regular y Secular, 181 exp. 6, Apr. 1808). At the time de la Rosa first went to Nativitas the church reportedly had the benefit of two small bequests producing 60 reales for an annual Mass and procession. One of the benefactors was Joan Sebastián, an Indian (BN AF, caja 120, doc. 1588).

30. Although de la Rosa insisted on calling the statue a representation of Nuestra Señora del Patrocinio (Our Lady of Intercession), he knew that the church and image were known locally as Nuestra Señora de Nativitas. The bilingual text of Christian doctrine he began to write at Nativitas in December 1744 identifies the place as "Convento y santuario de Nuestra Señora del Patrocinio nombrado Nativitas en el pueblo de Tepetlaltzingo extramuros de dha ciudad" (Convent and shrine of Our Lady of Intercession, named Nativitas, in the *pueblo* of Tepetlatzingo on the outskirts of said city) (Bancroft Library M-M 100).

31. Vetancurt, *Teatro mexicano*, 87, identified brick making; Villaseñor y Sánchez, *Suplemento*, 116, mentioned that people of Nativitas sold hay, salt, and saltpeter in the city. He briefly described the filtration and evaporation processes used to make the salt cakes there. Nativitas's property dispute with a rival salt miner and processor is recorded in AGN, Tierras, vol. 1415, exp. 4 (1815).

32. BN AF, caja 109, doc. 1494, parag. 6.

33. Archivo del Cabildo Catedral Metropolitano de México, acta de cabildo for Dec. 7, 1739, and AGN, Alcaldes Mayores 10, fols. 11–12 (1740). The willingness and ability of communities within the district of Nativitas to litigate political disputes should also have given de la Rosa pause in his estimation of Indian ignorance and lethargy. For example, in 1709 the subject villages of San Simón Ticomán and San Andrés Tetepilco complained to the archbishop of "grave extortions and interference" from the people of Nativitas and sought to separate from the doctrina and have their own resident priest.

34. Throughout his career de la Rosa was quick to report to the Inquisition on suspicious practices and literature that smacked of the devil's work. For example, AGN, Inquisición, vol. 820, exp. 5 (1741), vol. 899 unnumbered expediente, fols. 254–56 (1747), and vol. 1520 exp. 10 (1767). That the Inquisition no longer had jurisdiction over Indian affairs must have disappointed him.

35. In the Nativitas narrative Father de la Rosa was quick to criticize the record-keeping practices of others and touchy about criticism of his own records.

36. An example is his well-researched brief of 1772 in defense of his province's right of *patronato* over the main chapel of its Mexico City monastery (patronato basically meant the authority to administer chapel affairs and appoint its chaplains) (BN AF, caja 54, doc. 1137). In 1765 he was appointed to a team of inspectors of the property and archives of the twenty *conventos* (monasteries) that remained to his province (BN AF, caja 109, exp. 1499).

37. These changes are discussed in Taylor, *Magistrates of the Sacred*, esp. ch. 1.

38. In the early 1770s he wrote at length about the threat to Christianity in New Spain posed by the new language policy and closely followed the work of the regalist Fourth Provincial Council in 1771. See Bancroft Library M-M 101and M-M 69–70.

39. In another manuscript written after Easter in 1745 (near the end of his service in Nativitas), Father de la Rosa noted that for the first time many of his parishioners living in Mexico City had returned to confess and take communion in Nativitas (Bancroft Library M-M 135, exp. 28). This added interest by nonresidents in the life of the parish may be another sign of a desire to keep the statue there.

40. University of Texas, Benson Library, Manuscript No. 1641 (G-25).

41. In addition to the account of Nuestra Señora del Patrocinio, two versions of the catalog of deceased members of the province, and various other indexes and catalogs for the *menología* project now in the Benson Library, his writings included a 608-page text of Christian doctrine in Spanish and Nahuatl begun during his second appointment at Nativitas (which he hoped to publish) (Bancroft Library, M-M 100); a scathing treatise from the early 1770s on the regalist program to eliminate native languages from Christian practice in Mexico (Bancroft Library, M-M 101); a Nahuatl grammar; five volumes of sermons; a volume of poetry in Latin and Spanish; and various indexes and lists of proscribed books and the holdings of the library of his monastery. The grammar, sermons, poetry, and indexes are mentioned in José Mariano Beristáin de Souza, *Biblioteca hispanoamericana septentrional, o catálogo y noticias de los literatos que o nacidos o educados, o florecientes en la América septentrional española, han dado a luz algún escrito, o lo han dejado preparado para la prensa, 1521–1850*, 3rd ed. (Mexico: Ediciones Fuente Cultural, 1947), II:258. Beristáin de Souza located these manuscripts in the archive of de la Rosa's monastery in Mexico City. Elisa Sampson Vera Tudela adds a two-volume manuscript, "Crónica sucinta del convento de Santa Clara de México," dated 1755, that she located in the INAH library of the Museum of Anthropology in Mexico City, *Colonial Angels: Narratives of Gender and Spirituality in Mexico, 1580–1750* (Austin: University of Texas Press, 2000), 189.

42. In addition to the rebuilding project that began in 1807 there was at least one more major restoration, completed in 1944. The latter project is commemorated with a marble plaque on the right-hand wall at the entrance of the church. The cloister area, so prominent in de la Rosa's plans, has been rebuilt and converted into a school; a taller annex has been added behind the church.

43. I am indebted to María Isabel Estrada Torres for sharing her account of the annual fiesta and conversations with parishioners.

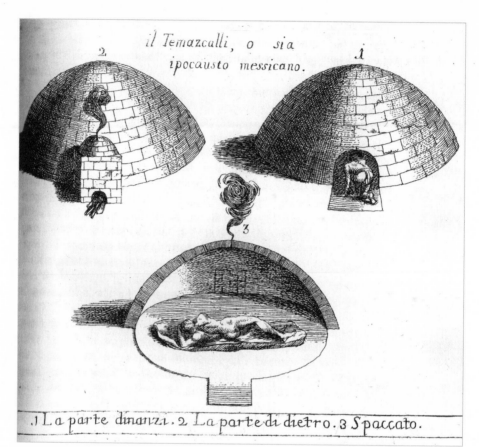

FIGURE 9. A temazcal

Drawing of a temazcal, or bathhouse. As part of his recreation of pre-Hispanic history, Clavijero commissioned artists to draw images of cultural phenomena of the Mexica. Taken from Francisco Javier Clavijero, Storia antica del Messico *(Cesena: Gregorio Biasini, 1780). Courtesy of Mandeville Special Collections Library, University of California, San Diego.*

CHAPTER FIVE

Autonomy, Honor, and the Ancestors

Native Local Religion in
Seventeenth-Century Oaxaca

David Tavárez

On Wednesday, September 15, 1700, don Juan Bautista and Jacinto de los Ángeles, two Zapotec men who would be beatified by the Catholic Church three centuries later, huddled in the back rooms of the Dominican house of San Francisco Cajonos, hours away from their deaths at the hands of their fellow townspeople.[1] Something had gone very wrong the night before in this usually peaceful town, located in the southern reaches of the jurisdiction of Villa Alta, in a mountain range to the northeast of Oaxaca City in southeastern New Spain.[2] It was too late for compromises: a throng had surrounded the church as they beat on wooden boxes shouting, "You cuckolds! You friars! You are about to die right here" [¡A cornudos, a frailes, aquí avéis de morir!].[3] Trapped inside were eleven Spaniards and mestizos, two Dominicans, at least twenty native allies from four neighboring towns, and don Juan and Jacinto, who had triggered the riot after leading their siege companions to an unorthodox ceremony held at the home of a local resident the previous evening. The mob then threw stones at the church; its defenders—four of whom had arquebuses—shot into the air first, and then

into the crowd, killing at least one rebel. After the Spaniards ran out of gunpowder, a desperate negotiation conducted in Spanish ensued. The rioters
were not appeased when their vicar displayed an image of the Virgin; they
then refused an offer of money and stated that, unless the two informants
were turned over to them, they would burn the church and its defenders and
flee to the mountains. In the end, the besieged Spaniards decided to surrender the two wanted men despite the friars' protests.

It is tempting to offer a well-rehearsed explanation that reduces this
confrontation to a clash of opposing sides: idolaters versus Dominicans,
native subjects against Spanish authorities, "folk" religion versus "official"
religion, a "little" rural tradition speaking out against a "great" urban,
hegemonic tradition—to use Robert Redfield's terms—or one cultural
system battling another, if one prefers Clifford Geertz's early but influential characterization of religion as a circumscribed cultural system.[4] This
essay, however, argues that a fuller understanding of local indigenous religious practices in colonial Spanish America calls for an analytical stance
and a detailed historical narrative that goes well beyond embracing and
defining one's choice of meaningful dichotomies—"beyond simplicity," as
Carlos Eire argues in the first essay in this volume. What lies beyond this
"beyond" is the resolve to examine local religious practices as complex,
independent social and symbolic phenomena that interdigitate with
metropolitan and transatlantic practices in myriad ways that cannot be
adequately analyzed through the deployment of antipodal categories.
Such a stance is inspired in part by William Christian's insistence on
studying both the institutional impact of Catholicism on rural communities and specific peasant religious practices as components of a social
sphere that may be termed "local religion"—a designation which, as
William Taylor notes in this volume, challenges received dichotomies
without dissolving the concreteness of the local and the institutional.[5]

Moreover, this essay proposes a careful, microsociological consideration of the actors involved in the production of local religion. This approach
is indebted to Pierre Bourdieu's notion of "the religious field of practice"—
a circumscribed sphere of symbolic practice that is not a discretely bounded
cultural system, but an ever-expanding or contracting social sphere that reg-
ulates itself through the interested interaction of its participants.[6] In his
analysis, Bourdieu stressed two properties of the religious field: the inherently dialectical nature of the process of religious production, and the limits placed by the logic of the field on the nature and type of discourse that

its participants deploy. To return to the confrontations between Zapotec villagers and their ministers, this essay proposes that the logic of their local field of religious practice—or "what was at stake," to use a more lapidary characterization—involved the convergence of local autonomy aspirations, the honorable defense of local forms of identity, and the preservation of ancestral devotions. This essay examines these three terms—autonomy, honor, and devotion—through the prism of three confrontations that took place between 1666 and 1704 in the jurisdiction of Villa Alta in Oaxaca.[7]

The practices that will be discussed here may be unfamiliar to many historians, as their study is a part of an emerging body of literature located at the intersection of historical anthropology and social history. Sources in Spanish and in native languages are both scarce and crucial; the colonial record of native religious practices in New Spain, as Taylor noted in an erudite survey of this topic, "is most striking for its patchiness."[8] Thus, this essay probes local orientations toward native religious practices by focusing on small but rather thick "patches" that encapsulate distinct local attitudes toward traditional and Christian ritual practices in three native communities in Villa Alta: San Francisco Cajonos, Lachirioag, and Betaza, all of which spoke Cajonos Zapotec.[9] Our close scrutiny of local religion in the Villa Alta region is not incidental, since a series of measures taken by ecclesiastic and civil authorities in the first decade of the eighteenth century not only resulted in idolatry trial records and collective confessions, but also yielded an unusual collection of documents—about 101 booklets with alphabetic transcriptions of the Zapotec 260-day ritual calendar, and four songbooks containing alphabetic transcriptions of Zapotec ritual songs. After a brief appraisal of confrontations over native ritual practices in New Spain, I explore local factionalism through two examples—an inconclusive idolatry case in Lachirioag, and the spontaneous riot at Cajonos. Finally, I examine the failed defense of a local system of parallel devotions—one directed toward Christianity, the other toward local ancestors—in Betaza.

The Struggle Against Local Zapotec Religion in Oaxaca, 1660–1704

Unlike the seventeenth-century idolatry campaigns in the Archdiocese of Lima, which were conducted through a partnership among Jesuits, Episcopal authorities, and seculars in a single diocese where a standardized variant of Quechua was embraced as the main linguistic vehicle for doctrinal education, idolatry extirpators in New Spain conducted their campaigns in an episodic manner across a variety of regions characterized by great linguistic diversity and variable demographic density.[10] From an institutional perspective, extirpation attempts in the diocese of Oaxaca may be divided into four stages: a first period of "apostolic" extirpation led primarily by Franciscans, Dominicans, and other members of the regular clergy between 1527 and 1571; a second period between 1571 and the epochal 1660 native rebellion at Tehuantepec (Oaxaca), characterized by extirpation attempts conducted by secular ecclesiastical judges; a third period between the 1660s and the 1720s noted by an increase in violent confrontations and novel punitive experiments; and a fourth and final stage that began in the 1720s, led the establishment of hundreds of Spanish-language schools, and introduced the medicalization of sorcery investigations.[11] After natives were removed from inquisitorial jurisdiction in 1571, only bishops and their associates were entitled to prosecute natives for crimes against the Christian faith, and inquisitors redirected accusations against native specialists to the Episcopal jurisdiction. Therefore, from 1571 onward, the Episcopal authorities of Mexico and Oaxaca delegated the faculty of conducting native idolatry and sorcery proceedings to a select group of priests with relevant experience and linguistic aptitudes. Although the extant documentations on ecclesiastical judgeship appointments in Mexico and Oaxaca containing faculties to act against native idolaters is scant, it seems to be the case that the Episcopal authorities in these two dioceses had a conservative approach to the granting of these faculties, which contrasts with the more liberal appointment policy for vicars and ecclesiastical judges in the bishopric of Yucatán.[12]

Any consideration of Zapotec struggles for local autonomy in midcolonial times must begin with the indigenous rebellion of Tehuantepec in 1660, which is the most visible event that predates a period of confrontations between natives and colonial authorities in Oaxaca that culminated with the 1700 Cajonos rebellion. On March 22, 1660, a large group of Zapotecs who had congregated in the town of Tehuantepec for Holy Week celebrations rioted against and killed their alcalde mayor (regional administrator and magistrate), along with two of his associates. Exactly two months later, the Zapotecs of Nexapa also rose up in arms, forcing a military standoff resolved only through the mediation of Bishop Alonso de Cuevas Dávalos. During 1660 and 1661, the rebellion spread like wildfire—to use its chroniclers' simile of choice—through several

Chontal, Huave, Mixe, Zapotec, and Zoque communities. This sequence of events occupies a unique place in the historiography of Spanish America due to its multiethnic character and its territorial scale. Two complementary analyses have explored the motivations for this rebellion.[13] One view—presented by Hector Díaz-Polanco in the only extant collection of historical essays devoted to the Tehuantepec rebellion—embraces a cumulative theory: taxation abuses related to the *repartimientos*, which were compounded by the punishment and humiliation of recalcitrant native elites, may have provided a spark for the Tehuantepec uprising.[14] By contrast, Marcelo Carmagnani has argued that, rather than a rebellion, this movement was a confrontation against the expanding political role of the alcalde mayor.[15]

Carmagnani's observations about the expanding powers of alcaldes mayores may account for the fact that, between 1665 and 1736, Villa Alta's alcaldes mayores and deputy governors, or *tenientes de alcalde*, presided over at least a dozen trials of natives accused of idolatry or sorcery, four of them occurring in the decade of the 1660s.[16] Dominican Bishop friar Tomás de Monterroso (1665–78) and Bishop Nicolás del Puerto (1679–81) both held in high esteem the cooperation of civil authorities in inaccessible regions regarded as prone to rebellion, as was the case in Villa Alta. In fact, during del Puerto's tenure, the Cajonos township in Villa Alta regained its saliency as a stronghold of idolatry in the extirpators' minds. For instance, in a 1679 letter to the crown, del Puerto reports the discovery of a "high priest" who, along with four others, received the deferential treatment accorded to Christian priests.[17]

Bishop Isidro Sariñana (1683–96), del Puerto's successor, established a novel punitive institution in Oaxaca City: a "perpetual prison of idolaters."[18] After arguing that such a prison was required to curb native idolatry, Sariñana obtained a substantial grant from the crown and completed a new building only a few streets west of the cathedral in 1692. Bishop friar Ángel Maldonado (1702–28), a member of the order of Saint Benedict, turned Sariñana's punitive project into a supporting pillar for an innovative but exacting extirpation campaign he carried out in Villa Alta.[19] In 1704, Maldonado issued an unusual offer: in exchange for denouncing its ritual specialists, turning in its ritual texts, and making a full confession about ritual practices, each native community would receive amnesty from any formal trial. Consequently, between November 1704 and February 1705, the elected authorities of about one hundred native communities journeyed to the jurisdictional seat of Villa Alta to register a communal confession. Through this innovative strategy, Maldonado harvested an exceptional set of ritual texts: 101 manuscript booklets, many of which contained local versions of the *piyè*—the 260-day Zapotec ritual calendar—and four booklets containing more than thirty Zapotec ritual songs. Although the transcription, translation, and interpretation of this unusual set of records is still in its early stages, some preliminary observations from these sources are discussed in the section below.

Clandestine Zapotec Devotions in Colonial Oaxaca

In recent years, a detailed portrayal of colonial Zapotec ritual practices has begun to take shape. A highly promising line of evidence is represented by two distinct ritual genres transcribed by literate Zapotec devotional specialists in northern Oaxaca in the seventeenth century: calendrical texts and ritual songs. About 101 separate booklets or booklet fragments containing partial or full lists of the *biyè gue xotao xoci reo*, or "time count of our fathers and ancestors," were turned in to Bishop Maldonado in 1704.[20] This *biyé* was the northern Zapotec version of a 260-day pre-Columbian divinatory calendar, which is widely attested throughout the Mesoamerican culture area. In contrast with the 365-day count or vague solar year, the 260-day count was used in pre-Columbian Mesoamerican communities—and in some colonial indigenous communities—for assigning calendrical names to individuals based on their assumed or actual birth date. Moreover, ritual specialists interpreted this count in order to indicate to their clients propitious days for undertaking both quotidian and life-cycle activities. According to the information collected by the Dominican friar Juan de Córdova for his 1578 grammar of Valley Zapotec, the Zapotec 260-day count was composed by two cycles: a 13-day cycle identified by the numbers between 1 and 13, and a 20-day cycle, identified by a fixed sequence of names that referred to animals, plants, and forces of nature.[21] This count had four major subdivisions, called *gocio* or *pitao* in Valley Zapotec, each of which was composed by 5 groups of 13 days, or 65 days.[22]

The second set of sources is the *dij dola nicachi*, or "wooden drum songs," and is represented by a surviving corpus of about twenty-two ritual songs that were performed during communal ceremonies to the beat of a wooden, cylindrical drum, called *nicachi* in Zapotec and *teponaztli* in

Nahuatl, which bear genre markers—such as stanza boundaries and transcription of percussion patterns—similar to those found in the sixteenth-century *Cantares Mexicanos*, written in Nahuatl. This corpus is contained in two separate booklets written in the Cajonos variant of colonial Zapotec, currently labeled with the numbers 100 and 101, and preserved at the Archivo General de Indias in Seville. Booklet 100 was sold by Pedro de Vargas, a renowned ritual specialist from Betaza, to Fernando López of Lachirioag, and contains a cycle of thirteen ritual songs; Booklet 101 was surrendered by Pedro Gonzalo of Lachirioag, and contains a nine-song cycle.[23] Both song cycles may have a number of rich symbolic associations with colonial Zapotec notions about the cosmological order, which is depicted in Calendar 11 from Villa Alta as a structure featuring nine layers between the House of the Underworld (*yoo gabila*) and the House of Earth (*yoo yeche layo*), and nine layers between the House of Earth and the House of the Sky (*yoo yaba*).[24] This map of the cosmos that resembles the multi-layered view of the Nahua cosmos displayed, for instance, in the late sixteenth-century Codex Ríos.[25] Furthermore, another local song genre designated as *libana*, or "Elegant Speech," attests to the efforts of Dominican missionaries. This second corpus—also performed to the beat of a hollow drum—contains songs with strong didactic overtones that revolve around the worship of Christian entities.

A tentative appraisal by this author of some of the songs from the *dij dola nicachi* corpus lends partial support to Joyce Marcus' characterization of Zapotec religion as oriented toward the propitiation of local deified ancestors.[26] Some of the entities mentioned in the corpus appear to have been worshipped locally or regionally and have names that link them to the ritual calendar. In Booklet 100 from the town of Betaza, several songs seek the favor of Lord 1 Cayman (*Coque Yagchila*)—a name that designates either a founding ancestor mentioned in the Genealogy of Quiaviní, a colonial pictographic manuscript with glosses in Valley Zapotec, or the divine Zapotec entity that presided over the first 65-day period in the 260-day count.[27] There are other entities that have the same calendrical or personal names as that of founding ancestors whose names were recorded in other colonial Zapotec alphabetic sources, but it is unclear at this time whether the songs refer to those particular ancestors or to namesake entities. For instance, Booklet 100 contains references to 10/7 Knot the Great (*Bilatela Tao*), who is named as the founding ancestor of the Villa Alta town of San Juan Tabaá in a colonial historical narrative written in Cajonos Zapotec, and to Great

Eagle (*Bicia Tao*)—a personal name shared by two ancestors in the afore-mentioned Genealogy of Quiaviní.[28] By contrast, this song corpus also refers to four Zapotec deity complexes that were also mentioned by Córdova's sixteenth-century informants from the Valley of Oaxaca, and by the renowned seventeenth-century ritual specialist Diego Luis from the south-central Oaxacan township of Sola: *Liraa (qui)tzino* or *Betao (gu)ichinoo*, or "God Thirteen," an entity that presided over all other deities; *Bezelao Dao* or *Coquie Cabila*, a deity associated with the Zapotec underworld; *Nohuichana* or *Huichana*, a goddess associated with birth-giving and with fish and rivers; and *Cozàana* or *Nosana*, a deity associated with procreation and with the animal world.[29]

Moreover, the confessions compiled by Maldonado in 1704 and a number of idolatry trials from at least eight Villa Alta Zapotec communities suggest that local Zapotec religious practices were grounded in the local memory of founding lineages. A ubiquitous category of effigies, which may have ranged in appearance from carved or painted representations of individuals to "hanks of hair"[30] tied to pieces of cotton,[31] was called in Cajonos Zapotec *quiquiag yag tao*, a term that was very loosely glossed in trial records as "the heads of our grandparents."[32] Communal ritual celebrations took place on geographical locations with specific local names, usually in the outskirts of a village, and evidence from Betaza suggests that these celebrations were tied to specific dates in the 260-day ritual calendar. Accordingly, one may ground the potentially broad rubric of "local religion" in a particular social terrain in this region: that in which ancestors, local foundational accounts, and sites for communal ceremonies converged within the social and spatial boundaries of a specific Zapotec *gueche*, a sociopolitical unit with its own foundational narrative, former ruling lineage(s) and territory, comparable to the Mixtec *ñuu* and to the Nahua *altepetl* (or indigenous community land and social unit, discussed at greater length in the essay by Edward Osowski in this book).[33] The following section explores a divisive public struggle over the preservation of these ancestral religious practices in the Zapotec village of Lachirioag in the late seventeenth century.

The Enigma of Idolatry in Lachirioag

The trial of eleven idolatry suspects from Lachirioag in 1666 by alcalde mayor Diego Sandoval Castro provides some evidence about local factions that held opposing views on traditional ritual practices within a single *gueche*.[34] This complex case involved ethnic tensions between an African slave and Zapotec villagers, as well as nagging questions about credibility.[35] Pursuing the recurrent policy of employing informants, the alcalde mayor asked Antonio de Cabrera—a black slave belonging to don Gaspar Calderón, the encomendero (or owner of royal land grant with Indian peon-servants attached to the land) of Lachirioag—to keep a watchful eye on any suspect local activities as he and his owner visited Lachirioag to collect tribute.[36] In May 1665, Cabrera provided the alcalde mayor with a detailed narrative of two strange events. A month earlier, Cabrera had seen some natives enter the house of one Gerónimo López late at night; they came in, went past two women who stood guard at the door, placed a coin of moderate value—a half real—on the ground, and sat around two pots in which deer meat was being boiled. A week later, Cabrera came across López and many town residents as they were coming down Yaguisi Hill toward the town center early at night. Around four in the morning, Cabrera returned to López's house and saw that the people inside were once again dividing up the deer meat. An Indian whistled, warning others about Cabrera's approach, and everyone left the house again. However, Cabrera saw them return to the house later as they took away the deer meat in small containers.[37]

Neither Cabrera nor the civil authorities had a clear idea about the significance of these gatherings; thus, a local spy was asked to inquire into this matter, to no avail. However, in February 1666, civil authorities decided to arrest six of the presumed idolaters—former catechism teacher Gerónimo López, Lachirioag's cacique and governor don Juan Martín and his wife, along with three other town officials.[38] As the trial began, a striking development occurred: none of the defendants admitted to the meetings described by Cabrera, in spite of intense questioning and veiled threats.

At this point, the failed spy brought to the court's attention the involvement of two influential men with a difference of opinion on traditional practices. One of them was the cacique don Diego Martín, a prominent Lachirioag resident with kinship ties to two of the arrested officials; he was Gerónimo López's nephew, and a second cousin to don Juan Martín. The second group was led by Gerónimo López and don Juan Martín. Don Diego Martín depicted himself and the cacique don Francisco Gutiérrez as devoted Christians who were despised by the commoners, "because they take away their pulque and their drunkenness."[39]

This rivalry was confirmed by a breakthrough in incriminatory information. About two weeks after don Diego Martín's first deposition, a mestizo
official from a neighboring community accused López, don Diego's oppo-
nent regarding ritual matters, of baptizing children with Zapotec calendrical names, and reported a confidential conversation he had had with
don Diego, triggering a second summons. In his second deposition, don
Diego provided a number of details he had not included previously, fearing local reprisals. Don Diego asserted that it was he who had steered
Cabrera to specific locations in town where he could observe the nocturnal encounters. Moreover, don Diego described an exchange with his own
uncle, who had branded him with a most dishonorable epithet:

> About a year ago, [don Diego] told Gerónimo López:
> "Turn away from those fiendish things that belong to the
> Devil! Your son has told me about them," and López answered
> him by saying: "Go away, you who go around licking the
> Spaniards' plates [*lambeplatos de los españoles*]; you are no
> longer my nephew!"[40]

However, a day after his second deposition, don Diego was said to have
galloped away from Lachirioag on his horse. At that point, he disappeared
from the trial records.[41]

Don Diego's disappearance was a prime factor in the unraveling of
the trial, as López and the remaining defendants clung to their denials.
Even when confronted in court with the slave Cabrera, an old man in
poor health who had to be carried on a hammock from Oaxaca to San
Ildefonso in order to face López and his associates, the defendants questioned his credibility by claiming he had raped three local women, thus
invoking the specter of uncontrollable African sexual lust. Moreover, one
of the defendants challenged Cabrera by asking why he had not seized
their ritual implements when he had the chance, and by punctuating
his responses with the phrase, "You lie, black man!" [*mentís, moreno*].[42]
Curiously, Cabrera did not directly contest the rape accusations, leading
the alcalde mayor to conclude the trial in April 1666 by stating that, since
"it [had] not been possible to prove and examine the contents of the initial accusation," he absolved the Lachirioag defendants, with the stern
admonishment that they were to avoid any activity that invited suspicions
of idolatry.[43] At the end of this confrontation, a faction that may or may

not have performed communal ceremonies, but which certainly held stern views regarding external influences, had successfully challenged the testimony of a slave and forced a local cacique into temporary exile. A generation later, the stakes in a similar confrontation had grown: this time, the lives of Dominicans, Spaniards, and native allies were at play.

Two Opposing Views of the Cajonos Revolt

We now return to the riot scene at San Francisco Cajonos in September 1700. After don Juan Bautista and Jacinto de los Ángeles were handed over, they were taunted, whipped at the pillory, and taken away to a nearby mountain, where they were executed. Some local witnesses would later claim that the dead informants' hearts were extracted and thrown out to the dogs. In any case, their corpses were disposed of in such an effective manner that no traces of them were ever found by colonial authorities. Two days after the riot, the residents of San Francisco appeared before the Dominicans to ask for their pardon and received an absolution on their knees. For the last two weeks of September, an apparent calm descended on the Cajonos region as natives, Dominicans, and Spaniards returned to their quotidian tasks. Until this point, and excluding the fact that two native informants were now missing, the Cajonos events bore a strong resemblance to a short-lived confrontation that had mobilized many residents from the neighboring towns of Zoogocho and Zoochila a decade before. On March 30, 1691, the Dominican José de Castilla, minister of Zoogocho, requested the support of the alcalde mayor don Juan Manuel de Quiroz in order to carry out an ecclesiastical legal procedure. Castilla wanted the imprisonment of four town officials and the choirmaster of Zoogocho, among other defendants. On April 1, 1691, after celebrating Mass in Zoogocho, Castilla closed the church's doors and then had the *comisionado* (deputy) Francisco Calvo arrest six native officials, who were then locked in the prison of neighboring Zoochila. Early in the morning of April 2, a native mob swarmed into Zoochila, liberated the officials, and threw Calvo in prison; Castilla and his supporters—which included a Zoogocho *principal* (or, indigenous community elite/noble)—barricaded themselves in the local church. However, friar Alonso de Vargas—the vicar of San Francisco Cajonos— appeared the following morning and convinced the rioters to free Calvo. Afterward, Castilla said Mass, and the native crowd kneeled to kiss his hands, asking for and receiving his pardon. In both Zoochila and Cajonos, an uncertain point of equilibrium shortly after a riot was achieved through a strategy that involved an organized show of unity and strength and a subsequent public act of repentance.[44]

Given that the threat of violence at Zoogocho was expediently dismantled, one may ask what led the natives of Cajonos to call for the blood of two fellow residents nine years later. Much in the way that don Diego had dared to tell an African slave where to observe communal practices in Lachirioag, Jacinto de los Ángeles had committed the transgression of alerting a handful of Spanish tradesmen about a communal celebration that was being held in the home of Joseph Flores, the head of the local confraternity of Saint Joseph. The Spaniards had reported this to the Dominicans, and don Juan Bautista—who had been a former *fiscal* but no longer held that office—came along with the group.[45] It is instructive to inspect two opposing views about the ceremonies that took place at Flores's home that evening. A day after the riot, four Spanish and mestizo witnesses made the following statement:

> [T]hey arrived at the house they said belonged to Joseph
> Flores, where they saw many natives, both men and women,
> and young boys, with many torches and in a great silence.
> Having seen this, in a loud voice, [Vargas] said, "What is this
> shameful thing?" [*qué desverguensa es ésta*], and Joseph de
> Valsalobre went into the house sword in hand, and all the
> Indians fled . . . and in the house they found a doe that they
> had apparently been bleeding, as it had not died yet, and on a
> table there were some images of saints placed face down, and
> on top of them some bowls filled with blood, and they also
> found some turkeys, plucked and headless, and much diabolic
> filth in two woven containers, and inside a cane case.[46]

A different perspective is evident in sixteen testimonies supportive of the Cajonos defendants, which alcalde mayor Juan Antonio de Mier y Tojo collected in May 1701 by order of the viceroy. The declarations of these natives of San Mateo, San Miguel, Yatzachi, and San Francisco— several of which were local notables—displayed quite a different outlook on the celebration at Flores's home, and the informants' motivations. While the scene that unfolded before the friars and their associates appeared to be a veritable catalog of bona fide idolatrous sacrifices—beheaded turkeys, a bleeding doe, offerings of tortillas and tamales, and the sacrilegious use of saints' images—some witnesses offered an alternative explanation. Consider the deposition of Francisco Luis, who had been alcalde of San Francisco in 1699:

> On the night of September 14 of last year, this witness and his five-year-old son, called Joseph, took one peso as a contribution to the confraternity of Saint Joseph to the house of Joseph Flores, who had invited his friends, compadres, and barrio neighbors to have dinner, because he was finishing [his term] as [the head of] said confraternity. Around eight o'clock at night, as everyone was gathered there . . . the two parish ministers came into the house with some Spaniards who had swords . . . and with another official called Juan Bautista, and Jacinto de los Ángeles. They came into one of the houses of Joseph Flores, in which they had turkeys, tamales, tortillas, and a deer, and the blood they had extracted from it in order to make blood sausages. . . . Father friar Gaspar de los Reyes and Jacinto de los Ángeles came into the kitchen in which this witness and another man were, and the said Jacinto seized a piece of pork . . . and threw it to the dogs. This witness asked him, "Jacinto, what are you doing?" Then, the people who were in the other room ran away in fright, but this witness and the people who were with him went home.[47]

These witnesses also asserted that the subsequent acts of violence against the convent occupants were inspired by indignation at the meddling of Bautista and Ángeles, who were depicted as former town officials who had embezzled some money from communal funds, by public apprehension about armed Spanish presence, and by the fact that a native had been shot and killed.[48] By contrast, these witnesses omitted crucial details from their declarations, such as their knowledge about the ultimate fate of the two informants. Furthermore, the original motivation for the gathering at Flores's house remains unclear: the gathering took place on September 14 of the Gregorian calendar, which fell on the day 12 Death (*benelana*) in the 260-day ritual Zapotec calendar. The celebration could have been linked to the end of Flores's service as head of the confraternity, to a celebration linked with the end of a thirteen-day period in the ritual calendar (marked by the interval between the days 12 Death and 13 Deer), or to the convergence of these two circumstances. Although the exact nature of this celebration remains elusive, the fracture lines between the informants and their neighbors were clear: once a local resident was suspected of collaboration, he could be attacked by those who saw themselves as the guardians of ancestral practices in domestic and public realms.

The Cajonos investigation had a redoubtable end after alcalde mayor Mier y Tojo began an investigation into the fate of the informants. Initially, it was claimed that they had fled the area, but after the imprisonment and interrogation of about thirty-four revolt leaders and participants, the alcalde mayor obtained a full confession. In a cruel departure from common legal protocol, he extracted the ratification of testimonies through torture at the rack. After a protracted trial for rioting, murder, idolatry, and insubordination that lasted from November 1700 until January 1702, Mier y Tojo handed down an especially inclement form of exemplary punishment. On January 11, 1702, after being sentenced to death without the right to an appeal, fifteen of the Cajonos rebels were hanged and quartered. Their remains were exhibited in San Francisco Cajonos and along the main road to Oaxaca. The following day, two more defendants were paraded in an *auto de fe* (literally, "act of faith"—a public punishment by religious court authorities), receiving two hundred lashes each. The remaining seventeen defendants were sentenced to death, but Mier y Tojo allowed them to present an appeal. Eventually, Maldonado would secure the commutation of these sentences as a prelude to his extirpation campaign.[49]

Serving Two Lords at Betaza

In late 1702, Bishop Maldonado brought his message of amnesty to San Melchor Betaza and Santo Tomás Lachitaa, but his visit bore little fruit.[50] According to Agustín Gonzalo Zárate, a former town official and ritual specialist, hardly a month had passed after the bishop's visit before the town engaged in another communal ritual celebration. Through the mediation of two experienced interpreters of the visions produced by the hallucinogenic seeds of the *cuana betao* plant, Betaza officials asked their own ancestors what would befall them.[51] The specialists were said to have reported that "they had fallen into the hands of God the Father, [*que ya habían dado en manos de Dios Padre*] . . . and that the Spaniards would come in and take away their parents and grandparents—meaning their idols."[52] In 1703, a visiting priest came to ask the people of Betaza to surrender their ritual implements, but the townspeople denied having any. After this visit, Betaza's officials called a meeting to discuss whether they would surrender their implements; the consensus held that they would not accept Maldonado's amnesty. Following a pattern of intercommunity communication—a local diplomacy of sorts that was also pursued by rebel communities during the Tehuantepec rebellion, Betaza's town council sent letters to neighboring towns informing them of their decision and asking them for support.[53]

Betaza's communal resolve was tested by an incident on December 17, 1703, during a local fair that some Betaza officials attended in Yalálag, a Zapotec town a few kilometers to the south.[54] Among the visitors who crowded the town square, Bernardo García, a Spaniard from Villa Alta, recognized Zárate, a Betaza ritual specialist whose arrest had just been requested by Bishop Maldonado. Another Betaza visitor was don Pedro de Paz, a former alcalde and *gobernador* who possessed such confidence about Betaza's defiance, that he approached one of the regidores of Yalálag and scolded him by saying:

> Perhaps the people of Yalálag are women, for they do not
> deserve to wear pants, and it would be better if they wore
> their women's petticoats [*las naguas de sus mugeres*], or else
> why should they have turned in their idols without resistance?
> They should not have turned them in without fighting to the
> last drop of their blood.[55]

After this exchange, Yalálag governor don Juan de la Cruz conferred with García, and arrested Zárate, Paz, and four other local officials who were at the fair. Initially, the people of Betaza interpreted these arrests as a direct attack on them from the community of Yalálag and promptly seized a Yalálag courier who was passing through town on his way to deliver a letter to alcalde mayor Diego de Rivera y Cotes. Cotes immediately sent an armed group of sixteen men into Betaza, who escorted the courier and the Betaza suspects to San Ildefonso. In January 1704, Cotes arrested and tried eleven Betaza residents for idolatry; all were current and former town officials, specialists who interpreted the visions triggered by ingesting *cuana betao*, or performers of ritual songs.

The ensuing idolatry trial revealed strong similarities between the financing of Betaza's ancestor worship celebrations and that of indigenous confraternities throughout New Spain. What set Betaza apart was the development of a parallel system, in which various methods were used to collect funds for two distinct budgets, one for Christian devotional practices, the other for clandestine communal ritual practices. First, Zapotec town officials took collections to satisfy the yearly demand for tribute to the crown. A group of twenty-four officials—replaced on a rotating basis—raised three pesos each in order to cover expenditures for the visiting priest and for the seven public Christian holidays held each year. Additional funds for Christian celebrations were raised by the only religious confraternity in town, the Confraternity of the Rosary. Then, whatever communal funds remained every year after satisfying the demands of crown and church—about 197 pesos on average—were devoted to communal ritual expenses.

Three former town officials described two other methods for raising funds for communal ritual practices. The first one was an outright collection of up to one and a half reales per household head. The second one involved a set of communal obligations and money-lending practices that mirrored the financial practices of native confraternities.[56] Three officials supervised the plowing of three land plots that may have corresponded to a tripartite lineage divisions and maintained three houses used in communal celebrations. After the maize obtained from these plots was sold, profits were lent to Betaza residents at a 37.5 percent interest rate—three reales for each borrowed peso.[57] Through the accumulation of communal funds earmarked for communal ritual practices, the town bought ten teams of oxen that were used primarily to plough the three communal land plots.[58]

On February 1704, as the interrogation of Betaza defendants began, friar Joseph Cardona pronounced a communal absolution from idolatry in Betaza. However, the town authorities began punishing those they deemed as local traitors on the day after Cardona's visit. Betaza resident Juan Mateo would later report that he was intercepted as he walked down the street by Juan Luis, who brought him forcibly into the local holding cell:

> The morning after, the [town's mayor] came in, and told him:
> "Now you will suffer, you who betrayed the pueblo"; [Juan
> Mateo] asked him to show them a witness of his betrayal, and

the alcalde answered that he would do so after his pants came off [*quitados los calsones*]. Then, [the mayor] had him tied to the pillory; as he whipped him, he asked how many of his associates had gone to Villa Alta to give accounts about their customs. Favián Gonzalo and Francisco Suárez then said that it was best to kill him, as the people of San Francisco Cajonos had done [with their informants], for on what account was he a [*bendedor del pueblo*], someone who sold his town away. . . . They kept on whipping him, saying that he had uncovered everything, and that he had a very loose tongue [*la lengua muy larga*].[59]

Conclusion

The social composition of a realm of ritual and devotional practices that may be termed "clandestine"—since its practitioners limited their activities to carefully delimited social and spatial domains and faced the possibility of public exemplary punishment—was a complex process in Villa Alta. Although the rhetoric that issued from colonial authorities and various local factions had a rather sharp edge to it, the struggles fought over the observance of ancestral devotions cannot be reduced to common bipolar oppositions, such as natives against Spaniards, elites versus commoners, or native lineages against political parvenus. However tempting, idolatry accusations cannot be reduced to a mere superstructural manifestation of local rivalries; rather, they become integrated into the thick web of alliances and rivalries within native communities, among residents and officials of various native communities, and between native representatives and the alcalde mayor.[60]

We can now turn to a final assessment of the meanings of autonomy in Lachirioag, San Francisco Cajonos, and Betaza. Autonomy may be seen as analytical shorthand for several forms of political action—such as secession, the spontaneous organization of local confraternities, or the defense of communal lands—that were articulated in different ways within different native communities. In Lachirioag and San Francisco, there seemed to be a consensus of sorts—led by local practitioners such as Gregorio López and Joseph Flores—that communal practices were to be performed in domestic spaces, and in ritually meaningful sites beyond the layout of public space at the town's center. Given this compromise of sorts, a dissenting local minority—such as the caciques don Diego and don Francisco, or the former fiscal don Juan Bautista—could avert their eyes from these nocturnal activities even as they chided their neighbors, and a pretense of harmony could have been kept.[61] By contrast, the consensus among Betaza officials allowed the emergence of a dual arrangement for local religious practices that rested on financial contributions from each head of household—an arrangement that reconfigured the religious field at Betaza, leading to individual participation on ancestor propitiation through the collection of royal and ecclesiastical tribute. Nevertheless, in these three communities, a minimal definition of autonomy with respect to communal devotions seems to include the absolute refusal to involve any foreigners—not simply Spaniards, but also natives from neighboring communities—in what may have been a heated local discussion over the proper social and spatial realms in which local religion was articulated. Giving information about these practices to an African spy, leading a group of armed Spaniards into the house of an official, or using a local fair in a neighboring town to entrap local officials were interpreted as intolerable breaches.

Although the sharp rhetorical acts that comment on this breach come down to us through Spanish translations, they remain vivid enough: those who reneged traditional devotions threatened the pride vested in them; they were described as servile beings who obtained their sustenance from licking the Spaniards' plates. Moreover, the masculinity of those who refused to defend their ancestors was put into question by denying them an iconic masculine garment—a pair of pants—which was substituted, in a symbolic rhetorical flourish, with their women's petticoats. Through a series of well-chosen epithets and characterizations, a rhetorical line was drawn between the servile, the feminized, those with loose tongues, and those who sold their towns away, from those who proudly kept their representations of lineage heads and baptized their children with calendrical names. The rioters even used shame as a rhetorical weapon, by referring to the besieged friars and Spaniards as "cuckolds." This local pride in the defense and veneration of lineage lines coexisted with other forms of honor and shame in colonial Spanish America—such as the honor that attached to legitimate birth, and the shame that issued from sexual impropriety, public insulting words or gestures, and illegitimacy—and may be placed alongside them as another permutation within the continuum of colonial honor.[62]

The Cajonos revolt has an interesting epilogue. In the 1880s, the narrative about the last two days in the life of don Juan Bautista and Jacinto de los Ángeles was reclaimed by Archbishop Eulogio Gillow. Gillow promptly located a "local tradition" that held they had been fiscales when they denounced Flores's celebration, identified an alleged beneficiary of a miracle achieved through their intercession, authored an account of the rebellion, and promoted a beatification inquiry.[63] This process, which yielded little in the 1880s, was restarted in the 1980s and came to fruition in 2001 with the beatification of the two Zapotec villagers by Pope John Paul II. In the end, it took three hundred years and thousands of pages of ecclesiastical and civil proceedings to travel the space in San Francisco Cajonos that separated the domestic realm—José Flores's house—from a public space legitimized by Christian orthodoxy—the church erected by the Dominicans. This distance, which is almost negligible in spatial terms, separates two highly distinct forms of organizing local devotions that underwent a paradoxical convergence: the clandestine worship of ancestors in colonial times, and the public veneration of ancestors proclaimed and celebrated by the Catholic hierarchy in the twenty-first century.

NOTES

1. Research for this essay was carried out under the auspices of a National Endowment for the Humanities fellowship tenable at the John Carter Brown Library, a grant from the Foundation for the Advancement of Mesoamerican Studies, and research funds from Vassar College. The abbreviations used for archival depositories in this essay are as follows: Archivo General de Indias (AGI), Archivo Judicial de Villa Alta (AJVA), Archivo Histórico del Arzobispado de Oaxaca (AHAO), the Archivo Parroquial de Nuestra Señora de la Merced (APMO), and Archivo Luis Castañeda (ALC).

2. Villa Alta was an *alcaldía mayor* (local administrative unit of colonial Mexico similar to a county, parish, or district) located to the northeast of the Valley of Oaxaca. The town of Villa Alta de San Ildefonso was the administrative center for more than one hundred Zapotec, Mixe, and Chinantec communities in the Sierra Zapoteca. See Peter Gerhard, *A Guide to the Historical Geography of New Spain* (Norman: University of Oklahoma Press, 1972), 369.

3. Testimony of Joseph de la Trinidad, October 26, 1700, APMO, 1700–1702 Cajonos trial records, 183r.

4. See Robert Redfield, *The Little Community: Viewpoints for the Study of a Human Whole* (Chicago: University of Chicago Press, 1955); and Clifford Geertz, *The Interpretation of Cultures: Selected Essays* (New York: Basic Books, 1973).

5. See William A. Christian Jr., *Local Religion in Sixteenth-Century Spain* (Princeton, NJ: Princeton University Press, 1981).

6. Pierre Bourdieu, "Genèse et structure du champ religieux," *Revue Française de Sociologie* 12 (1971).

7. For a thorough discussion of the establishment of colonial institutions in this region, see John K. Chance, *The Conquest of the Sierra* (Norman: University of Oklahoma Press, 1989).

8. William B. Taylor, *Magistrates of the Sacred: Priests and Parishioners in Eighteenth-Century Mexico* (Stanford, CA: Stanford University Press, 1996), 48.

9. There were three major colonial Zapotec language variants spoken in Villa Alta: Cajonos, Nexitzo, and Bijanos Zapotec. Cajonos Zapotec was spoken in the three towns in question. See Chance, *Conquest of the Sierra*.

10. See Nicholas Griffiths, *The Cross and the Serpent* (Norman: University of Oklahoma Press, 1995); Sabine MacCormack, *Religion in the Andes: Vision and Imagination in Early Colonial Peru* (Princeton, NJ: Princeton University Press, 1991); Luis Millones, "Religion and Power in the Andes: Idolatrous *curacas* of the Central Sierra," *Ethnohistory* 26 (1979); and Kenneth Mills, *Idolatry and its Enemies: Colonial Andean Religion and Extirpation, 1640–1750* (Princeton, NJ: Princeton University Press, 1997).

11. See David Tavárez, "La idolatría letrada: Un análisis comparativo de textos clandestinos rituales y devocionales en comunidades nahuas y zapotecas, 1613–1654," *Historia Mexicana* 194, no. 49 (1999).

12. See John Chuchiak, "The Indian Inquisition and the Extirpation of Idolatry: The Process of Punishment in the Ecclesiastical Courts of the Provisorato de Indios in Yucatán, 1563—1812" (Ph.D. dissertation, Tulane University, 2000); as well as his article "Pre-Conquest Ah Kinob in a Colonial World: The Extirpation of Idolatry and the Survival of the

Maya Priesthood in Colonial Yucatán, 1563—1697," in *Maya Survivalism: Acta Mesoamericana*, vol. 12, ed. U. Hostettler and M. Restall (Munich: A. Saurwein, 2001).

13. See Hector Díaz-Polanco and Araceli Burguete, "Sociedad colonial y rebelión indígena en el Obispado de Oaxaca (1660)," and Hector Díaz-Polanco and Consuelo Sánchez, "El vigor de la espada restauradora. La represión de rebeliones indias en Oaxaca (1660–1661)," in *El Fuego de la inobediencia. Autonomía y rebelión india en el obispado de Oaxaca*, ed. H. Díaz-Polanco (Mexico: CIESAS, 1996).

14. *Repartimientos* governed the appropriation of local goods by colonial authorities through a mandatory exchange for goods manufactured elsewhere that natives rarely needed and at unfavorable exchange ratios. See Chance, *Conquest of the Sierra*. A dissenting view holds that this process had an integrative effect on regional markets; see Jeremy Baskes, *Indians, Merchants, and Markets: A Reinterpretation of the Repartimiento and Spanish-Indian Economic Relations in Colonial Oaxaca, 1750–1821* (Stanford, CA: Stanford University Press, 2000).

15. See Marcelo Carmagnani, "Un movimiento político indio: La 'rebelión' de Tehuantepec, 1660–1661," in Díaz-Polanco, *El Fuego de la inobediencia*. This perspective on the Tehuantepec rebellion is partially based on Carmagnani's focus on the revitalization of local and regional indigenous identity in Oaxaca in the second half of the seventeenth century. See Marcelo Carmagnani, *El regreso de los dioses: El proceso de reconstitución de la identidad étnica en Oaxaca, siglos XVII y XVIII* (Mexico: Fondo de Cultura Económica, 1988).

16. Diego de Villegas y Sandoval Castro, alcalde mayor of Villa Alta in 1653–55, and again from late 1665 until late 1667, appeared to be an especially active civil extirpator of idolatries under the aegis of Bishop Monterroso (1665–78), for he presided over at least three idolatry trials in 1665 and 1666; see AJVA Criminal 19, 22, 23. Moreover, at least three of Sandoval Castro's successors are known to have presided over idolatry trials in Villa Alta between 1667 and 1684.

17. The link between Villa Alta and idolatry was not a novel one at this point. The Dominican friar Pedro Guerrero began one of the first systematic extirpation campaigns in the region in 1560, when he convinced scores of natives to turn in their idols. Del Puerto's activities are discussed in AGI México 357.

18. AGI México 357. Sariñana was probably inspired by inquisitorial precedent.
    In Mexico City, in the early seventeenth century, the Holy Office erected
    a prisión perpetua for proselytizing Jews and heretics; see Solange Alberro,
    Inquisición y sociedad en Mexico, 1571–1700 (Mexico: Fondo de Cultura
    Económica, 1988). In the Archdiocese of Lima, a prison for idolaters
    called Casa de Santa Cruz existed between 1618 and 1639. See Iris Gareis,
    "Repression and Cultural Change: The 'Extirpation of Idolatry' in Colonial
    Peru," in *Spiritual Encounters: Interactions Between Christianity and Native
    Religions in Colonial America*, ed. N. Griffiths and F. Cervantes (Lincoln:
    University of Nebraska Press, 1999), 234.

19. Sariñana's prison lasted only a few years: first, an earthquake damaged
    it in 1696; later that year, Sariñana died, leaving the prison's finances in
    a state of uncertainty. After 1702, Bishop Maldonado abandoned the
    original prison building, erecting instead a new building funded by a
    bequest from a former extirpator of idolatries on a piece of land ceded
    by the Dominican order.

20. An extremely useful survey of the pocket calendars and the communal
    ritual practices of Villa Alta appeared in the first monograph devoted to
    the topic is José Alcina Franch, *Calendario y religión entre los zapotecos*
    (Mexico: UNAM, 1993); see also Arthur Miller, "Transformations of
    Time and Space: Oaxaca, Mexico, circa 1500–1700," in *Images of Memory*,
    ed. Susanne Küchler and Walter Melion (Washington, DC: Smithsonian
    Institution Press, 1991). However, it bears noting that recent developments
    in colonial Zapotecs linguistics and philology may yield significant revisions
    of the transcriptions and interpretations offered by Alcina Franch. For
    an influential appraisal of the Zapotec calendar and Zapotec religion,
    see Joyce Marcus, *Mesoamerican Writing Systems* (Princeton, NJ: Princeton
    University Press, 1992).

21. Fray Juan de Córdova, *Arte en lengua zapoteca* (Mexico: Pedro Balli, 1578).
    There is an 1886 reprint of this work (Morelia: Imprenta del Gobierno),
    and a 1987 facsimilar reprint of the Morelia 1886 edition (Mexico:
    Ediciones Toledo, 1987).

22. The epigraphic evidence regarding the origins of this calendrical
    system reaches as far back as late Formative times (600 BCE). See
    Javier Urcid Serrano, *Zapotec Hieroglyphic Writing* (Washington, DC:
    Dumbarton Oaks, 2001).

23. For further details on the activities of ritual specialists in Betaza, see
    David Tavárez, "Colonial Evangelization and Native Resistance: The
    Interplay of Native Political Autonomy and Ritual Practices in Villa

Alta (New Spain), 1700–1704," in *Interpreting Colonialism*, ed. Byron Wells and Philip Stewart (Oxford: Voltaire Foundation, 2004).

24. AGI México 882, 384v.

25. For a review of Nahua and Mesoamerican cosmology, see Alfredo López Austin, *Tamoanchan, Tlalocan: Places of Mist* (Niwot: University of Colorado Press, 1997).

26. See Kent Flannery and Joyce Marcus, *The Cloud People: Divergent Evolution of the Zapotec and Mixtec Civilizations* (New York: Academic Press, 1983); and Joyce Marcus and Kent Flannery, *Zapotec Civilization* (London: Thames and Hudson, 1996).

27. AGI México 882, Calendar 100. The Genealogy of Quiaviní was found in 1996 by the archivists of the Archivo de la Reforma Agraria in Oaxaca City. For a discussion of its contents, see Michel Oudijk, *Historiography of the Bènizàa. The Postclassic and Early Colonial Periods (1000–1600 A.D.)* (Leiden: CNWS Publications, Vol. 84, 2000), 141–52.

28. This narrative, known as the Primordial Title of San Juan Tabaá, is kept in the local archives of this community. The purported author of the earliest section of this title is native ruler Thiadela, said to be the son of 10/7 Knot the Great, who baptized and received the Christian name of don Juan de Mendoza y Velasco after the arrival of Spaniards to Villa Alta in the 1520s. A transcription of the original Cajonos Zapotec title and of a 1953 translation by Tabaá residents appears in Oudijk, *Historiography of the Bènizàa*, 295–310. The Zapotec calendrical name *Bilatela* can be read as either "10 Knot" or "7 Knot."

29. A review of sixteenth-century philological evidence regarding Zapotec deities in the Valley of Oaxaca appears in Thomas Smith-Stark's "Dioses, sacerdotes, y sacrificio—una mirada a la religión zapoteca a través del *Vocabulario en lengua Çapoteca* (1578) de Juan de Córdova" (paper delivered at the III Conferencia de Estudios Oaxaqueños, Oaxaca City, 1998).

30. See the declarations of Joseph Hernández from San Pablo Cajonos, AGI México 882, 301v, and Pedro Gonzalo from Yaa, AGI México 882, 305v.

31. See, for example, AJVA Criminal 49.

32. In Betaza, three communal houses called *Yoo Yagtao*—which may have been linked to three distinct lineages—were built for the sole purpose of hosting divination practices. See AJVA Criminal 117.

33. For an erudite discussion of the former, see James Lockhart, *The Nahuas After the Conquest: A Social and Cultural History of the Indians of Central Mexico, Sixteenth Through Eighteenth Centuries* (Stanford, CA: Stanford University Press, 1992); for a ground-breaking discussion of the latter, see Kevin Terraciano, *The Mixtecs of Colonial Oaxaca: Ñudzahui History, Sixteenth Through Eighteenth Centuries* (Stanford, CA: Stanford University Press, 1991).

34. See AJVA Criminal 23.

35. A detailed discussion of this trial appears in David Tavárez, "Idolatry as an Ontological Question: Native Consciousness and Juridical Proof in Colonial Mexico," *Journal of Early Modern History* 6 (2002).

36. It is unusual to find an encomienda—an arrangement that allowed a former conqueror and his heirs to collect tribute in a territorial unit in exchange for assuming the religious and civil stewardship of its native inhabitants—as late as the 1660s in Villa Alta. However, the fact that at least another encomienda lasted into the eighteenth century in Villa Alta suggests that Lachirioag was not an isolated survival. See Gerhard, *Guide to Historical Geography*, 372.

37. AJVA Criminal 23, 42v–44r.

38. *Cacique* was a term used in colonial Spanish America to designate a native lineage ruler and his descendants. By the mid-seventeenth century, this term indicated a claim to being descended from an indigenous ruling lineage, rather than political office, unless the title was "cacique and governor."

39. AJVA Criminal 23, 14r.

40. AJVA Criminal 23, 38v.

41. Since don Diego's own wife reported his flight, it is unlikely that he suffered the same fate as the two Cajonos informants.

42. AJVA Criminal 23, 45r.

43. AJVA Criminal 23, 71r; my emphases.

44. AHAO Mártires de Cajonos S–1.2. The exact nature of the transgressions committed by Zoogocho's officials cannot be ascertained, although the actions and language of Castilla suggest an idolatry scenario, as these proceedings were incomplete even in 1889.

45. A *fiscal* was a native official who worked with church authorities to ensure native compliance with church precepts on a regular basis.

46. APMO Cajonos, 95v.

47. AHAO Mártires de Cajonos, 265v–66v.

48. Pascual Martín, one of the community's witnesses, reported that Don Juan Bautista had previously served as a fiscal, and that he still owed the community some of the funds he had received during his administration. AHAO Mártires de Cajonos, 269r.

49. ALC 1270, 161v–69v; AHAO Mártires de Cajonos, S–4, 615–31.

50. Betaza was a relatively large town, with an estimated population of 935 residents in 1703; the neighboring community of Lachitaa shared numerous political and kinship links with Betaza and had an estimated population of 178 individuals in 1704. See Chance, *Conquest of the Sierra*. AJVA Criminal 117, 28v, 27v.

51. According to multiple testimonies, certain Zapotec specialists drank a beverage made with the ground seeds of a plant called *cuana betao*, which may be *Turbina* (or *Rivea*) *corymbosa*, a vine of the morning glory family with hallucinogenic properties.

52. AJVA Criminal 117, 39v–40r; my emphasis.

53. AJVA Criminal 117, 60r.

54. Yalálag held an important place among the Zapotec communities of southern Villa Alta due to three factors: its role as a regional market hub; its location on the road to Oaxaca; and its position as the largest town in southern Villa Alta, with an estimated population of 1,577 residents in 1703. See Chance, *Conquest of the Sierra*, 48.

55. AJVA Criminal 117, 9r.

56. Central Mexican indigenous sodalities routinely constituted themselves as money-lending enterprises. A particularly well-documented operation during the 1760s at the Nahua community of Tlapa is described in Danièle Dehouve, "The 'Money of the Saint': Ceremonial Organization and Monetary Capital in Tlapa, Guerrero, Mexico," in *Manipulating the Saints*, ed. A. Meyers and D. E. Hopkins (Hamburg, Germany: WAYASBAH, 1988).

57. AJVA Criminal 117, 17r–v.

58. AJVA Criminal 117, 28v.

59. AJVA Criminal 117, 51r–v.

60. This web of mediations for Yatzona, Yatee, and other Villa Alta towns is analyzed in Yanna Yannakakis, "Indios Ladinos: Indigenous Intermediaries and the Negotiation of Local Rule in Colonial Oaxaca, 1660–1769" (Ph.D. dissertation, University of Pennsylvania, 2003).

61. For a treatment of consensus building in a contemporary Sierra Zapotec community, see Laura Nader, *Harmony Ideology: Justice and Control in a Zapotec Mountain Village* (Stanford, CA: Stanford University Press, 1990).

62. See Lyman Johnson and Sonya Lipsett-Rivera, eds., *The Faces of Honor: Sex, Shame, and Violence in Colonial Latin America* (Albuquerque: University of New Mexico Press, 1998).

63. Eulogio Gillow, *Apuntes históricos sobre la idolatría e introducción del cristianismo en Oaxaca* (Graz: Akademische Druck-u Verlagsanstalt, 1978).

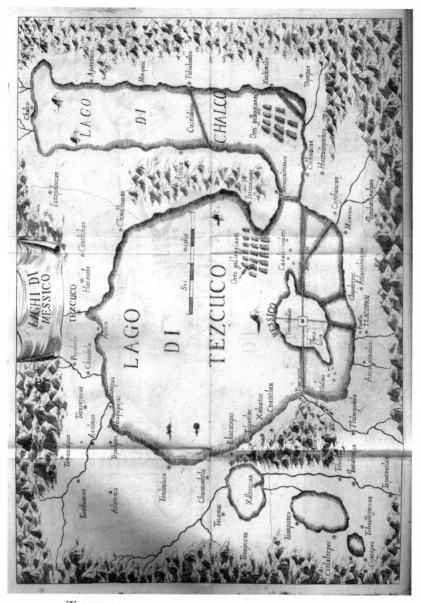

FIGURE 10. Texcoco

*Map of the valley of Mexico with depictions of important Mexica imperial areas.
Taken from Francisco Javier Clavijero,* Storia antica del Messico *(Cesena:
Gregorio Biasini, 1780). Courtesy of Mandeville Special Collections Library,
University of California, San Diego.*

FIGURE 11. Priests traveling

Image of priests traveling by horseback. Taken from Robert Wilson, Mexico and Its Religion *(London: Sampson Low, Son, and Co., 1856). Courtesy of Mandeville Special Collections Library, University of California, San Diego.*

148

have lost half its attractiveness had it been the stiff and clumsy thing which the pictures represent it to be.   I had admired it in pictures from my childhood for what it was not; but I now admired it for what it really was —the finest Indian mound on this continent; where the Indians buried the bravest of their braves, with bows and arrows, and a drinking cup, that they might not be unprovided for when they should arrive at the hunting-grounds of the Great Spirit.   A little digging, a few years ago,* has furnished the evidence on which I base this assertion.   This digging has destroyed the old monkish fiction to reinstate the truly Indian idea of the dead, and of the necessity of mounds for their burial.

PYRAMID OF CHOLULA.

By going round to the north side, I obtained a fine view of the modern improvements which have been con-

* The living witnesses of the result of this excavation are still at Cholula, and the fact is mentioned in several American works; my inference from the fact is the only novelty in the matter.

FIGURE 12. Cholula

The Catholic Church on top of a pre-Hispanic pyramid in Cholula, just outside of Puebla. Taken from Robert Wilson, Mexico and Its Religion *(London: Sampson Low, Son, and Co., 1856). Courtesy of Mandeville Special Collections Library, University of California, San Diego.*

FIGURE 13. Historia de Nueva España

In addition to editing and publishing the 1555 and 1565 Mexican church councils, Archbishop Lorenzana published an edition of Hernán Cortés letters to Charles V in support of the Spanish conquest of Mexico. This is frontispiece from that edition. Note the use of the eagle and nopal cactus, symbols of the foundation myth of Mexico-Tenochtitlan, incorporated into the official Catholic iconography of the Mexican church at the highest levels. Taken from Historia de Nueva España, escrita por su esclarecido conquistador Hernán Cortés, aumentada con otros documentos, y notas, por el ilustríssimo señor don Francisco Antonio Lorenzana *(Mexico: Joseph Antonio de Hogal, 1770). Courtesy of Mandeville Special Collections Library, University of California, San Diego.*

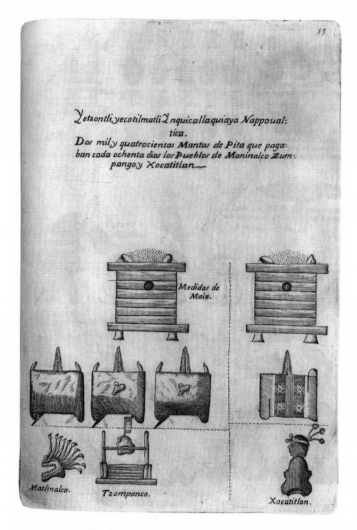

FIGURE 14. Malinalco tax rolls

One of the most intriguing components of the 1770 edition of Cortés' letters is the incorporation of Nahuatl pictographs representing pre-Hispanic tax rolls of dependent cities and provinces of the Mexica empire. This image represents the tax roll from Malinalco, the pre-Hispanic site of an important military shrine and near the Catholic pilgrimage site of Chalma. Taken from Historia de Nueva España, escrita por su esclarecido conquistador Hernán Cortés, aumentada con otros documentos, y notas, por el ilustríssimo señor don Francisco Antonio Lorenzana *(Mexico: Joseph Antonio de Hogal, 1770). Courtesy of Mandeville Special Collections Library, University of California, San Diego.*

FIGURE 15. Catalina de Alejandria

Taken from Devocionario mexicano. Pequeños grabado novohispanos,
introducción de Alicia Gojman (Mexico: Backal Editores, 1998).
Courtesy of Backal Editores.

S. HYPOLITO M.

FIGURE 16. San Hipólito Mártir

Taken from Devocionario mexicano. Pequeños grabado novohispanos, *introducción de Alicia Gojman (Mexico: Backal Editores, 1998). Courtesy of Backal Editores.*

FIGURE 17. San Juan de Sahagún

Taken from Devocionario mexicano. Pequeños grabado novohispanos, *introducción de Alicia Gojman (Mexico: Backal Editores, 1998). Courtesy of Backal Editores.*

FIGURE 18. Santiago

Santiago was the patron saint of Spain, associated with the Reconquest of Iberia from the Muslims and often depicted as a patron of the conquest of Mexico.
Taken from Devocionario mexicano. Pequeños grabado novohispanos, *introducción de Alicia Gojman (Mexico: Backal Editores, 1998).*
Courtesy of Backal Editores.

CHAPTER SIX

Carriers of Saints

Traveling Alms Collectors and Nahua Gender Roles

EDWARD W. OSOWSKI

In 1791, doña Ana Ventura Gómez, a member of the indigenous elite, was forced to defend her leadership of a collective effort to finance devotion to Our Lady of Loreto at the ex-Jesuit Colegio de San Gregorio in Mexico City. Starting in 1586, the Jesuit secondary school had educated the sons of Nahua lords, and in the eighteenth century, daughters of the indigenous upper class took catechism classes there as well.[1] With the expulsion of the Society of Jesus from New Spain in 1767, the Colegio came under crown sponsorship. Ventura sought to renew her license from the archdiocese's Provisorato de Indios y Chinos, the Indian Tribunal, but the Audiencia of Mexico's indigenous appeals court, the Juzgado General de Indios, refused. As part of the larger historical trend of secularization, the Juzgado General de Indios, which was a royal law court, had just recently gained the authority as the final arbiter of whether to grant indigenous people approval. Reviewing this highly capable legal wrangler's appeal, the viceroy's special legal advisor on native matters, the *fiscal de lo civil*, questioned Ventura on how she would raise funds for the image. She assertively responded that she would designate collectors who would travel throughout the entire viceroyalty of New Spain to collect alms (*limosnas*). The license forms permitted the holder, the mayordomo, to use the alms to finance the decoration and restoration of chapels and churches where catholic religious images were housed or to purchase fine clothes, jewelry, and golden crowns that adorned effigies and statues. The fiscal de lo civil's final legal opinion, which he addressed to Viceroy Juan Vicente de Güemes Pacheco y Padilla, the Conde de Revillagigedo (1789–94), stated that allowing the woman a license would encourage the participation of women as coordinators of alms gathering:

> This would be a disorder, opposed to the express intentions
> that have motivated the correct opinions and very just oversight
> that your excellency has dictated in order to extirpate similar
> abuses so prevalent in all of the kingdom, and it would occasion
> to impede such holy ends. In addition to this, the cult of Our
> Lady of Loreto for which they intend to ask for offerings is in a
> state of florescence, that much is public; therefore, there is no
> need for such a campaign.

He continued by specifically noting that Ventura was one of many female indigenous petitioners for alms whom the court officials were attempting to control. The rule against the practice indicates that it was prevalent in reality:

> She is of the same class of other women that have collected for
> this higher authority, and in light of this fact, it is such political
> inconveniences and public damages that motivated the general
> resolution of your excellency and as the civil official, I need not
> repeat what has been reproduced many times.[2]

Ventura's court record does not specifically state if the people that she had been directing in the past were male or female, elite or nonelite, but evidence from alms collection licenses and judicial commentaries regarding other cases show that both sexes and all social classes were involved in taxing the faithful. Two visions of proper public religious leadership—the indigenous view that included women and the Spanish courts that did not—caused the disagreement between the native woman and the Spanish officials in this particular case and others discussed here.[3]

This essay follows the stories of two indigenous alms collectors and will visit the mixed Spanish-indigenous cultural environments through which they traveled. Doña Ana Ventura Gómez from the capital of New Spain and Gregorio Aparicio from a rural town called Ecatepec, both acted as spiritual leaders when they cared for their communities' holy images as mayordomos. They relied on unofficial networks of nonelite community members who acted as ambling solicitors and, by extension, shared with the elite this leadership function of financing local religion. An anonymous third character who worked in the Juzgado General de Indios also plays a role in this essay. In the eighteenth century, the fiscal de lo civil who was the crown attorney acting in the capacity of protector of the Indians, wrote the viceroy's legal opinions on the alms collectors and all other native legal matters. The men who held this position simply signed their opinion papers with their title, fiscal de lo civil, which then received the viceroy's final signature stamp. These lawyers behind the scenes, whose evaluations of the reports of Spanish provincial magistrates and indigenous petitions stood for the will of the viceroy, supply the main plot here.

In the 1790s the Juzgado General de Indios documented these stories when the court was flooded with alarming reports of social disorder from the provinces and Mexico City. In the case of Gregorio Aparicio, indigenous municipal officials fought amongst themselves, but mostly with Spanish provincial magistrates and curas over the proprietorship of images and the issue of how best to finance their decoration and ceremonies. The Juzgado General de Indios gathered the stories for the purpose of writing legal sanctions in order to control what it viewed as social disorder. Indigenous people, however, were legally entitled to respond to legal sanctions. Therefore, reports on conflicts over alms collectors illustrate divergent indigenous and Spanish attitudes about the practical ways that good leaders organized their community members, which included different views on women's participation. Administrators in the Juzgado were primarily concerned with the dissolution of the *pueblo de indios* (Indian town/village) and the improper use of pueblo finances, which were intended for religious purposes only. From the administrators' point of view, reports of the alms collectors' long-distance travel and the participation of powerful women like doña Ana were two pieces of evidence that major disruptions of public order were occurring within indigenous communities. After these explorations into the practical organization of people, the final analytical section of this essay presents linguistic evidence that allows us to delve into the abstract cultural concepts of the indigenous elite. Concepts of community order that had their roots in non-European social practices justified the practice of alms collectors carrying images of saints. Corroborating the Juzgado General de Indios' reports on alms collectors from the 1790s, antedated Nahuatl-language sources suggest that mobility and female participation were adaptation strategies that the male indigenous elite encouraged in order to maintain community cohesion and their own power within the pueblo de indios.

A higher religious purpose can be a powerful source of community solidarity. I argue that these indigenous leaders depended on formal and informal networks of their community members who aided them in collecting a "tax" that financially supported local saint cults. Women unofficially collected or directed the collection of alms on the local municipal level; male collectors who were named on licenses ranged further afield throughout the regions of central Mexico. The goal was to finance emblems of spiritual protection, thus bolstering worldly, indigenous municipal sovereignty. Both the Mesoamerican and Spanish worlds produced the practice of itinerant alms collection. In the 1790s, Bourbon administrative pressures, punitive measures, and patriarchal attitudes pushed up against native organizational methods, which included more women's participation than the Hispanic community allowed. Thus, forces from below and above, both internal and extraneous to the indigenous community, shaped the practice of native people traveling with saints during the last century of Spanish colonial rule.

The Eighteenth-Century Stage for the Traveling Show

The historical outcomes of the Spanish Conquest and the indigenous people's experience of it created these internal and external cultural forces. Although the Spaniards militarily destroyed the Mexica's great imperial edifice in 1521, many of the core Nahua communities survived and were incorporated into the Spanish Catholic global order, which included the viceroyalty of New Spain. The Nahuas called the fundamental indigenous community the *altepetl* in Nahuatl, which included a town and surrounding agricultural lands. Indigenous people successfully maintained this local structure of human organization and culture, which the Spaniards called the pueblo de indios, because they were able to adapt to the new order of the Spanish Catholic monarchs. However, survival through adaptation required a gradual acceptance of aspects of Hispanic culture.

During the colonial period, an upper class of indigenous men monopolized offices in the first level of colonial government, the town council, which held sway over ancient territorial settlements. These officeholders represented the *república de indios* (the Indian spatial and legal world) and the first wrung of a legal and administrative ladder that was separate from that of the *república de españoles* (the Spanish spatial and legal world). The viceroyalty of New Spain's Juzgado General de Indios and various diocesan Provisoratos de Indios (Vicarates of Indians) were the two colonial bureaucracies that had exclusive judicial and administrative functions in regulating religious and civil matters of people legally classified as indios, including the practice of transporting and financing saints. Because Spaniards and mestizos were the ethnic minority in the vast rural areas of New Spain, the república de indios had a degree of political autonomy and corporate bargaining power on the local level. In central Mexico, native notables conducted business, administered the lands of the altepetl, and led Catholic catechism classes in Nahuatl. Indigenous notaries wrote wills, tax records, village histories, and land titles, leaving a paper trail of indigenous-language documents, which modern historians can plumb. The predominantly Hispanic Catholic clergy depended on native leaders as intermediaries to help them in the laborious work of shaping the Indian population into good Catholics with "correct" beliefs. Nahua lay-religious leaders and town council officials had to project positive public images of their towns as Catholic places if they were to preserve their power and ensure the survival of their communities.

Catholic images located in altepetls were a necessary means of communicating to Spanish authorities that the people were steadfast believers. Miraculous events such as mysteriously moving stone crosses, paintings that restored themselves after natural disasters and statues that disappeared from homes and reappeared in chapels were further proof that God favored the Indian towns that displayed so much faith.[4] Indigenous leaders set aside communal crop and cattle lands to produce funds to pay for the adornment of images and paid priests to say Mass in their chapels. By the mid-eighteenth century, however, land had become scarcer because of rapid demographic growth. Royal administrators also began to pressure indigenous officials to cease using the land they had left for financing the devotion to religious images of intercession in their towns.[5] In the rapidly changing

New Spain, soon to be the independent Republic of Mexico, indigenous leaders resorted to seeking revenue through itinerant alms solicitation.

Every year in the 1790s, hundreds of indigenous alms collectors from central Mexico removed holy paintings, crosses, and effigies from rural and urban chapels and churches located in pueblos de indios (the altepetl). With the blessings of their community leaders and *curas* (the latter who signed their printed licenses to carry), these men would enclose their paintings, crosses, and effigies up in wooden chests, strap them to the backs of donkeys and mules, and set off on highway journeys lasting one year or more. They often rode into rural towns, mining camps, and the outskirts of Mexico City with a carnival parade of musicians playing the popular secular tunes of the day. The traveling show attracted crowds of onlookers in the streets, including conspicuous throngs of indigenous women who gathered around the images. The local men and women who came to see the arriving icons donated their money and joined the spectacle of ritual giving. During these pious performances, alms collectors and donors alike took steps together toward salvation. They practiced good works, which were acts of Christian sacrifice that the Counter Reformation Catholic Church proclaimed to be soteriologically as valuable as faith. Often after the parade, the saints or crucifixes would be placed on top of altars that many indigenous women maintained in their houses. Visitors who came to pray at these domestic altars left money as well, which some Spanish authorities believed the wandering male collectors and female altar-keepers split. After the images had sat on the home altars for several days or weeks, the alms gatherers safely locked them back up in their cases, and with their pack animals jingling with coins, they set off to another destination, eventually returning to their hometowns with the images and a supply of cash to fund local religion.

The particular types of Catholic religious images that these men transported were important political and social symbols for indigenous people. Today, many people automatically associate Mexican Catholicism, especially as practiced by indigenous people, with images of Saint Mary, the virgin mother of Jesus, especially the Virgin of Guadalupe. However, late eighteenth-century native itinerants carried a substantial number of graphic depictions of the Passion of Christ. The Passion refers to the story of the suffering of Jesus on his way to crucifixion on the cross and Saint Mary's anguish witnessing this event, which was celebrated during Semana Santa (Holy Week), the week before Easter Sunday.

Table 6.1. Alms-Funded Images from the Regions of Mexico City, Chalco, Ecatepec, Zumpango de Laguna, and Cuautitlan, 1789–1801

Images	Number	Percentage
Passion of Christ	50	28
Mary's Suffering at the Cross (Our Lady of the Sorrows and Solitude)	22	10
Christ (Holy Christ)	11	5
Saint Anthony of Padua	6	3
The Virgin of Guadalupe	25	12
Other Various Saints	88	41
Total Number of Licenses:	**212**	

Sources: Achivo General de la Nación, Mexico City, Clero Regular y Secular, vols. 22, 116, 123, 151, 155.

The alms licenses, which the archdiocese of Mexico's Provisorato de Indios issued, show that passion devotions were found in chapels and churches of indigenous doctrinas in the regions of Mexico City (including Santiago Tlatelolco), Chalco, Zumpango de Laguna, Ecatepec, and Cuautitlan.[6] Out of a total of 212 licenses permitting indigenous people to collect alms to adorn images from 1789 to 1801, there is a high percentage (43 percent) of mayordomos' requests to collect funds for icons of the suffering of Christ and his mother at the cross, as well as other Christ images such as Jesus of Nazareth. (See Table 6.1.)

Prior to the eighteenth century, Passion images had been historically important to the indigenous elite as symbols of political legitimacy within the global Catholic order and local political empowerment under Spanish rule. Since the sixteenth century, the Nahua elite had embraced Passion devotions, which the Franciscan order had originally brought, as divinely ordained signs that they had an active role to play in the reception of a new Catholic monarchical order. During Easter Week in the eighteenth century, native communities in Mexico City and surrounding rural provinces such as Chalco held vigils and processions with bloody crucifixes and life-size effigies of Jesus faltering on shredded knees as he made his way to his death at the hill of Calvary or laying dead in his tomb. Through annual ritual reenactments of the cycle of death and resurrection, native communities publicly affirmed their Catholic faith, and by extension the Spanish monarchy, which was charged with defending the faith. Men from the indigenous town councils who organized Easter festivals, community members dressed in Roman Centurion costumes, and nonelite confraternity members "witnessed" the suffering and death of Jesus. In spite of the morbid motifs of the festival, the overall spirit was triumphal and fairly inclusive. The people of New Spain believed that on the first Easter Sunday Jesus Christ the King rose from the dead and extended the beneficence of his universal kingdom of salvation to all of humanity. Easter Week pageants in colonial Mexico were steeped in the mythologies of the conversion of the Indians of the New World and the early Christian church under the Roman Empire. The indigenous people were cast as the pagan but civilized Romans who crucified Jesus, but then rapidly accepted the truth of Jesus's divinity and kingship.

The native elite politically capitalized on their work organizing their community members' participation in these festivals, which were often funded with alms. Neither indigenous leaders nor Spanish rulers objected to the political use of religion, nor viewed mixing religion and politics as incompatible with true faith. In fact, under the Laws of the Indies, indigenous leaders' demonstrated Catholic faith and their lay religious stewardship of their community members were basic legal conditions for maintaining positions in the local municipal councils and holding entitled estates. Thus, when the elite patronized and were present at Easter Week performances and alms collection rituals, they publicly affirmed that they were making the good-faith effort to honor their contractual obligations to the King of Spain and Christ the King.

Despite the fact that Passion devotions bolstered elite interests, in the late eighteenth century, significant numbers of nonelite people helped to collect alms for them. In the 1790s community members who did not serve in municipal councils and did not possess entitled estates helped to pay the debts owed to Christ the King in the spiritual currency of good works by funding local religious practices. Doña Ana Ventura Gómez's license was just one of an estimated seventy printed forms and handwritten letters that the Archdiocese of Mexico's Provisorato de Indios issued to indigenous alms collectors every year in the 1790s. The Juzgado

General de Indios confiscated the licenses when there were violations of the rules printed on the forms. One hundred thirty-five of these forms survive today. Out of the ninety-eight mayordomos whose names appear on the licenses, 38 percent can be classified as members of the indigenous elite, meaning the upper-class men who held a monopoly on the highest positions in the local town council and lay-religious offices, as well as being the wealthiest natives. Thirty-five percent of the alms collectors were from middle of the social hierarchy, not occupying the highest status positions in town council and employed in trades, petty marketing, and highway transportation. The remaining 26 percent of license-holders were at the bottom of the indigenous social scale, occupied as landowning small farmers and temporary agricultural workers on haciendas.[7] In the closing years of the colonial period, Passion images and the social status that being an alms-collecting patron afforded belonged to both native elite and popular culture. Indigenous patronesses had a hand in creating this popular culture as well. This was revealed in the early 1790s when the Juzgado General de Indios attempted to suppress women's involvement. The investigations, from which the stories of Gregorio Aparicio and doña Ana emerged, documented that indigenous women had been routinely acting as collectors of alms in their homes, neighborhoods, and provinces. Indigenous council members, such as gobernadores and alcaldes, acted as executive patrons of local religious devotions and the male mayordomos who were legally registered on the alms licenses were responsible to the councilmen. In Aparicio's experience, these men in local government officially sanctioned by the church and state in turn delegated alms collection to women.

Itinerant Alms Collector Gregorio Aparicio and His Network

Gregorio Aparicio, a Nahua from Santa Cruz Tecamac, a rural town within the province of Ecatepec and roughly fifteen miles northeast of colonial Mexico City, was a legally sanctioned indigenous alms seeker. Tecamac was situated at the crossroads of two major colonial highways, one of which went north to the great silver mines of Zacatecas, and the other to the Atlantic port of Veracruz in the east. Just south of Tecamac were Chiconautla and Ecatepec, and these three towns were transportation hubs for the mule trains that carried goods from region to region.[8] On July 18, 1789, Aparicio embarked from Tecamac on a journey with an image of Nuestra Señora de la Concepción (Our Lady of the Immaculate Conception) and a license from the Archdiocese of Mexico to travel. Although the record only indicates that he carried an image, Aparicio probably carried a painting depicting the belief that Saint Mary, the mother of Jesus, was conceived without the taint of original sin, which the rest of humanity suffered from. As the mayordomo of his town, he was the lay-religious leader and keeper of the finances for a group of people who were devoted to this particular image of Saint Mary. During a twenty-month period, Aparicio collected alms, roaming through at least twenty-three towns, mining camps, and haciendas with the image of the saint encased in a chest. The mayordomo solicited donations in the prosperous agricultural zones of Chalco and Xochimilco where Nahuatl-speakers worked, and he traveled to his farthest destinations in modern-day Guerrero and Michoacán, where he displayed the image of his patroness in towns composed of Chontal, Otomí, and Matlazincan ethnic majorities.

After Aparicio returned to his home in Tecamac in March 1791, the region became embroiled in a conflict over who would next take charge of the saint, and the subsequent investigations of Spanish magistrates revealed that women were illegally collecting alms with the support of the male leadership of indigenous town councils. According to the rules of the license, each mayordomo was allowed only one year of collection time, after which he was required to relinquish the image, collection box, and license to the next mayordomo in his district under the supervision of the Spanish provincial magistrate. Discord in the region began when don Juan Antonio Jímenez Frenero, provincial magistrate of Ecatepec, intervened in the normal process of transferring the image. Suspicious that the natives were violating the legal ban on women's participation in alms collection, Jímenez took custody of Tecamac's Nuestra Señora and the license and refused to surrender them to Aparicio's successor in the neighboring community of San Cristóbal Ecatepec.[9]

In August 1791, months after Aparicio's return, Jímenez gave the license to some Nahua alcaldes—magistrates and members of the indigenous town council—of the municipality of San Cristóbal Ecatepec. The two alcaldes planned to use the image to solicit funds to build a new church. Alcalde don Felipe de Jesús supervised the gathering of materials and indigenous laborers for construction that was already underway. Mayordomo don Felipe de Jesús possessed the printed license form issued by the archdiocese's Provisorato de Indios, but in a petition addressed to the viceroy in the Juzgado General de Indios, he complained he could not proceed with collection. A deputy *corregidor* (or, local administrator, similar to an alcalde), simply referred to as "el teniente," and his sons from neighboring Santiago Tianquistenco had taken the image in her case and would not return it despite the alcaldes' repeated protests and visits to Tianquistenco. According to the terms of the license, without the image and its box, the native alcaldes could not legally march in a procession that would dazzle potential donors and entice people to make contributions for the building.

Responding to don Felipe de Jesús's request that he be able to collect alms without being in physical possession of the image, the fiscal de lo civil ordered the *teniente* (or, deputy alcalde) of Santiago Tianquistenco to produce a license that gave him and his sons the legal right to keep the representation of Saint Mary.[10] Then, in an attempt to discredit the seemingly pious alcaldes of Ecatepec, the teniente and his sons in Tianquistenco retaliated by revealing the prohibited activities of dishonest female alms collectors in Ecatepec. Soon the fiscal de lo civil received a damning report from magistrate Jímenez concerning the abuses of two communities over which the Nahua municipal councilmen of Ecatepec had jurisdiction as dependent towns. The dependencies appeared to be completely out of their control. For the magistrate, the seemingly independent behavior of native women was compelling proof of social disorder. In the parishes of Santo Tomás and Santa María Chiconautla, women were collecting alms under false pretenses and breaking the license's ban on women gathering alms for images:

> There are more than thirty women, widows without really
> being them, due to being ignorant of each of their husband's
> whereabouts, that have gone out with rented licenses; and
> for around two years the mayordomos have not contributed
> to their pension that they normally give them; they remain
> hidden without knowing their whereabouts.[11]

The district magistrate verified that the women were not only subsisting on alms collected in the name of the Virgin but also pretending that their husbands were dead. Subsisting on alms was illegal on two counts. The collections licenses specified that indigenous people were only permitted to use the alms to finance the adorning of effigies and paintings and the decoration of the chapels where they were normally housed. Secondly, the license only sanctioned the mayordomos named on the license—or, if not named on the form, approved by local priests—to solicit donations in their hometown streets and in distant villages down the highways.

Feigning widowhood was a third deception on top of the two violations of the legal provisions of the license. In Chiconautla, local custom dictated that indigenous widows were entitled to a pension that the mayordomos of the cult of the Virgin Mary withdrew from the treasury and distributed to them.[12] The mayordomos were not dispersing the pensions to the women because they were not really widows. By renting the licenses to the women, the mayordomos were not only breaking the law but also defrauding gullible givers who thought that they were either contributing to beautifying the chapel of the Virgin Mary or aiding impoverished widows. Continuing investigations revealed that, in truth, eighteen of the indigenous women's husbands had left them and joined a veritable colony of thirty-two former Chiconautla and Ecatepec families in the City of Puebla de Los Ángeles. The Spanish officials investigating the scandal blamed the husbands who "abandoned their wives on account of alms," but it is not clear whether the women consented to their husbands leaving.[13] According to the assessment of the Juzgado General de Indios, the men became vagabonds who shirked their commitments as husbands because they had contracted wanderlust when they traveled to other towns to collect alms.

The court was most outraged that the absent men had fled Ecatepec knowing that their wives could survive or possibly profit in their husbands' absence. The women rented the licenses because they stood to gain in some way, either financially or in social standing, and in the court's opinion they were not gathering alms primarily to save their souls. Mayordomos also benefited from this scheme because they secured finances for their religious activities through rental fees. With no husbands in evidence, the "widows" were free to collect the money in environs of Ecatepec, undoubtedly benefiting from the public pity caused by their abandonment. Despite the blatant fraud, the Juzgado de Indios took pity on the women and ordered that they not be forced to pay back what they had collected in the past two years. In the end, the court ordered the men of Tianquistenco to return the image of the Immaculate Conception to the alcaldes of Ecatepec despite the improper use of alms in their jurisdiction.[14]

In Ecatepec, male alcaldes who served in the town council were aware of women's illegal participation, and they either actively encouraged or felt ambivalent about it. The Spanish bureaucrats in the Juzgado General de Indios viewed native women's community authority as distinctly inappropriate, whereas male indigenous councilmen did not. As in many indigenous communities in central Mexico, alcalde was a position of great social status in the local indigenous hierarchy of Ecatepec. The Spanish legal bureaucracy also recognized the men who served in the position as legitimate royal officials. Spaniards and indigenous people publicly acknowledged Ecatepec's alcaldes as community leaders, and the councilmen used this authority to insure that their community maintained ownership of the image of the Immaculate Conception. They acted as guardians and protectors of the holy object when they officially coordinated their mayordomos but also when they unofficially employed women in the endeavor. Women's participation in alms collection was illegal, and, if discovered, the community risked losing its alms license. Yet town councilmen continued to rely on women to succeed as the financial protectors of local religion.

Finally, a case from Mexico City displays a similar pattern as in Ecatepec. A male member of indigenous municipal government, serving in the capacity of mayordomo, worked with male and female solicitors who were not licensed to gather offerings, creating a large informal network of devotees that alarmed the crown attorneys of the Juzgado de Indios. Don Antonio Ortega, who was the official mayordomo named on two collection licenses and identified as an "Indian Cacique and resident of Mexico City," had been financing the image of San Antonio de Las Huertas, which was the titular saint of his parish in Mexico City. Throughout the fall of 1790, he had been collecting along a route that took him through seven towns in the Mexicalcinco, Coyoacán, and Xochimilco districts, which were all close to Mexico City. In October 1790 Ortega petitioned the Juzgado General de Indios and requested that he be allowed to collect alms within the limits of Mexico City as well, which, as stated on the printed licensing form, was legally closed to indigenous alms collectors. He also asked that he be able to work with don Ramos Gómez, mayordomo of Nuestra Señora de la Piedad of Salto de Agua within the city. Ortega proposed to the court that he would give Goméz one of his licenses and they would share offerings and split collections for their separate devotions. In December 1790, the fiscal de lo civil's responded to Ortega's request by confiscating his two licenses and denying him the privilege of acting as mayordomo of the indigenous community of Salto de Agua. The crown attorney's legal brief attached to the confiscated licenses articulated why he believed that the indigenous alms collectors were fomenting disorder, and this statement is the most succinct articulation of Viceroy Revillagigedo's official policy toward itinerant alms collectors. The fiscal de lo civil believed that granting such requests as Ortega's would lead to an uncontrolled proliferation of unregistered alms collectors whose sheer numbers should "not be permitted in a civilized Republic." The presence of so many outsiders in native towns would create a situation where whole communities felt that they were being coerced to pay offerings: "If each saint or avocation had a mayordomo and alms solicitor, the result would be that the pueblos [de indios] would be full of them and they would suffer from very serious extortion."[15] In his mind, women's participation and the lack of decorum were emblematic of the breakdown of social order in the indigenous community. Commenting on the crude entertainment of the traveling shows and the mixing of municipal finance with piety, the irritated fiscal de lo civil barely contained his scorn and suspicion of the indigenous women's morals:

> Essentially, the first constant is the indecency with which
> they convey the images in cases carried by beasts of burden,
> as if they were any kinds of goods being transported.
> Sometimes the images are accompanied by profane music
> and suspect women who put altars in private houses and it
> is even worse in other places in which excess and vice turn
> veneration into an outrage. In addition, these petitioners
> turn collection into a business, making a pact and agreement
> with the curas to withdraw their salaries and pensions from
> the collection and in this way they convert and act of piety
> into business. They are commonly a vagabond people who,
> with that pretext, go with impunity wherever they want
> to, converting the excess time on their hands to their
> own advantages.[16]

The viceroy's policy statement equated the collectors' free movements and the hidden household shrines of the women with public disorder in the indigenous pueblo. Social order depended on indigenous women adhering to proper gender roles. As for Ortega's opinion on the matter, his petition displayed an unawareness of the ban on indigenous people collecting within the city limits, and he did not comment at all on employing female solicitors. His was a silent approval.

Doña Ana: Alms Collector for a Complicated Domestic Symbol

Doña Ana Ventura Gómez, whose story opened this essay, brashly confronted the Juzgado General de Indios, which indicates that she felt entitled to the position of chief alms collector for her community of urban indigenous devotees to Our Lady of Loreto. As in the court investigations that revealed Ortega and Aparicio's informal networks of collectors, the intervention of the Juzgado de Indios into doña Ana's organization impinged on her and other indigenous people's assumption that it was normal for women to act as public patronesses of religion. This norm was rooted in an older indigenous Mesoamerican worldview. Doña Ana had to constantly navigate a mixed cultural environment, not a purely indigenous context, which was a typical experience of members of the eighteenth-century Nahua elite in the city and provincial towns. Indigenous societies in central Mexico were far from closed to the outside world, especially in the case of the elite. Native people bought and sold in regional provincial marketplaces, traveled the highways in the name of Christian good works or employment, went to seek justice in the capital at the Juzgado General de Indios, and attended schools run by the Catholic clergy. Such everyday contact experiences acted as cultural transmitters that communicated Hispanic values, including gender norms, which influenced the indigenous elite's outlook.

In the late eighteenth century, indigenous people encountered, and partially accepted, the value that women should be confined to the private domain of the home. The image of Our Lady of Loreto at the Jesuit Colegio de San Gregorio in Mexico City, which was one of the colony's premier centers of education of the sons and daughters of the indigenous upper class, encouraged dedication to the Holy Family (Jesus, Mary, and Joseph) among the Nahuas. This devotion spread the patriarchal value of the male-headed household among the indigenous elite, albeit to a limited degree because of the translation process of Spanish concepts and the fact that Mary was a far more popular saint than her husband, Joseph.

In 1586, the Society of Jesus founded the Colegio de San Gregorio with the mission of educating the sons of the Mexica elite, in a location minutes away from the two architectural symbols of Spanish religious and worldly hegemony—the cathedral and viceroy's palace—in the center of

Mexico City. This secondary school facilitated the transformation of young indigenous men into loyal subjects of the Spanish sovereigns by teaching skills that would aid in spreading the habits of correct Catholicism and imperial administration to rural towns and urban barrios. In the seventeenth century, one church historian reported, "At the Colegio or Seminary of San Gregorio . . . the Indian sons of the native leaders learn to read, write, and sing, and from there many catechism teachers, skillful organists and musicians have gone out to many Indian towns."[17] A description of Mexico City from 1768 relates that the teachers at the school had taught the canonical doctrines of the faith to both boys and girls.[18]

Through the exchange of culture, San Gregorio aimed to create mutual respect among local indigenous rulers in the Valley of Mexico and the clergy that trained them. Like all educational institutions for indigenous people during the colonial era, the Colegio was also a training center for Spanish priests to study indigenous languages such as Nahuatl. Ignacio de Paredes was a learned Jesuit at the Colegio who was a prolific author of Nahuatl sermons, catechisms, and literature dedicated to the spreading of devotion to the Holy Family. In 1758 Paredes wrote in his Nahuatl translation of the *Catechismo Mexicano* that the Nahuas should be instructed to sing litanies to the Virgin Mary "at her home of Loreto" (*ichantzinco de Loreto*) at the Jesuit secondary school of San Gregorio in Mexico City.[19] According to legend, the Casa de Loreto (House of Loreto) was the original house in Nazareth where the Holy Family of Jesus, Mary, and Joseph had lived, which had been miraculously transported to Italy. Our Lady of Loreto, whose effigy was depicted in her home with the baby Jesus, was one of six miraculous images of Saint Mary in Mexico City that residents increasingly associated with the apparition of the Virgin of Guadalupe during the eighteenth century. In the great plague year of 1737, the most important Spanish and indigenous officials of the city councils led an all-night procession of three hundred lights through the streets in order to implore God through Saint Mary to grant the capital a reprieve.[20] Today, in the town of Tepotzotlan on the northern outskirts of sprawling Mexico City one can visit a full-scale red-brick replica of the house in the gilded church of the Jesuit Colegio de San Francisco Javier.

When Paredes translated the Spanish phrase "Casa de Loreto" in the *Catechismo Mexicano*, Paredes used the Nahuatl word -*chan* that made a specific reference to family relations instead of architecture. Paredes had two possible words from which to choose: *calli* and -chan. Calli translates as "house," and it signifies the building itself. -Chan means "home" or "residence," referring to an individual's membership in a group of people who lived together in an altepetl. Nahuatl does not have a general word for "family" (*familia* in Spanish), so, at times, Nahuas wrote -chan in order make a more general statement about the people who lived in a home that was roughly equivalent to "family" in English. Paredes's exhortations using -chan in the phrase *ichantzinco de Loreto* signified that Saint Mary belonged with her two most important domestic relations, Jesus and Joseph, but not necessarily confined in a house structure.

During his tenure at the Colegio de San Gregorio, Paredes also wrote and preached in Spanish about the merits of the Holy Family. In his *Día Diez y Nueve, que Veneran los Devotos en cada uno de los doze Meses del año, à Gloriosisimo Protector el Patriarcha Sr. San Joseph* (The Nineteenth Day: That the Devoted Will Venerate the Glorious Protector, the Patriarch Saint Joseph on Each of the Twelve Months of the Year), Paredes conceptually linked devotion to Saint Mary with that of Saint Joseph, her husband, and explained that human beings could communicate their needs to God through a network of heavenly family members. The Jesuit explained that the value of praying to Saint Joseph was that he and Saint Mary were the immediate family of Jesus and thus the most able to convey a petitioner's needs to the God. The priest asserted that the mother of Jesus was most certainly the best advocate for human beings, but Joseph "being this great saint, after Mary, the person closest to Christ, his intercession must be the most powerful after Mary." Paredes lauded the power of Saint Joseph because it was far more impressive than the average saint, although not as powerful as his wife's: "Saint Thomas asserts that his power is not limited to particular necessities as is other saints; but that he embraces all of them without differentiation: he sends rain, contains frosts, multiplies harvests, protects [us] in storms, on the roads, in shipwrecks."[21]

Paredes taught that Mary should be understood as a member of the Holy Family, and not as a power unto herself. He also encouraged Nahua choirs in Mexico City to sing litanies "at her home of Loreto." With these two exhortations the priest attempted to assert that the presence of the male authority of Jesus and Joseph in the home. Regarding the symbolism of Marian devotion at the Colegio de San Gregorio, male authority over the domestic space of Holy Family was possible, whereas in images of Mary that did not include Joseph or Jesus, male power was not. "At her home of Loreto," Saint Joseph was the patriarchal presence among the ubiquitous duality in Mexican Catholic culture of Jesus, the suffering son, and his compassionate mother, Mary, who anguished beside the cross.

How might doña Ana have interpreted the meaning of Mary in her home for her own life? The interpretive position from which indigenous people understood and learned to accept Hispanic concepts was non-European, so Spanish priests and civil administrators were often exasperated with the results of their efforts. If doña Ana and her cohorts thought in terms of -chan, then the home referred to a social network of men and women, but not necessarily the geographical confinement to a house structure. Clearly, in the case of doña Ana, who was a member of the native upper class, the image of the house of Our Lady of Loreto at the Colegio de San Gregorio did indeed inspire devotion to the Holy Family among her social circle of urban indigenous people. However, the fact that doña Ana had coordinated a network of alms collectors who ranged outside of the confines of the Colegio suggests that she did not interpret the portrayal of Mary as a domestic icon to mean that women should be excluded from an active public role in the religion of the community. In 1791, when doña Ana petitioned to the Juzgado General de Indios that she be allowed to continue to work as chief alms coordinator, the value that her indigenous community placed on women's leadership emboldened her to face the court. However, as the record of her defense in the Juzgado General de Indios shows, she also drew strength from her familiarity with the Spanish judicial process in which the power to judge her fitness as a ruler ultimately rested with men.

Since the 1500s, the Colegio de San Gregorio had been a powerful mechanism of spreading colonial values to the indigenous elite that guarded Spanish ideas about civic order. Educational and governmental institutions taught the native rulers about patriarchal gender roles and the way to habitually use law courts to mediate disputes among themselves. Doña Ana was astute at navigating Hispanic legal institutions, which Spanish education had encouraged. Simultaneously, she interpreted her proper role as a loyal Catholic subject of the divine and worldly king in a way that the Spanish legal counsel viewed as rebellious to patriarchal social order. In 1790, Ventura held a license from Archdiocese of Mexico's Provisorato de Indios that gave her permission to be the chief organizer of the Nahua alms collectors who were devoted to Our Lady of Loreto despite the fact that the spirit of the law banned women from financing the adoration of community images. Perhaps doña Ana and other women were aware of the exact wording of the licenses that stated in relation to sacred images that "woman will not accompany it" because, taken literally, the regulation does not bar women from acting as executive coordinators of ambling solicitors who would physically accompany statues of saints, paintings, and crosses. The court record does not specifically state if the people that she was directing were male or female, but it appears that as a leader of alms collectors she was cleverly circumventing the literalism of the printed regulation.

In the exchange of legal correspondence between the fiscal and Ventura's lawyer, it is obvious that doña Ana had been fully informed of the rules and procedures of obtaining a license. Documents from the Juzgado General de Indios always note when an indigenous petitioner required an interpreter. Because the record of the exchange between the women's lawyer and the viceroy's representative does not mention the use of an interpreter, we may assume that Ventura was fluent in Spanish and not limited by being monolingual in Nahuatl. As an urban woman, a member of the indigenous upper class, and a visible supporter of the religious activities at the Colegio de San Gregorio, she optimized her chances of accessing the avenues that led to the centers of Hispanic colonial power in the capital of the Kingdom of New Spain—the Juzgado General de Indios located in the viceroy's palace and the Provisorato de Indios in the archbishop's palace.

Her privilege as a Hispanized Indian gave her the freedom to move through the legal procedures of the court, access the corridors of colonial power, and make choices. Doña Ana had more authority than most indigenous women in New Spain; consequently, Spaniards were more likely to listen to her plea than if she were an average indigenous woman. However, there was a limit to the extent that male authorities would listen to indigenous women petitioners in the late eighteenth century. Patriarchal gender expectations negated the rewards that doña Ana received from access to Hispanic privilege. The license did not literally ban women from organizing itinerant collectors. Even though the license did not literally ban women from organizing itinerant solicitors, in the minds of the Spanish bureaucrats that judged her case, she had transgressed a cultural value that it was unseemly for a woman to command such public power. On the contrary, doña Ana interpreted the motherhood, which the image of Mary at

the House of Loreto represented, as a call to public action. She took
responsibility to care for the image of Our Lady of Loreto who watched
over the indigenous boys and girls at their school. She stayed at home but
coordinated a network of collectors; thus, the Juzgado General de Indios
judged her actions to be far too public, powerful—in short, too masculine—
for a proper woman.

The Indigenous Vision of Community Order

When doña Ana petitioned for the license to coordinate the activities of the
religiously enthusiastic members of the native community of Mexico City,
she faced a larger trend toward a strongly articulated patriarchy in the mentality of Spanish officials that had been brewing since the 1760s. At the
time, native women were engaged in many public activities in their local
rural and urban communities such as market work, tribute collection, and
religious leadership. In 1768, the renowned eighteenth-century archbishop
of Mexico Francisco Lorenzana y Buitrón preached that only the authority
of indigenous *padres de familias* could prevent the dissolution of the pueblos de indios (synonymous with altepetl). In his pastoral letter called
"Regulations that will make the Natives Happy in Spiritual and Worldly
Life" ("Reglas para que los Naturales de estos Reynos Sean Felices en lo
Espiritual, y Temporal"), Lorenzana advocated that men control the marriage choices of their children so that they would marry only pure Indians
or Spaniards and not those of mixed race. The indigenous governors of
town councils, whom the archbishop viewed as fathers of pueblos, should
compel young men and women to marry and build a house (*xahcalli*) by the
age of twenty-five in order to prevent them from fleeing their traditional
communities. The archbishop believed they were tempted to abandon their
towns when they traveled to work as day laborers on large estates that
engaged in commercial agriculture on haciendas.[22] The mobility of the
indigenous population and uncontrolled women created anarchy in indigenous communities and threatened to destroy them.

As the story of Aparicio and the widows illustrates, indigenous people on the move did use the roads as an opportunities to avoid regulations
regarding alms collection and to deceive the authorities who attempted to
enforce them. However, they did not do it for the sake of rebellion against
order. Traveling with images and women's participation in leadership
activities such as mobile alms collecting may have been extensions of

older altepetl concepts of social order. Thus, contrary to what the Bourbon reformers like Archbishop Lorenzana and Viceroy Revillagigedo believed, indigenous leaders likely understood these two activities not as a signs of disorder, but as logical attempts to maintain community.

The Nahuatl documents that are available for constructing the indigenous view of gender, leadership, and travel do not contain direct statements about women and the mobility of indigenous people the way that the statements of the Bourbon reformers do. Reformers self-consciously worked within a larger program of centralizing monarchical power, filling the royal treasury, and pushing a patriarchal vision of more rational social order. As a result, they made direct statements about women's participation in religion. Indigenous leaders and native people who could write did not. Furthermore, during the period of the 1760s and 1770s, Nahuatl writing was in decline.

We are forced to use scattered written sources in order to piece together abstract, indigenous cultural concepts that explain the meaning of community leadership. Two cultural concepts found in these sources were the metaphors of traveling and parenting. They explained the moral qualities of good leaders and appear to have run parallel to the way that late eighteenth-century leaders actually coordinated social networks of male and female collectors, thereby informally sharing with the wider community of women and nonelite men the leadership duty of acting as patron of local religion.

Indigenous people's enthusiasm for the penitential ritual of traveling with sacred statues, crosses, and paintings in the late eighteenth century may have been inspired by an ancient Mesoamerican metaphor that characterized community leaders as parental guardians who carried their human subjects and holy objects. Nahuatl-language sources dating from the sixteenth to the early eighteenth centuries describe virtuous guardians of the altepetl as those who displayed the traits of good parents. Thus, theoretically, women could have public leadership roles as guardians of local religion and ethics.

In writing Nahuas used the metaphors of travel/rest and mother/father in order to explain the proper power relationship between a dynastic ruler of an altepetl, called a *tlatoani*, and his people. For example, fray Bernardino de Sahagún's *Florentine Codex* of the 1540s to 1570s and the anonymous *Coyoacán Codex* from the early 1700s depict rulers of altepetls as stationary trees that provided shaded protection to their people.[23] In the text of the *Florentine Codex*, the ruler is described as gum, cypress, and silk-cotton trees, all of which have large shading canopies. Opposed to the idea that the leader provides rooted protection like a tree, we find that the performance of governing duties also may have suggested images of transportation to Nahuatl speakers. A passage that explains that a tlatoani was obligated to "take responsibility for people and matters" consists of several verbs, which translated more literally mean the leader is one who "carries things" and "carries people in the folds of his garment."[24]

Nahuatl grammar does not have gender-specific third-person pro-nouns, objects, and subject prefixes of words. Single words of these types can signify "he," "she," or "it." Unlike Spanish and other Latin tongues, the language does not have masculine and feminine endings for nouns. Therefore, in Nahuatl texts such as Sahagún's in which the nouns for "woman," "man," "lady," "nobleman" and other gender-specific nouns are absent, descriptions of the proper behavior of leaders are linguistically ambivalent when it comes to gender. The words used to explain the cor-rect use of political power were not explicitly male terms, but instead could be characterized as parental. However, one should not jump to the conclusion that indigenous society was gender inclusive because Nahuatl is gender neutral. Much of the political power, land, and wealth were con-centrated in the hands of males.

Just as the metaphor of ruler as traveler who carried burdens was compatible with the figure of speech that the ruler was a stationary shade tree, Nahuas sometimes described male leaders as both the mothers and fathers of the community. In the Cuernavaca region as late as the eigh-teenth century, Nahuas referred to the members of the all-male town council as *in tonantzin in totatzin*, "our mother and our father."[25] They also combined the metaphors of mother and child with that of travel. In Sahagún's book the common people are those whom leaders cradle in their arms.[26]

The Nahuas commonly referred to the spiritual protectors of their communities and homes with the parental terms of mother (-*nantzin*) and father (-*tatzin*) as they did in reference to human guardians. In eigh-teenth-century Nahuatl wills from the Chalco region, for example, indigenous notaries wrote such honorific words when they recorded upper-class people addressing their patron saints on their deathbeds. In 1777, doña María Theresa Antonia left monetary offerings that she hoped would maintain the images of her most cherished saints: "her precious and revered mother, Lady Saint Mary of the Assumption," and "My precious father Saint John the Baptist."[27] In 1721, don Blas de los Reyes claimed his personal patron saint as "my precious father Señor Santiago." In the closing statement of this will, when the notary named don Blas's town, he called it the "Altepetl Señor Santiago Chalco." Therefore, in addition to the saint being don Blas's personal guardian, Santiago was also the patron saint of the town of Chalco, the man's altepetl of residence.[28] The forms of address found in the Chalco testaments were more than just honorific titles for personal spiritual guardians. "Mother" and "father" were also political terms to address community advocates in heaven. Spiritual advocates of towns were just as often female as they were male.

The most famous use of a parental term for a saint occurs in Luis Laso de la Vega's *Huei tlamahuiçoltica* (By a Great Miracle) of 1659, which calls the Virgin of Guadalupe "Our Precious Mother." De la Vega's text also refers to the Virgin of Guadalupe as "the Heavenly Queen" (*ilhuicac tlatocaçihuapilli*) using a form of tlatoani (*tlatoca-*) reserved for compound words.[29] As the wills from eighteenth-century Chalco suggest, parental titles were not unique to Guadalupe because Nahuas applied them to many different male and female Catholic saints. Both the wills and the account of the apparition of Guadalupe demonstrate the Nahuas used parental metaphors that had political meanings to describe the beings that they believed protected their sedentary communities. They did not, however, envision their political and spiritual parents as only stationary fathers who provided for "stay-at-home" mothers. Good female or male protectors dynamically provided for their dependents by transporting them as well as shading them.

As merchants and settlers, Nahuas had traveled long before the Spaniards had arrived in Mexico, but indigenous people had always been wary of moving along roads. Just as it was physically dangerous to travel Mexico's roads, metaphorically speaking, moving through life was morally perilous outside of the protection of the leaders of the altepetl. The *Florentine Codex* describes a disobedient person as a "rabbit" or a "deer" who goes wandering to avoid facing parental criticisms of moral comportment.[30] In another passage from the *Codex*, prostitutes are described as women who stray along roads, and they are portrayed in the accompanying illustrations as standing at the crossroads. People avoided wandering aimlessly on the road like grazing animals or wayward women by maintaining ties to the rulers of their local communities, whose moral guardianship was described with parental, travel, and transportation metaphors.

Leaders attempting to adapt to the rapid changes of the late eighteenth century could draw on community maintenance strategies that involved the mobility of its members such as insuring the financial solvency of local religious devotions through traveling alms collection. Indigenous society had always been mobile, and we should not mistakenly interpret colonial Nahuatl documents as providing a complete record of communities because they can sometimes give the impression that these were closed, locally focused societies only. The physical movements of eighteenth-century Nahuas also facilitated transformations in the altepetl. In the 1760s and 1770s Nahuas made a rapid transition from writing in Nahuatl to writing in Spanish. They substituted the term pueblo for altepetl in their town documents, but this did not mean that the structures of the altepetl disappeared overnight. Instead, gender and leadership concepts in late colonial indigenous communities were the product of both local, indigenous altepetl structures and regional, Hispanic forces. Colonial highways, which linked transportation-oriented towns and Spanish institutions in Mexico City that educated members of the indigenous upper class, were two major conduits of change in indigenous society. Mexico City, the terminus of all regional trade, was the origin point of Hispanic ideals for women and men that they carried back and forth to the surrounding regions in New Spain. The interplay of contact among local pueblos, provincial transport hubs, and the capital shaped people's understanding of gender, the ethical commitments they had to their communities, and how they believed God intervened in their world.

From the local perspective of the Nahuas of colonial Mexico, the material representations of God's presence such as miraculous images of saints and crucifixes belonged to specific, territorial communities that had dual names—one a Christian European patron saint, the other an ancient Nahuatl word. The names of Nahua communities often made reference to a prominent topographical feature or element from the natural world to designate the organization of people who controlled the territory. For example, "Ehecatepec," the name of the preconquest Mexica altepetl, means "The Settlement Near Wind Mountain." After the Spanish Conquest, "San Cristóbal," was added, and the name of the town in the Christian era became "San Cristóbal Ecatepec." These territorial settlements were further distinguished as places by the landmarks of agricultural plots, each of which were often named after an indigenous family's saints.[31] Spiky maguey plants sprouted on the borders of private and communal land, as did small rivers, oddly shaped rocks, and wooded hills sweeping up toward snow-capped mountains. From birth to death, landscapes unique to every individual town were the horizons of experience that framed rural people's lives and set the boundaries of their spiritual habitats where they enacted yearly cycles of Catholic ritual.

Although local identity was the foundation of colonial indigenous society, regional commerce also shaped the local sense of community, which Catholic images represented, because roads that eventually led to Mexico City bisected many colonial towns. The indigenous towns that produced the largest numbers of indigenous alms collectors were transportation hubs and provincial markets. Many of the collectors probably worked as muleteers. The people who transported their local community saints to distant towns reinforced the idea that their saints belonged to their hometowns because they had an outside audience to acknowledge it. Alms collectors who considered themselves primarily residents of specific indigenous communities had countless opportunities for daily interactions on roads, in transportation-oriented towns, and in the capital.

Alexander von Humboldt, the European demographer and geographer who traveled extensively throughout New Spain during first years of the nineteenth century, was impressed by the high volume of commerce that was made possible by brave indigenous and mixed-race muleteers who traveled along these roads:[32]

> [I]n the present bad state of the roads, waggons [*sic*] are not
> established for the conveyance of goods. They give preference
> to the employment of beasts of burden; and thousands of horses
> and mules cover in long files [*requas*] the roads of Mexico.
> A considerable number of Mestizoes and Indians are employed
> to conduct these caravans. Preferring a wandering life to
> every sort of sedentary occupation, they pass the night in the
> open air, or in sheds, [*tambos*, or *casas de communidad*] which
> are constructed in the middle of villages for the convenience
> of travellers [*sic*].[33]

In addition to the petty traders who led their mules through town, a host of other characters came down these treacherous tracks. Archbishops sent inspectors to pen reports of the conditions of parish churches, and on rare occasions, the viceroy dispatched squads of black militiamen who passed through town on their way to defend the coast against pirates.[34] In preconquest Mesoamerica, Mexica *pochtecatl*, traveling merchants, who were depicted in the *Florentine Codex* carrying their wares on their backs with tramp lines slung around their foreheads, traversed many of these roads, such as the highway that stretched from the Gulf coast (near the present-day port of Veracruz) to Tenochtitlan (Mexico City).[35] Conquistadors such as the Spaniard Hernán Cortés in 1519 and the American General Winfield Scott in 1847 led their armies along the Veracruz-Mexico City road.

What Humboldt viewed as evidence of the virtue of industry in the people on the move, Spanish officials in the Juzgado General de Indios saw as the vice of vagabondage. High officials of the court, as well as the church, feared that indigenous people were becoming detached from their traditional towns. Within the context of this concern, in the early 1790s, the legal bureaucrats in the court began to aggressively revoke the licenses of itinerant alms collectors, which in the past the archdiocese had freely granted indigenous people.

Late colonial indigenous men and women from Ecatepec, Chiconaulta, Chalco, and Mexico City had many different experiences that shaped their understanding of their social obligations as leaders. They were people bounded by the local landscapes of the traditional altepetl and legal subjects of the Catholic monarchy that astutely operated in the Spanish courts of justice. They were also traveling hacienda workers and ambling alms gatherers of high- and low-social class. Contradictory ideas about appropriate behavior guided the movements of the alms gatherers as they traveled through a hybrid, colonial society. In the case of the widows of Chiconautla, we find echoes of the Mesoamerican perspective that good leaders had the moral traits of both mothers and fathers of communities. Male town council members worked with informal networks of nonelite men and women, including multiple community members in their leadership endeavor of acting as patron. Officials of the Juzgado General de Indios, who were determined to legally bring indigenous women under control in the 1790s, reported that the majority of women involved in the alms collection networks maintained home altars that attracted donations for the male itinerant collectors who placed their images there when they arrived in town. Consequently, Nahua women, acting more like sheltering trees in their local communities, worked with male mayordomos who gathered alms further afield. The predominately male travelers who carried the saints acted more like mothers cradling their dependent children in their arms than the rooted role models of earlier times.

The gravitational force that bound the mayordomos to their female partners was a compromise between the demands of Hispanic patriarchy and the conception of the indigenous leader as parent—a conception that did not deny public leadership roles to women. As guardians of the most important religious symbols of their local communities, indigenous women acted politically in public, but patriarchy literally limited their geographic range of activity within the vicinity of local home communities. Through educational institutions like the Colegio de San Gregorio, patriarchal ideas spread to the rural areas from Mexico City, the center of Hispanic culture, while Nahua conceptions of gender balance may have been more prevalent in local, rural communities. [36]

At the end of the eighteenth century, strong economic and demographic forces threatened to fragment the ancient sedentary life of the Nahua altepetl in the countryside, but the roaming of the alms collectors did not contribute to local community dissolution. Traveling was a survival mechanism that helped to preserve the social obligations necessary for reconstituting the local community during difficult times. Unlike the situation of rural, indigenous women who migrated to Mexico City and lost their culture when they became part of the great *casta* underclass, community social obligations remained strong cords that drew male and female itinerant collectors back to their local communities.[37] Furthermore, the people of Chiconautla who relocated to the city of Puebla did not disperse when they moved, but instead formed a transplant colony and remained together.

Thinking of the widows of Chiconautla as "abandoned," implies that they had no intrinsic value or power independent of their husbands, which was the assumption of the Spanish magistrate who reported the incident. Nahuas did not necessarily view the women this way. It is likely that the women agreed to the arrangement when their husbands left for the city of Puebla and enjoyed some autonomy that was a fitting role for an indigenous woman. The "widows" themselves were never allowed to tell their own tales, but the fragments of information—the reticence and complicity of Nahua males, the horror of Spanish officials when confronting upstart women, and the linguistic evidence—offer a convincing profile of these women. Indeed, the "widows" of Chiconautla narrate a tale of a fragmenting community that strove to remain in tact. When far from home on perilous journeys, people could still carry the internal maps of moral obligation that would allow them to reconstitute the community of the future. These indigenous survival mechanisms of community cohesion prompted native people to collect money for the adornment of Roman Catholic images.

Long before the Nahuas carried their Catholic saints, they told stories about people navigating dangerous passages. In one of founding myths of the Mexica city of Tenochtitlan recorded in the *Codex Boturini*, three men and one woman lead a migration of people from Aztlan, their original island home. Each of the four leaders carries a bundle on his back that contains images of their god Huitzilopochtli.[38] On their long, meandering journey, they are not yet rooted to an altepetl, the rock that anchors a temperate and measured ethical life, but the three men and the woman ensure that they will reach their destined, stable home by the lake.

NOTES

1. Fray Agustín de Vetancurt, "Tratado de la ciudad de México y las grandezas que la ilustran despues que fundaron españoles [1698]," in *La Ciudad de México en el siglo XVIII (1690–1780), Tres crónicas*, prólogo y bibliografía Antonio Rubial García, notas a Juan de Viera, Gonzalo Obregón (Mexico: Consejo Nacional para la Cultura y las Artes, 1990), 111; Charles Ronan, *Francisco Javier Clavigero, S.J. (1731–1787), Figure of the Mexican Enlightenment: His Life and Works* (Chicago: Loyola University Press, 1975), 32; Juan Manuel de San Vicente, "Exacta descripción de la magnífica corte mexicana . . . [1768]," in *La Ciudad de México*, 159.

2. Archivo General del a Nación (hereafter AGN), Clero Regular y Secular (hereafter CRS), vol. 22, exp. 15, fs. 250v–51r.

3. For more information on this structure that is sometimes called "gender parallelism," which was common to indigenous Latin America, see Susan Kellogg, "From Parallel and Equivalent to Separate but Unequal: Tenocha Mexica Women, 1500–1700," in *Indian Women of Early Mexico*, ed. Susan Schroeder et al. (Norman: University of Oklahoma Press, 1997); and Susan Kellogg, *Law and the Transformation of Aztec Culture, 1500–1700* (Norman: University of Oklahoma Press, 1995). Regarding the structure among the Yucatec Maya, see Marta Espejo-Ponce Hunt and Matthew Restall, "Work,

Marriage, and Status: Maya Women of Colonial Yucatan," in *Indian Women*; Matthew Restall, "'He Wished it in Vain': Subordination and Resistance among Maya Women in Post-Conquest Yucatan," *Ethnohistory* 42 (1995), 589–90; and Matthew Restall, *The Maya World: Yucatec Culture and Society, 1550–1850* (Stanford, CA: Stanford University Press, 1997), 136–39.

4. AGN, Bienes Nacionales, vol. 992, exp. 23, Pablo Antonio Peñuelas, *Breve Noticia de la Prodigiosa Imagen de Nuestra Señora de los Ángeles, que por espacio de dos siglos se há conservado pintada en una pared de adove, y se venera en su Santuario extramuros de México* (Mexico: F. de Zuñiga y Ontiveros, 1781); Francisco de Florencia, *La Milagrosa Invención de un Tesoro Escondido en un Campo que Halló en Venturoso Cacique, y Escondió en su Casa, para Gozarlo à sus Solas...* (Seville: Imprenta de las Siete Revueltas, 1745 [1685]), 6–7.

5. For more on how colonial Mesoamerican people privately and communally funded their saint cults with land, see James Lockhart, *The Nahuas After the Conquest: A Social and Cultural History of the Indians of Central Mexico, Sixteenth Through Eighteenth Centuries* (Stanford, CA: Stanford University Press, 1992), 232–33; S. L. Cline "The Spiritual Conquest Reexamined: Baptism and Christian Marriage in Early Sixteenth-Century Mexico," *Hispanic American Historical Review* 73 (1993). Regarding the erosion of land-based funding see, William B. Taylor, *Magistrates of the Sacred: Priests and Parishioners in Eighteenth-Century Mexico* (Stanford, CA: Stanford University Press, 1996), 303–11; John Chance and William B. Taylor, "Cofradías and Cargos: An Historical Perspective on the Mesoamerican Civil-Religious Hierarchy," *American Ethnologist* 12 (1985); and Stephanie Wood, "Adopted Saints: Christian Images in Nahua Testaments of Late Colonial Toluca," *The Americas* 47 (1991).

6. AGN, CRS, vols. 22, 116, 123, 151, 155.

7. AGN, CRS, vols. 22, 116, 123, 151, 155. The licenses cover the period of 1789 to 1799.

8. Charles Gibson, *The Aztecs Under Spanish Rule: A History of the Indians of the Valley of Mexico, 1519–1810* (Stanford, CA: Stanford University Press, 1964), 361.

9. AGN, CRS, vol. 155, exp. 6, fs. 122–36.

10. AGN, CRS, vol. 155, exp. 6, fs. 122–36v.

11. AGN, CRS, vol. 155, exp. 6, f. 125r. "[Q]ue hay mas de treinta mugeres vuidas sin ser lo por ignorarse el paradero de los Maridos, respecto, a que haviendo saliendo con Demandas arrendadas y tal vez no teniendo a los dos años con que contribuir la pencion con que se les dan los Mayordomos se quedan incognitos, sin saver su paradero."

12. I use the term *cult* because many indigenous communities did not have legally chartered confraternities, but instead had more ad hoc organizations of people devoted to *cultos* of particular images or festivals.

13. AGN, CRS, vol. 155, exp. 6, f. 136.

14. AGN, CRS, vol. 155, exp. 6, f. 131r.

15. AGN, CRS, vol. 155, exp. 6, f. 202r.

16. AGN, CRS, vol. 155, exp. 6, fs. 201r–v. "Efectivamente es constante lo primero la indecencia con que conducen las Imagenes en cajones sobre una bestia de carga, como si fuera qualesquiera otro genero o efecto de transporte. Tal vez son acompañadas de musicas profanas, Mugeres sospechosas; se ponen altares en casas particulares y aun lo que es peor en otros (201r) lugares en que la desemboltura y el vicio hacen ultrage a la veneracion. Ademas de esto los demandantes hacen comerico la colectacion, pactando y comviniendo con los curas el salario o pencion que han deducir, y de esta suerte un acto de piedad lo comvierten en negociacion. Ellos por lo comun son gente vagamunda, que con tal pretexto trancitan impugnemente por donde quieren."

17. Ventancurt, "Tratado de la ciudad de México," 111; Ronan, *Francisco Javier Clavigero*, 32.

18. San Vicente, "Exacta descripción de la magnífica corte mexicana," 159.

19. Ignacio de Paredes, "Letanías de Nuestra Señora la Virgen María, que se le cantan en su Casa de Loreto. In itlatlauhtilocatzin, in Itoca Letanía, in Tlátocaichpotzintli in Santa María, in quimocuicaehuililiã in Ichantzinco de Loreto," in *Catechismo Mexicano* (Mexico: Imprenta de la Bibliotheca Mexicana, 1758), 137.

20. Cayetano de Cabrera y Quintero, *Escudo de Armas de México* (Mexico: Impresso por la viuda de d. J.B. de Hogal, 1746), 99–103.

21. Un Sacredote de la Compañía de Jesús [Antonio de Paredes], *Día Diez y Nueve, que Veneran los Devotos en cada uno de los doze Meses del año, à Gloriosisimo Protector el Patriarcha Sr. San Joseph. Devocion para celebrar su Dia, en èl implorar la proteccion del Santo* (Mexico: n.p., 1755).

22. Archbishop Francisco Lorenzana y Buitrón, "Reglas para que los Naturales de estos Reynos Sean Felices en lo Espiritual, y Temporal," June 20, 1768 (John Carter Brown Library).

23. Fray Bernardino de Sahagún, *Florentine Codex: General History of the Things of New Spain*, trans. and ed. Arthur J. O. Anderson and Charles E. Dibble (Santa Fe, NM, and Salt Lake City: School of American Research; University of Utah Press, 1969), book 10,

ch. 4, 15; and Anonymous, *Coyoacán Codex* [ca. 1700–43], John Carter Brown Library, Codex Ind. [F] 1 [R].

24. Sahagún, *Florentine Codex*. This is my literal translation of the printed Nahuatl: *tlatqui tlamama tecuexanoa*.

25. Robert Haskett, *Indigenous Rulers: An Ethnohistory of Town Government in Colonial Cuernavaca* (Albuquerque: University of New Mexico Press, 1991), 100.

26. Sahagún, *Florentine Codex*, book 10, ch. 4, 246.

27. AGN, Civil, vol. 1055, exp. 7, f. 1: "[Y]tlaço Mahuiztic Nantzin Cihuapilli Santa María de la Asunción ytlaço" and "Notlaço Tatzin San Juan Bautista." The 1736 will of Josepha María of Santiago Apostol Chalco also employs mother/father terms. AGN, Civil 1067, exp. 2, fs. 1–9. Two Nahuatl sources that Lockhart transcribed and translated have examples of the mother/father title for other saints than Mary. It was apparently a common practice throughout the colonial period. A land and house grant document from 1583 refers to Saint Michael as "totlaçotatzin y santo sa migel" ("our precious father, her saint, San Miguel"). See Lockhart, *Nahuas*, 456. In the "Testament of Angelina, San Simón Pochtlan (Azcapotzalco), 1695," there is the following example: "notlaçomahuiznantzin candelaria, notlaçomahuiztatzin Sto. Domingo." The will identifies Santa Catalina as "notlaçonatzin sta catalina," and also "ylhuicac ychpochtli" ("[her] Heavenly Virgin"), which was supposed to refer to the Virgin Mary. See Lockhart, *Nahuas*, 464. For more seventeenth-century examples, see Arthur J. O. Anderson, Frances Berdan, and James Lockhart, *Beyond the Codices: The Nahua View of Colonial Mexico*, Latin American Studies Series, vol. 27 (Berkeley: University of California Press, 1976), 70–71, 112–13.

28. AGN, Civil, vol. 2215, exp. 1, fs. 11r–v: "notlaçotatzin Señor Santiago."

29. *The Story of Guadalupe: Luis Laso de la Vega's Huei tlamahuiçoltica of 1649*, ed. and trans. Lisa Sousa et al. (Stanford, CA: Stanford University Press, 1998), 41, 48. At one point in the story, Mary rhetorically asks Juan Diego, "Are you not in the security of my lapfold, in my carrying gear?" 79.

30. Sahagún, *Florentine Codex*, 253.

31. Wood, "Adopted Saints."

32. Alexander von Humboldt, *Political Essay on the Kingdom of New Spain*, vol. IV, trans. John Black (New York: AMS Press, 1966 [1811]), 2–14.

33. Ibid., 2.

34. Ben Vinson III, *Bearing Arms for His Majesty: The Free-Colored Militia in Colonial Mexico* (Stanford, CA: Stanford University Press, 2001).

35. "The vanguard merchant" illustration no. 115 in Sahagún, *Florentine Codex*.

36. For more information on indigenous women and Hispanic honor codes, see Sonya Lipsett-Rivera, "A Slap in the Face of Honor: Social Transgression and Women in Late-Colonial Mexico," in *The Faces of Honor: Sex, Shame, and Violence in Colonial Latin America*, ed. Lyman L. Johnson and Sonya Lipsett-Rivera (Albuquerque: University of New Mexico Press, 1998).

37. Juan Javier Pescador, "Vanishing Woman: Female Migration and Ethnic Identity in Late-Colonial Mexico City," *Ethnohistory* 42 (1995).

38. This image can be found in Elizabeth Hill Boone, "Migration Histories as Ritual Performance," in *Aztec Ceremonial Landscapes*, ed. David Carrasco (Niwot: University of Colorado Press, 1991).

Altissimo Dios, y Señor Nuestro Trino, y uno Criador, y Conservador de todas las cosas yo te doi mil
gracias, por aver criado a tu Siervo San Homobono, tan lleno de Caridad, humildad, y demas
virtudes, que merecio se hallase su nombre escrito, con letras de oro en el cathalogo de los
Santos; te pido por sus meritos tengas misericordia de mi, librandome de todos los males, y
plantando en mi todas las virtudes conque lo ilustraste, para que como San Homo bono te
sirba en esta vida, y te goze en la otra Amen.

SUMARIO DE LAS GRACIAS,
E INDULGENCIAS PERPETUAS QUE GOZAN LOS HERMANOS
DE LA ILUSTRE COFRADIA
DEL SEÑOR SAN HOMOBONO,

Fundada en nuestra Iglesia de la SANTISIMA TRINIDAD, por el Alcalde, Veedor, Guardianes
de la Ilustre Archicofradia, y demas Maestros del Arte de la Sastreria de la muy Noble é
Imperial Ciudad de México, agregada á dicha Ilustre Archicofradia, y aprobada por nuestro Santisimo Padre el Señor Inocencio Duodecimo, quien se dignó concederlas por su Apos-
tólico Breve, dado en Santa María la Mayor, debaxo del Anillo del Pescador, el dia veinte y quatro de Enero de mil seiscientos noventa y ocho, al séptimo de su Pontificado.

FIGURE 19. San Homobono

The frontispiece of a license/summary of indulgences and privileges for a confratnernity.
Taken from Devocionario mexicano. Pequeños grabado novohispanos, *introducción*
de Alicia Gojman (Mexico: Backal Editores, 1998). Courtesy of Backal Editores.

CHAPTER SEVEN

Confraternities and Community

The Decline of the Communal Quest for Salvation in Eighteenth-Century Mexico City

Brian Larkin

On February 9, 1717, don Jacinto de Silva Ortuño, a priest and chaplain in Mexico City's cathedral, called José de Anaya y Bonillo, a notary public, to his home to write his last will and testament. The priest lay in his bed, dying. As a good Catholic, he had decided to put his worldly affairs in order and to firm up his relationship with God before death by composing his will. As with all wills written in Mexico City in the eighteenth century, don Jacinto de Silva Ortuño's testament began with an invocation of God's presence: "In the name of God Almighty, Amen." Silva Ortuño then confessed his faith and selected the Virgin Mary, Saint Joseph, and his two special patron saints—Saint Cajetan and Saint Nicholas—as his special intercessors to plead for his salvation before God. After this opening prayer, the priest, like all other contemporary testators, arranged his funeral. He asked to be buried in the Monastery of San Bernardo in Mexico City. Immediately following his funeral request, Silva Ortuño declared his membership in five confraternities, or pious organizations dedicated to the veneration of a patron saint and other religious activities. The priest belonged to the

Congregations of the Immaculate Conception, housed in the Jesuit school of San Pedro y San Pablo; to the Congregation of Our Lady of Antigua, located in a side chapel of Mexico City's cathedral; to the Congregation of Saint Peter, housed in the Church of the Holy Trinity; to the Congregation of Saint Barbara, located in the Monastery of San Bernardo; and to the Archconfraternity of the Holy Trinity. He ordered his executors to deliver his patents, or proof of membership in the confraternities, to the directors of each organization "so that they perform suffrages for me and say the masses for me that they are obligated to do, for I have performed those that I was obligated to do."[1]

In short, Silva Ortuño looked to confraternities to which he belonged for spiritual aid. He attested that he had celebrated masses (lay confreres, or confraternity members, requested priests to celebrate masses) and performed other good works for confreres who had passed away. Now that his end was drawing near, he asked the surviving confreres to perform good works for his soul. Through the prayers they offered and the masses they requested, he expected to accrue merit for his soul and thus shorten the time it had to reside in the purifying flames of purgatory before God allowed it to pass into heaven. Membership in confraternities in colonial Mexico, then, was a method to help ensure salvation. Confreres could always count on the prayers and masses offered by the confraternity to ease their final passage.

Confraternities were a central feature of Mexican colonial Catholicism, and they performed a number of religious activities, including distribution of charity, sponsorship of religious festivals and processions, and promotion of the cult of saints. One of their most important functions, however, was participation in the rites of death and dying. In and through all of their activities confraternities cultivated a sense of Christian unity and fellowship among their diverse memberships. This essay analyzes how Spanish conceptions of the role of confraternities in death rites and in the memorialization of the dead changed during the eighteenth century in Mexico City. This analysis calls into question dichotomous scholarly understandings of colonial and early modern religion.[2] In this sense, this essay corroborates the thrust of Carlos Eire's discussion in this collection: sharp binary distinctions in the analysis of religion often obscure as much as they clarify. Furthermore, this essay sheds light on the dissolution of the collective quest for salvation, or the belief that the Christian community could help an individual soul enter heaven, that underlay communal forms of traditional Catholicism.

In his classic study of Spanish piety, *Local Religion in Sixteenth Century Spain*, William Christian Jr. proposed a new framework for the study of early modern religion. In this work, Christian questions the utility of the concept of popular religion. He insists that "magical" and instrumental religious practices that historians had previously ascribed solely to the common people actually extended throughout all levels of society, from the peasantry to the monarchy. For this reason, Christian formulates the concept of local religion, or religion as practiced and understood on the local level. He argues that local religion in early modern Spain primarily consisted of the veneration of saintly relics and images at local and regional shrines. Typical practices included pilgrimages and communal vows pledged to saints by entire villages for protection and aid. Devotion to saints was widespread because in early modern Spain God was viewed as a distant and stern judge who was best approached through saintly interme-diaries who pleaded humanity's case before the divine throne. After the Council of Trent (1545–63), the synod of the church that codified Catholic theology and reformed ecclesiastical discipline and religious practice in response to the Protestant challenge, elements of the universal church— bishops, theologians, and concerned lay people—began to assault local practices. But according to Christian, these attempts, though they invigo-rated the activities of the universal church at the local level, were mostly unsuccessful in dislodging local religion.[3]

As this study of Spanish perceptions of confraternities and their role in death rituals in eighteenth-century Mexico City makes clear, my under-standing of Catholicism differs in two significant ways from Christian's. Although Christian's emphasis on Catholic practice in the local setting is admirable, the concept of local religion privileges the study of extraliturgi-cal practices to such an extent that it ignores the powerful influence of the liturgy.[4] Early modern and colonial Catholics certainly participated in extraliturgical activities, such as collective vows, pilgrimages, and other devotions to saints and their images, but they also regularly participated in liturgical events, such as the Mass. Moreover, they received communion at least once a year—probably more frequently—and took part in the other sacraments of the universal church at significant turning points in their lives. Thus, early modern and colonial religion consisted of both local and uni-versal practices. These practices could even overlap in time and space; for example, the faithful could participate in a procession for a saint that cul-minated with the celebration of the Mass. Second, Christian views early

modern religion as primarily an instrumental tool that Catholics employed
to ensure their health and livelihood in an unpredictable and potentially
dangerous environment. Spanish villagers and townspeople turned to their
saints in times of dearth, drought, and plague to implore their advocacy
before an irate God. In essence, the concept of local religion presents early
modern piety as a means to control the natural forces of climate, disease,
growth, and reproduction. This perspective ignores Catholics' concerns
about death, judgment, and resurrection. Yet the devotions performed by
confraternities in eighteenth-century Mexico City demonstrate that the
faithful were intimately concerned with questions of death and the afterlife
and devoted much of their spiritual energies toward these ultimate issues.
The liturgical and eschatological nature of many confraternal practices indicates that a more ample understanding of early modern and colonial
Catholicism—one that accounts for both local variation and the universal
church's liturgy and investigates the instrumental and ultimate nature of
religious practice—is in order.

The role of confraternities in the rituals surrounding death and dying
also reveals the fundamentally collective nature of religious devotion in
New Spain. Of course, Mexican Catholics could and often did worship
individually, but the rites and institutions of colonial Catholicism fostered
collective devotions. The Mass and other aspects of the liturgy were
designed to bring diverse segments of the social hierarchy together at one
moment in one act and foster a sense of community by suspending social
divisions and tensions that divided the faithful.[5] Even salvation was not
left entirely to the lone Catholic. In Catholic practice, salvation depended
on the "community of saints," or the community of church members both
living and dead. The living could receive grace from Christ and the saints
and could pray for the repose of souls in purgatory. A person's eternal fate
did not rest entirely on his or her own merits. The community of the
faithful prayed for individual Catholics during the transition between life
and death and continued to perform suffrages for their souls after death.
The highest expression of this concept of Christian community was the
confraternity. Confreres joined together in regular worship and obligated
themselves to pray for all confraternal members, both living and dead, in
the knowledge that after their deaths, new and remaining members would
perform suffrages for their souls. Joining a confraternity was a way to
ensure salvation through a set of mutual religious obligations that bound
individual Catholics together in a devotional community.

What made this collective religion possible was a communal subjectivity, or a sense of personhood in which the self is porous, open to outside influence, and subsumed under a larger, collective identity. The pioneering work of a handful of European historians reveals that the sense that Western individuals have of being one autonomous, wholly integrated personality throughout a lifetime emerged to varying degrees throughout the West in the late medieval and early modern eras, the period during which Europe colonized the Americas.[6] Before the emergence of the individual, bounded self, Europeans in both the Old and New Worlds perceived themselves primarily as part of larger groups, such as families, lineages, guilds, estates, and religious communities that were situated within a hierarchical yet integrative social order.

During the second half of the eighteenth century, an individual understanding of the self began to emerge strongly among some sectors of Mexico's Spanish population. Pamela Voekel, in a masterful study of burial practices and religious change in late colonial Mexico, argues that a sense of the autonomous individual arose as the hierarchical society of estates collapsed. In the late eighteenth century, some members of the clergy and laity began to promote cemetery reform, calling for burials to take place in cemeteries outside the city rather than under church floors as had been the practice. Burial in churches allowed for the ecclesiastical sanction of hierarchical order, for those of high status marked their privilege by burial close to the main altar or other important sites, whereas commoners and the poor rested far from altars or outside the confines of church entirely. Voekel contends that this reform movement shattered the traditional social order because it undermined church-sponsored display of social rank. In suburban cemeteries, individual Catholics lay in eternity together without distinction.[7]

The history of confraternities in eighteenth-century Mexico City reveals a decline of communal piety. This situation in turn strongly suggests the rise of the individual at the end of the colonial period. It is impossible to measure the degree to which residents of eighteenth-century Mexico City experienced their own individual sense of self. But statements about confraternity membership made in a corpus of almost one thousand last wills and testaments written by the propertied, largely Spanish faithful from the late seventeenth to the early nineteenth centuries in New Spain's capital indicates that the bounded, autónomous self was emerging.[8] By the end of the century, Spanish testators and notaries downplayed the confraternity's responsibility for collective memorialization of the dead, indicating that the communal quest for salvation at the heart of much confraternal activity faded as the colonial era came to a close. Now, the individual Catholic stood alone at judgment.

Confraternities in Context

Confraternities arose in Europe during the twelfth and thirteenth centuries, increased rapidly in number, and became an important feature of late medieval piety.[9] In the fifteenth and sixteenth centuries they witnessed a period of accelerated expansion at first in response to incipient stirrings of Catholic reform and later to the church's advocacy of these fraternal organizations to counter Protestant assaults on Catholic doctrine.[10] Of course, lay enthusiasm was a necessary ingredient for the rapid growth of confraternities. The laity founded, joined, and participated in numerous new fraternities on their own initiative and under the aegis of the clergy.

The conquistadors and other early immigrants from Spain quickly established confraternities in Mexico. Hernán Cortés founded the first confraternity, the Cabelleros de la Cruz (Knights of the Cross), in the chapel of Santa Veracruz in 1526, just five years after the capture of Tenochtitlan, the Mexica capital and future site of Mexico City. Other settlers soon followed suit. Apparently, they founded many of these congregations in Mexico City on their own initiative because in 1555 the First Mexican Provincial Council observed that some people, "moved by well-intentioned zeal," established confraternities but never obtained Episcopal approbation of their statutes and constitutions, a situation that led to "many troubles [inconvenientes]."[11] The tension that existed between communal lay religiosity as expressed and formed by confraternities and the growing desire of the Catholic hierarchy, especially after the Council of Trent, to regulate all aspects of religious practice remained a constant problem in colonial Mexico City but never seems to have provoked a general crisis. Although the Council of Trent had mandated close Episcopal supervision of confraternal governance and finance, the archbishops of Mexico City generally allowed these institutions to function independently, only occasionally monitoring internal confraternal elections or auditing accounts.[12]

The confraternities of colonial Mexico City, like their counterparts in Europe, were largely concerned with death, burial, and the memorialization of the dead. Although not alone in their efforts, confraternities ensured that death was not a solitary process. As death approached and judgment neared, residents of colonial Mexico could find some solace in the almost constant presence of their Christian fellows, for during the majority of the colonial period few died truly alone. Death was a sacred and social affair that required the performance of specific public rites of passage. Priests visited the dying to administer the last rites consisting of the sacraments of confession, communion, and extreme unction. Many colonial Mexicans who possessed at least some wealth dictated wills before a public notary and witnesses, bequeathing their property to heirs and founding pious works during their last days. Family, friends, and clerics attended the bedside of the moribund, exhorting the dying to remain hopeful of God's mercy and mindful of the Christian promise of everlasting life and the resurrection of the body in the world to come.

Confraternities participated significantly in the rites of death. Although not all spiritual organizations provided aid for deceased members, many specified in their governing constitutions that confreres must attend the funerals of and perform other suffrages for fallen brothers and sisters. For example, confreres of the confraternity of Our Lady of Sorrows founded in the parish of Santa Catarina Mártir of Mexico City in the late seventeenth century had the obligation to provide a bier with twelve candles for the funerals of deceased members. They also were required to pay for a requiem Mass with a catafalque, or funerary monument usually consisting of a wooden frame draped in black cloth and adorned with numerous candles, every year during the octave of All Souls as a suffrage for all dead members.[13] The confraternity of Saint Benedict, founded in the main Franciscan monastery of Mexico City, offered members the option of having the friars from the community carry their cadaver in formal procession to the monastery church for a solemn requiem Mass and burial or receiving seventeen pesos for burial in a parish church. Beyond this, the confraternity promised an annual anniversary requiem Mass for the souls of all its departed members.[14] Members of confraternities, then, could count on the aid of their brothers and sisters during their final passage, for confraternities often arranged funerals and burials and prayed for the souls of the departed as they faced judgment and the purifying flames of purgatory.

Confraternities participated in a wide range of pious activities apart from memorialization of the dead. Funded by pious donations and membership fees, these organizations performed acts of charity to gain merit for both living and deceased members. They engaged in such acts as the founding and administration of hospitals for the care of the ill and lodging of pilgrims, the granting of dowries to poor or orphaned girls so they could marry honorably, the visitation of prisoners, and the distribution of alms to the poor. For example, the Congregation of the Immaculate Conception in Mexico City donated more than seventeen hundred pesos annually to the Hospital of Saint Hipólito, which was dedicated to the care of the insane. Most of these funds were allotted to provide food and clothing for the hospital's wards. Likewise, the congregation earmarked fewer funds to provide meals for the ill in the Hospital of Espíritu Santo (Holy Spirit) and for the inmates of Mexico City's three jails.[15]

Just as important as these charitable acts, confraternities encouraged the veneration of their patron saints and Catholic worship in general through processions, sponsorship of feast day liturgies, construction of chapels, the adornment of churches with religious art, and the purchase of liturgical and paraliturgical items for religious ceremony. The confraternity of the Precious Blood of Christ founded in the parish of Santa Catarina Mártir of Mexico City hired a chaplain to collect alms every day for the upkeep and adornment of its chapel in the parish church. The fraternity also sponsored masses every Friday in its chapel in honor of the crucified Christ and a Mass and procession every Thursday in honor Christ's first celebration of the Eucharist at the Last Supper. Furthermore, it patronized a lavish annual solemn Mass on the feast of the Transfiguration of Christ in November, paying up to fifty-five pesos for the priests, choir, musicians, wax, and fireworks necessary for the celebration. Lastly, it hired a preacher "of great reputation" to deliver a sermon from the door of the confraternity's chapel every Thursday during Lent.[16]

In all their activities, confraternities promoted sacred sociability between members both living and dead. As living institutions designed to unite diverse groups of Christians, confraternities sought to establish the mystical body of Christ on earth and invoke His presence among their members. The most evident expression of this function, other than the regular services to memorialize the dead, was the confraternal feast that usually followed liturgical services on select holy days throughout the year. The sharing of food in a ritual context encouraged conviviality and recalled the central tenet of the Mass, the communal consumption of Christ's body and blood in the form of bread and wine, and the early Christian ritual meal, or *agape*, that constituted an integral part of the liturgy in antiquity. The confraternal banquet was more than a simple secular affair; it sought both to express and induce the Christian virtue of charity—charity as understood as love of God and love of neighbor.[17]

The Late Colonial Reform

The eighteenth century was an era of reform—both civil and religious— in the Hispanic world. The Spanish crown attempted to centralize authority and wrest more wealth for the royal coffers from its subjects. At the same time, both the church and state sought to instill a greater sense of self-discipline and moderation in the population.[18] Confraternities, because of their popularity, wealth, and independence from oversight, naturally came under the scrutiny of reforming officials. The first sustained project to monitor the confraternities of New Spain occurred in the last quarter of the eighteenth century and was initiated by the Spanish crown. The monarchy's interest in confraternities was mainly financial. It viewed these organizations as reservoirs of untapped revenue and denigrated what it considered their wasteful expenditures on paraliturgical items, such as carriages, candles, and other adornments used in processions, for the celebration of an excessive number of feast days. Using an early seventeenth-century law that had ordered all confraternities to obtain royal approval of their constitutions, the crown in 1776 commissioned a report on the state and number of these organizations in Mexico. Although surveys were conducted of rural confraternities in New Spain on account of this order, the viceroy did not commission an examination of the confraternities of Mexico City until 1787, when he asked Alonso Núñez de Haro y Peralta, the archbishop of Mexico (1772–1800), to begin such an investigation.[19]

Ecclesiastical participation in the effort to monitor and regulate confraternities was far from reluctant, for many bishops in New Spain were already engaged in a significant campaign to transform religious culture. During the second half of the eighteenth century a group of reform-minded members of the clergy and laity attempted to eliminate what they considered "excesses" and "superstitions" from colonial Mexican piety. Among other practices, targets of reform included ornate adornment of sacred space, lavish liturgical ritual, exuberant and oftentimes raucous feast-day celebrations, ostentatious funerary rites, excessive devotion to images and relics, and in general, the easy commingling of the sacred and profane common in colonial Catholicism.[20] For example, Archbishop Núñez de Haro excoriated his flock in one sermon, admonishing the faithful to desist from sinking their wealth into ever more dazzling decoration of Mexico City's cathedral—decoration that he insisted only distracted them from the Mass and other sacraments. Instead, he urged them to focus their attention on the words and meaning of the Mass and to donate alms to institutions like workhouses that aided and reformed the poor.[21]

Not surprisingly, the reforming bishops of Mexico disapproved of many confraternal practices. Francisco Fabián y Fuero, the bishop of Puebla (1765–73), condemned confraternities for their "profane expenses, ostentation and gluttonous dissipation [of funds]."[22] His counterpart, Francisco Antonio Lorenzana y Buitrón, the archbishop of Mexico (1766–72), issued a more extensive castigation of brotherhoods in an edict he published in 1769. He wrote:

> Confraternities, brotherhoods, and congregations are founded only so that the faithful may partake, as brothers closely united together, in sacred functions and not for profane expenses, ostentation, or to provide incentives to gluttony. Even the gentiles venerated with great respect the places destined for the false worship of their gods and held graves as religious. Then should not we Christians [do the same] in our cemeteries, in which are deposited some bodies whose souls we piously believe are in God's presence [*gozando de Dios*] and [that] are to revive united [with their souls] from that sleep of the earth for the eternity of heaven?[23]

He later continued:

> We exhort all pastors of our diocese, particularly those of this city, that they take care that on feast days and other ecclesiastical solemnities that no one sell edible things nor beverages in the cemeteries of churches under the pretext of gatherings at them, nor that the brothers of any confraternity, brotherhood, or congregation hold lunches, suppers, refreshments, or other excesses with the motive or as a result of their processions, festivities, and meetings, especially during holy week.[24]

In these passages, the archbishop revealed his extreme distaste for the traditional activities of confraternities. He dismissed their paraliturgical functions designed to praise, thank, and promote veneration of their patron saints and increase the splendor of holy days as "profane expenses" and "ostentation." Rather than view confraternal banquets as mechanisms to promote Christian unity and participate in the mystical body of Christ, he condemned them as "incentives to gluttony." Moreover, he sought to distance these organizations from their close association with death and aid for the souls of deceased members in purgatory by banning confraternal functions from cemeteries. Confraternities held their meetings, commemoration ceremonies, and feasts close to gravesites precisely to emphasize the intimate connection between the living and dead and to increase the merit of their suffrages on behalf of the departed by performing them in proximity to their earthly remains. By declaring the cemeteries off limits, the archbishop undermined the traditional raison d'être of confraternities.

The reform-minded Mexican prelates never attempted to disband these organizations outright. They believed that confraternities could be useful in the dissemination of doctrine if they were properly regulated, participated in appropriately solemn religious practices, and contributed resources to parish expenses. In fact, during the eighteenth century the church hierarchy had promoted the foundation of confraternities dedicated to the Blessed Sacrament in each of the parishes of Mexico City. These confraternities, however, largely conformed to prescriptions concerning ecclesiastical supervision and often acted more as adjuncts to the parish than independent organizations for lay religious practice.[25]

Archbishop Núñez de Haro enlarged the Blessed Sacrament confraternities when he finally acted on the surveys he had commissioned at the insistence of the viceroy in 1787. According to the surveys, in 1794, the year they were completed, there were some 991 urban and rural confraternities in the Archdiocese of Mexico, 152 of which existed in Mexico City. Archbishop Núñez de Haro ordered the dissolution of more than 450 of these organizations, most of them rural confraternities, because of mismanagement and precarious finances. He suppressed at least 40 of Mexico City's confraternities either totally or by amalgamating them with other more vibrant ones, often fraternities of the Blessed Sacrament.[26] In this way, the hierarchy extended its influence and authority over lay devotions.

It is intriguing that at the end of the century the archbishop considered at least one-fourth of all confraternities in Mexico City either defunct or moribund. Did Núñez de Haro falsely justify the suppression of confraternities that he believed egregiously contravened the dictates of his somber reformed piety? Did the suppressed confraternities enjoy an active and large membership but simply suffer from poor financial management? Or did the extirpation of one-fourth of Mexico City's confraternities indicate that the laity had begun to view them with indifference and shun the communal religiosity they promoted? Although all three factors may have influenced the archbishop's decision, evidence from last wills and testaments written by the residents of Mexico City during the eighteenth century suggests that the last played a significant role in Archbishop Núñez de Haro's thinking. The wills reveal that the testator population of Mexico City grew increasingly disaffected with confraternities as the century progressed.

Toward the end of their lives, many propertied residents (who were mostly Spanish) of Mexico City called a notary public to their bedside to compose their last wills and testaments. During the colonial period, the will was as much a religious as a secular document: testators used it as much to set straight their relationships with God and to achieve salvation as to pass on property to family and friends. In addition to naming heirs, testators often bequeathed alms to the church, images of saints, and the poor; designed their funerals; and requested masses for their souls. They also commonly stated that they belonged to confraternities and asked that these brotherhoods perform their obligations to the deceased.

Confraternal clauses contained in wills shed light on how the faithful understood the role of these organizations in death, burial, and salvation. To investigate how the populace perceived confraternities, I analyzed a corpus of 960 last wills and testaments written by the population of Mexico City during the eighteenth century. I chose to examine wills written during four years—1696, 1737, 1779, and 1813—and read about 240 wills for each year.[27]

The sharp decline in percentage of testators who mentioned membership in a confraternity as the eighteenth century wore on strongly suggests that the populace of Mexico City increasingly viewed them as less essential than before in attaining salvation and therefore joined them with less frequency. In 1696, 25 percent of all testators stated that they belonged to one or more confraternities; in 1813 only 5 percent of testators claimed membership in a confraternity. We should not, however, take these figures as a fully accurate reflection of patterns of confraternal

Table 7.1. Confraternal Membership

Year	Total # of Testators	# of Testators in Confraternities	% of All Testators in Confraternities
1696	246	62	25
1737	248	50	20
1779	222	22	10
1813	244	13	5

membership during the eighteenth century in Mexico City. Changes in testamentary practice account for some portion of this decline. For some unknown reason, in the latter part of the century notaries must have stopped prompting testators to list the confraternities to which they belonged. In 1813 alone, five testators asked to be buried in the chapels of various third orders, suggesting that they belonged to these organizations, but never mentioned their membership in them in their wills.[28] Other testators in the latter part of the century mentioned their membership in fraternities only in an incidental way. For example, Marcos Francisco Maldonado, a bureaucrat in the office of tribute collection, stated that he was the treasurer of the confraternity of Our Lady of Loreto and that as its financial representative various people owed him money, after which he listed the sundry debts.[29] I have the impression that if it were not for the debts owed to the confraternity through him, Maldonado would not have mentioned his association with it.

Nonetheless, the decline in references to confraternities in testaments probably did mirror, if somewhat opaquely, a growing disaffection with these organizations. A decline in membership in Mexico City's confraternities would parallel a decrease in confraternal membership and in the number of confraternities themselves that occurred in areas of Catholic Europe at the same time.[30] It would also be congruous with other evidence concerning confraternities found in the wills of Mexico City. During the eighteenth century the number of gifts pledged to confraternities dropped significantly—nineteen in 1696, eight in 1737, eleven in 1779, and three in 1813—demonstrating a growing indifference toward them on the part of the testator population. Even if confraternal membership in Mexico City did not fall during the eighteenth century, the perception of these institu-tions and of the purposes they served changed dramatically.

At the beginning of the eighteenth century, the testators of Mexico City continued to view the function of confraternities along traditional lines, as sacred congregations devoted to the care of dead members' souls. It was the confreres' obligation to attend the funerals of their spiritual brothers and sisters, pray for their eternal repose, and commission masses for their souls. Almost all wills written by testators who declared their membership in a confraternity in 1696 and 1737 indicate such an under-standing. For instance, Félix Vela de Castillo, a physician, stated:

> I am a confrere of Señor Saint Peter and on account of having as all confreres [of this congregation] have the obligation to say for my soul the masses that are said for each confrere after they die, I leave no other masses for my soul.

At the end of his will, just before signing it, Vela de Castillo added:

> I am a brother of Saint Diego, Saint Michael, and of others. . . . Likewise [I am] a confrere of Our Lady of Antigua, and this confraternity has the obligation of attending my burial with acolytes [*monacillos*], processional cross, and choir [*capilla*].31

Vela de Castillo revealed many aspects of confraternal practice in these clauses. First, he belonged to at least six confraternities. Most people who mentioned membership in fraternities belonged to more than one. It is impossible, however, to count accurately the average number of confrater-nities to which confreres belonged because most listed only the one or two most prestigious confraternities of which they were members. Afterward they simply stated that they belonged to many others without naming them. Even Vela de Castillo listed only four confraternities by name but indicated that he belonged to more with the phrase, "I am a brother . . . of others." Second, confraternities provided various and sometimes different suffrages for the deceased. The Congregation of Saint Peter, a confrater-nity composed mainly of the archdiocese's secular clergy but which also invited the laity to join for an entrance fee of five hundred pesos, required each member to say or commission three masses for each confrere who died.32 The total number of masses said for each departed confrere must have been large for Vela de Castillo to desist from requesting any other mass for his soul. By contrast, the confraternity of Our Lady of Antigua, a fraternity whose chapel was located in the cathedral, participated in an extraordinary manner in the funeral and burial rites of confreres, providing acolytes and a choir to enhance the splendor of these ceremonies. The fact that the confraternity furnished a processional cross suggests that its members also marched in the funeral procession from the deceased's home to the church where the requiem Mass and burial were to take place. Confraternal participation in these processions must have been common, for the manual for priests written by friar Miguel Venegas in the early eighteenth century specifically mentioned the presence and precise placement of confreres in describing the proper arrangement and activities of funeral corteges.[33] Vela de Castillo remained silent about the obligations of the other confraternities to which he belonged, suggesting that their duties were more standard: participation in the funeral cortege, paying of funeral dues, and collective commemoration of the dead with masses and prayers.

Antonio de Aguilar, a priest and administrator of the Conceptionist nunnery of La Concepción, likewise dictated a telling confraternity clause in his will in 1696. He stated that he belonged to the Congregation of Saint Peter and faithfully fulfilled his obligation to say three masses for each departed confrere "within a week" of his or her death. But he lamented that since he had begun his work as administrator of La Concepción, "I do not attend the burials and suffrages of my brothers as I used to." In recompense for his breach of this sacred obligation, Aguilar said that he had given ten pesos a year to a hospital the confraternity had founded for the care of ill clerics to pay for food on the feast of Saint Joseph. He then asked that twelve members of the congregation carry his corpse during his funeral procession and asked his fellow confreres to each say or commission one Mass for his soul on the day of his funeral. Aguilar's admitted absence from the funerals and commemorative services of the congregation reveals that the participation of individual confreres in these rituals was not necessarily certain. Nonetheless, they were not obligations dismissed lightly. Aguilar felt compelled to make restitution to the confraternity for his dereliction of service by endowing the hospital it administered. In a separate clause, he stated that he belonged to at least five other confraternities and requested that the members of each of them "commend me to God and fulfill what may be of their obligation as I do for all [of them]."[34] In this phrase Aguilar encapsulated the basic logic of confraternities: mutual obligation between members to aid each other in the quest for salvation.

Most testators wrote less revealing confraternity clauses in their wills, but almost all of them in 1696 and 1737 made some reference to the obligation of members to perform suffrages for the souls of the departed. The vast majority of these clauses resembled one written by Felipa Juárez de Salazar. She stated in her 1696 will:

> I am a confrere of the confraternities of the Blessed Sacrament,
> of the Rosary, of the most Holy Trinity, of Saint Cajetan, of Jesus
> the Nazarene, and of other confraternities that are made known
> by their patents [certificates of membership given to confreres].
> I order that notice of my death be given to them so that they do
> the good for my soul that they are obligated to do.[35]

Even in this less revealing clause, it is evident that confraternities were obliged to perform suffrages of some kind on behalf of the deceased.

This was not the case in a new discourse on confraternities that appeared in a small number of wills by 1737 and more commonly by 1779. Testators who deployed this new discourse viewed confraternities less as sacred forms of Christian sociability founded to perform suffrages for the dead and more as mutual aid societies that provided financial assistance for the costs of burial and votive masses. Certainly, confraternity members even in the seventeenth century considered confraternities a source of material aid at death and in times of need. But the testamentary language they employed to describe their relationship to these organizations stressed its spiritual nature. The new discourse, by contrast, emphasized its monetary character.

The oddest articulation of this new discourse was expressed in a unique clause written by Marcos de Mendoza, a mestizo carpenter, in his 1737 will. He declared:

> I have four confraternities to which I understand I am not a
> debtor of any amount and in case I am it would be of very little.
> Understanding that said four are each worth 25 pesos, and
> independently of them, I have another worth 10 pesos. . . .
> It is my will that being dead, [these amounts] be collected and,
> with the sum, the costs of my burial be paid.[36]

Mendoza conceived of the confraternity as an asset with specific monetary value. Most likely, he was referring to the confraternal patent, the certificate that proved one's membership in a fraternity. Upon death, these certificates were returned to the issuing confraternity, which paid a specified sum to the bearer. It is noteworthy that Mendoza did not conceive of the fraternity as anything but a financial organization. He indicated that he did not owe any dues to the fraternities to which he belonged, or at most "very little." He never spoke of the suffrages the confraternities were obliged to perform on his behalf or mentioned the saints to whom the confraternities were dedicated. Instead, he only stated the amount of money each confraternity owed him. He did not even mention the purpose of these confraternal funds: to cover funeral and burial expenses. In this clause, Mendoza stripped confraternities of their religious nature and represented them as purely secular institutions.

Although no other testator conceived of a confraternity as something to be possessed, most who mentioned that they belonged to one in 1779 and 1813 viewed them primarily as sources of money for funeral expenses. For example, Josefa Rodríguez de Pinillos wrote in her 1779 will:

> I am a confrere of the cord [of Saint Francis?] from which
> I have 25 pesos and 20 for being a sister of the Holy Angels.
> Likewise 25 in Santa Cruz as is certified in their respective
> patents that may be found in my papers. Their sum is to
> be added to my goods to help pay for my funeral and burial
> [*para ayuda de mi funeral y entierro*].37

Josefa de Salcedo, the widow of a cobbler, listed the confraternities to which she belonged in the burial clause of her 1779 will, indicating their close association with death and burial rites. After stating that she wished to be interred in the chapel of the Holy Trinity in front of an altar dedicated to Our Lady of Sorrows with the "pomp that seems fitting to my executors," she informed them that they should pay

> their [the funeral's and burial's] costs from what the confrater-
> nities of which I am a confrere should give. [The confraternities
> I belong to] are that of the Souls [of Purgatory] founded in
> the holy Cathedral church, that of the most Blessed Sacrament
> in the parish of San Sebastián, that of Saint Homobono in the

church of the most Holy Trinity, that of Our Lady of Solitude
in the parish of Santa Cruz, and that of the Cord of our
seraphic father Señor Saint Francis, applying the remainder
[of the money collected] that there may be so that masses
may be said for my soul.[38]

All three testators still associated confraternities with death. The money
received from them was specifically to be used for funeral and burial
expenses, and once these had been paid, the remainder, as Josefa de Salcedo
indicated, was to be used for masses for the confrere's soul. But the sacred
nature of these organizations, the mutual spiritual commitments of confreres, was lost in this new discourse. Although these testators, especially
Josefa de Salcedo, continued to believe that suffrages were necessary for the
soul, they were no longer necessarily the obligation of confraternities.
Confraternities were seen as associations that provided money for suffrages,
but their actual performance was left to the testator's executors.

I do not mean to suggest that confraternities ceased to perform their
traditional acts of participation in funerals and the commemoration of
departed confreres during the last half of the eighteenth century. The passage from Archbishop Lorenzana quoted above leaves no doubt that confraternities still practiced festive and commemorative rites during this
period. Furthermore, the unique confraternity clause composed by María
Manuela Jiménez de Velasco, the daughter of a royal treasury official, in her
1813 will shows that confraternities still practiced suffrages for their
deceased members. She stated:

I order that the patents that I have as a member of a
third order [tercera] and the others be delivered to their
corresponding confraternities so that they may apply
suffrages to me. Those that should contribute some sum
of reales to me, [I order] my executors to collect it and
add it to my goods.[39]

Jiménez de Velasco, however, was the only testator in either 1779 or 1813
who mentioned the spiritual obligations of confraternities, and she was
quick to indicate that at least some of the confraternities to which she
belonged were obligated to compensate her monetarily.

By the end of the eighteenth century in Mexico City, testators rarely spoke of the religious duties of confraternities. Although these organizations continued to exist and participate in devotions, in the minds of Mexico City's Spanish property-owning residents, the confraternities no longer directly aided their fallen members with suffrages as they stood before God. Now the soul faced judgment bereft of the company and prayers of its fellow confreres.

Conclusion

The role of confraternities in the rites of dying offers valuable insight into the religious culture of colonial Mexico. It sheds light on the decline of communal piety as the self emerged in late eighteenth-century Mexico City. Even though confraternities still performed traditional ritual acts, testators in the second half of the eighteenth century deemphasized the sacred nature of these organizations by omitting mention of the mutual bonds of spiritual obligation that membership in them engendered. The transformation in discourse on confraternities was predicated on and represented a retreat from the collective subjectivity that formed the base on which the traditional conception of confraternities rested. The ties of sacred sociability that participated in the mystical body of Christ and the mutual spiritual obligations that depended on a communal understanding of salvation gave way to secular bonds of associational interests. During the eighteenth century, Christians joined confraternities less and less because confraternities structured and expressed sacred social bonds and promoted Christian charity. More and more, people joined them to ease the financial burdens that death placed on their families. The decline of the sacred character of the confraternity reveals the disintegration of the collective enterprise of salvation that occurred during the eighteenth century as the modern, bounded self emerged.

Apart from the decline of communal piety at the close of the colonial period, the study of confraternities highlights the limitations of the concept of local religion. Confraternal activities demonstrate that colonial Mexicans were greatly concerned with death and the afterlife. In fact, the fundamental purpose of most confraternities in New Spain for most of the colonial period was to provide Christian burial and suffrages for deceased members. Catholics joined confraternities precisely to ensure their salvation and a quick passage through the agonies of purgatory. Although colonial Catholics certainly looked to religion to alleviate mundane distresses and improve their material conditions in this world, they spent much of their spiritual energies preparing for the next.

Furthermore, confraternal participation in the rituals of death reveals the highly liturgical nature of colonial Catholicism. Upon the death of a confrere, living members of the fraternity attended and participated in the universal church's liturgical rites of funeral and burial. Moreover, the confraternities paid for and often required members to attend anniversary masses for the deceased. Beyond these rites performed in memory of the dead, confraternities sponsored weekly masses and lavish liturgical celebrations on the feast days of their patron saints. Granted, the paraliturgical activities of confraternities could be highly local in nature and often contradicted the precepts of the church universal as witnessed by the eighteenth-century attempt by royal and ecclesiastical officials to reign in the "excesses" of confraternal piety and better monitor fraternity finances and administration. But many of the devotions performed or commissioned by confraternities coincided with and funded liturgical celebrations of the universal church. In the end, the analytical categories—or to use Carlos Eire's language, the "binary opposites"—of local religion and the universal church are too stark to capture the fluidity and complexity of early modern and colonial religion.

NOTES

1. Will of Jacinto de Silva Ortuño, notarized by José de Anaya y Bonillo, Mexico City, 9 Feb. 1717, Archivo General de Notarías del Districto Federal, Mexico City [hereinafter AN], Notary #13, vol. 76, fs. 98–102.

2. "Early modern" refers to a period in European history between the Medieval and the modern eras, roughly from 1450 to 1800. Colonial refers to the period in which Latin America was ruled by European powers, roughly from 1500 to 1825. Although these time periods overlap to a great extent, these terms refer to different sociopolitical contexts.

3. William A. Christian Jr., *Local Religion in Early Modern Spain* (Princeton, NJ: Princeton University Press, 1981).

4. On the importance of the liturgy in late medieval and early modern Europe, see Eamon Duffy, *The Stripping of the Altars: Traditional Religion in England, 1400–1580* (New Haven, CT: Yale University Press, 1992); Ann W. Ramsey, *Liturgy, Politics, and Salvation: The Catholic League in Paris and the Nature of Catholic Reform, 1540–1630* (Rochester, NY: University of Rochester Press, 1999).

5. John Bossy, *Christianity in the West, 1400–1700* (New York: Oxford University Press, 1985). Of course, this does not mean that ritual events could not express or foment division. Many times they did. But their articulated and intended purpose was community formation.

6. See, for example, Philippe Ariès, *The Hour of Our Death*, trans. Helen Weaver (New York: Alfred A. Knopf, 1981); Bossy, *Christianity in the West*; David Warren Sabean, *Power in the Blood: Popular Culture and Village Discourse in Early Modern Germany* (New York: Cambridge University Press, 1984); Georges Duby, ed., *A History of Private Life II: Revelations of the Medieval World* (Cambridge, MA: Harvard University Press, 1988), especially 511–14; Lynn Hunt, "Psychoanalysis, The Self, and Historical Interpretation," *Common Knowledge* 6 (1997); and for a controversial account of selfhood and embodiment, see Morris Berman, *Coming to Our Senses: Body and Spirit in the Hidden History of the West* (New York: Simon and Schuster, 1989).

7. Pamela Voekel, *Alone Before God: The Religious Origins of Modernity in Mexico* (Durham, NC: Duke University Press, 2002). Voekel touches on confraternities, but, given her broader concerns, does not analyze them in depth.

8. Like the presence of planets in distant solar systems, the rise of the modern sense of the bounded individual is difficult to observe directly. But just as a planet's presence can be deduced by variations it causes in a star's movement, the bounded individual can be inferred by changes in more observable cultural practices—practices like participation in confraternities.

9. William Monter, *Ritual, Myth and Magic in Early Modern Europe* (Athens: Ohio University Press, 1984), 15.

10. Christopher F. Black, *Italian Confraternities in the Sixteenth Century* (New York: Cambridge University Press, 1989), 7.

11. *Concilios provinciales primero y segundo celebrados en la muy noble y muy leal ciudad de México...en los años de 1555 y 1565...* (Mexico: Joseph Antonio de Hogal, 1769), 150–51.

12. Alicia Bazarte Martínez, *Las cofradías de españoles en la ciudad de México* (Mexico: Universidad Autónoma Metropolitana, 1989), 31–32.

13. "Autos fhos sobre que se aprueben las constituciones de la Cofradía que nuevamente se a ynstituido y fundado en la Parrochia de Sta. Catharina Virgen y Martir...," Mexico City, 11 May 1694, Archivo General de la Nación, Mexico City (hereafter AGN), Bienes Nacionales, vol. 1028, exp. 40, f. s/n.

14. "Constituciones de la cofradía de Sn Benito sita en la Yglecia de Sn Francisco, Mexico," Mexico City, 1672, AGN, Templos y Conventos, vol. 160, exp. 35, fs. 731–35.

15. Asunción Lavrin, "Cofradías novohispanas: Economías material y espiritual," in *Cofradías, capellanías y obras pías en la América colonial*, ed. Pilar Martínez López-Cano, Gisela von Wobeser, and Juan Guillermo Muñoz (Mexico: Universidad Nacional Autónoma de México, 1998), 57.

16. "Autos fechos sobre la Aprovación de las nuevas constituciones reformadas de la cofradía de La presiosa Sangre de Xpto Señor Nuestro fundada en la Parrochia de Sta Catarina Mártir de esta ciudad," Mexico City, 1683, AGN, Bienes Nacionales, vol. 1028, exp. 1, f. s/n.

17. For a discussion of the diverse activities of confraternities, see James R. Banker, *Death in the Community: Memorialization and Confraternities in an Italian Commune in the Late Middle Ages* (Athens: University of Georgia Press, 1988); Black, *Italian Confraternities*; Maureen Flynn, *Sacred Charity: Confraternities and Social Welfare in Spain, 1400–1700* (Ithaca, NY: Cornell University Press, 1989). For the case of Mexico, Bazarte Martínez, *Las cofradías de españoles*. For the role confraternities performed in the creation of sacred communities, see Flynn, *Sacred Charity*, 13; and Bossy, *Christianity in the West*, 58–60. For ritual feasting, Sara Nalle, *God in la Mancha: Religious Reform and the People of Cuenca, 1550–1650* (Baltimore, MD: Johns Hopkins University Press, 1992), 158. For the *agape*, Theodor Klauser, *A Short History of the Western Liturgy: An Account and Some Reflections*, trans. John Halliburton (New York: Oxford University Press, 1979), 7–8.

18. The history of the Bourbon reforms is vast. For a good overview, see John Lynch, *Bourbon Spain, 1700–1808* (Cambridge: Basil Blackwell Inc., 1989). The best introduction to the Bourbon reforms in New Spain remains David A. Brading, *Miners and Merchants in Bourbon Mexico, 1763–1810* (New York: Cambridge University Press, 1971).

19. Clara García Ayluardo, "Confraternity, Cult and Crown in Colonial Mexico City, 1700–1810" (D.Phil. thesis, University of Cambridge, 1989), 248–68.

20. The historiography of religious reform is growing. For a good overview, see David A. Brading, *Church and State in Bourbon Mexico: The Diocese of Michoacán, 1749–1810* (New York: Cambridge University Press, 1994). For more detailed studies of particular aspects of reform, see Voekel, *Alone Before God*; and Brian Larkin, "The Splendor of Worship: Baroque Catholicism, Religious Reform, and Last Wills and Testaments in Eighteenth-Century Mexico City," *Colonial Latin American Historical Review* 8 (1999).

21. Alfonso Núñez de Haro y Peralta, *Sermones escogidos, pláticas espirituales privadas, y dos pastorales*...(Madrid: Hija de Ibarra, 1806), 1: 209–28.

22. García, "Confraternity, Cult and Crown," 258.

23. Francisco Antonio Lorenzana y Buitrón, *Cartas pastorales y edictos del Illmo Señor D. Francisco Antonio Lorenzana y Buitrón, Arzobispo de México* (Mexico: Joseph Antonio de Hogal, 1770), 75.

24. Lorenzana, *Cartas*, 76.

25. García, "Confraternity, Cult and Crown," 37, 181–82. Promoting the Blessed Sacrament confraternities, the Fourth Mexican Provincial Council mandated that they were always to be given precedence of place in processions, regardless of the date of their foundation, the criteria most often used to determine placement of confraternities in processions. *Concilio IV provincial mexicano celebrado año de 1771* (Querétaro, Mexico: Escuela de Artes, 1898), 67.

26. García, "Confraternity, Cult, and Crown," 276–78. I calculated the minimum number of confraternities suppressed in Mexico City from the table of all confraternities extant in the capital contained in Bazarte Martínez (in *Cofradías, capellanías y obras pías en la América colonial*, ed. Pilar Martínez López-Cano, Gisela von Wobeser, and Juan Guillermo Muñoz [Mexico: Universidad Nacional Autónoma de México, 1998], 64–67). I speak of a minimum number because this table significantly undercounts the number of confraternities in Mexico City in 1794. William Taylor has argued that the archbishop did not suppress rural confraternities but merely degraded their status to informal organizations; see his *Magistrates of the Sacred: Priests and Parishioners in Eighteenth-Century Mexico* (Stanford, CA: Stanford University Press, 1996), 307–11. Perhaps the same occurred in Mexico City. More research is needed on the issue.

27. In order to assure the validity of the sample, I employed an innovative sampling technique. I examined those wills proved by the most active notaries in terms of will writing who worked in Mexico City during the years when severe plagues struck the viceregal capital. The sample consists

of 246 wills from 1696, 248 from 1737, 222 from 1779, and 244 from 1813. I chose these four years using the demographic crises tables from Juan Javier Pescador, *De bautizados a fieles difuntos: Familia y mentalidades en una parroquia urbana, Santa Catarina de México, 1568–1820* (Mexico: El Colegio de México; Centro de Estudios Demográficos y de Desarrollo Urbano, 1992), 95, 103. Because each notary catered to a specific population of Mexico City, the inclusion of many notaries in the sample avoids the possibility of mistaking differences in the religious practices of particular notarial clienteles for more general changes in pious practice, a possibility that raises doubts about the validity of random samples of notarial documentation. I studied 68 percent of all wills written in 1696, 75 percent in 1737, 97 percent in 1779, and 87 percent in 1813. I consulted fifteen notaries (33 percent) of all active notaries for 1696; twenty-four (36 percent) for 1737; forty-four (67 percent) for 1779; and nineteen (42 percent) for 1813. I chose plague years under the assumption that the high rate of mortality in these years would increase the number of wills written. The unusually high number of wills composed in these years not only provided a large source base but, more importantly, yielded an unusually high ratio of wills per notary. In fact, of all the notaries sampled, none proved less that five wills per year, and most proved at least double that amount. The exception is 1779. I consulted all notaries who proved wills in that year. Twenty of these notaries proved less than three wills. This high ratio of wills per notary allowed for a thorough examination of notarial influence on the religious directives present in any given will. If no other reason for their presence could be determined, then identical or similar directives that appeared in many wills proved by the same notary could be attributed to his influence. In the case of confraternal clauses, notarial influence did not figure as a factor.

28. Will of María Luisa de la Puente y Becerra, notarized by Manuel Bravo Torija, Mexico City, 9 Aug. 1813, AN, Notary #93, vol. 587, fs. 2727–28; Will of Luis Martínez, notarized by Francisco Calapiz y Aguilar, Mexico City, 12 June 1813, AN, Notary #155, vol. 924, fs. 255–57; Will of María Bárbara Fernández, notarized by Francisco Calapiz y Aguilar, Mexico City, 12 Aug. 1813, AN, Notary #155, vol. 924, fs. 373–76; Will of Francisco Xavier Paez, notarized by José Cano y Moctezuma, Mexico City, 26 Feb. 1813, AN, Notary #158, vol. 950, f. s/n; Will of Ana María Andrade, notarized by Mariano González de la Rosa, Mexico City, 1 Sept. 1813, AN, Notary #610, vol. 4088, f. s/n.

29. Will of Marcos Francisco Maldonado, notarized by Bernardo de Rivera Buitrón, Mexico City, 16 Jan. 1779, AN, Notary #600, vol. 4055, fs. 143–48.

30. John McManners, *Death and the Enlightenment: Changing Attitudes to Death among Christians and Unbelievers in Eighteenth-Century France* (New York: Clarendon Press, 1981), 233; William J. Callahan, "Las cofradías y hermandades de España y su papel social y religioso dentro de una sociedad de estamentos," in *Cofradías, capellanías y obras pías en la América colonial*, ed. Pilar Martínez López-Cano, Gisela von Wobeser, and Juan Guillermo Muñoz (Mexico: Universidad Nacional Autónoma de México, 1998), 36.

31. Will of Félix Vela del Castillo, notarized by Miguel Leonardo de Sevilla, Mexico City, 22 Dec. 1696, AN, Notary #637, vol. 4407, f. s/n.

32. Asunción Lavrin, "La congregación de San Pedro: Una cofradía urbana del México colonial, 1604–1730," *Historia Mexicana* 29 (1980), 570–76.

33. Miguel Venegas, *Manual de párrocos para administrar los santos sacramentos y exercer otras funciones eclesiasticas conforme al ritual romano* (Mexico: Joseph Bernardo de Hogal, 1731), 92–98.

34. Will of Antonio de Aguilar, notarized by Antonio de Anaya, Mexico City, 16 Sept. 1696, AN, Notary #9, vol. 30, fs. 196–202.

35. Will of Felipa Juárez de Salazar, notarized by Martín del Río, Mexico City, 7 Dec. 1696, AN, Notary #563, vol. 3893, f. s/n.

36. Will of Marcos de Mendoza, notarized by José Caballero, Mexico City, [?] Nov. 1737, AN, Notary #132, vol. 832, fs. 23–25.

37. Will of Josefa Rodríguez de Pinillos, notarized by Antonio de la Torre, Mexico City, 15 Oct. 1779, AN, Notary #669, vol. 4530, fs. 698–701.

38. Will of Josefa de Salcedo, notarized by José Manuel Ochoa, Mexico City, 8 May 1779, AN, Notary #480, vol. 3264, fs. 35–38.

39. Will of María Manuela Jiménez de Velasco, notarized by José María Moya, Mexico City, 9 July 1813, AN, Notary #425, vol. 2820, fs. 98–101.

TEMPLE OF THE VIRGIN OF GUADALUPE.

FIGURE 20. Guadalupe shrine

In the nineteenth century, Anglo traveler Robert Wilson produced his reflections on his experiences in Mexico as well as on the nation's history and religion. Many of the images reflected an Anglo stereotype of Mexican and Catholic "degeneration" and "superstition," but others are fine examples of nineteenth-century reproductions of religious sites. Here is the Basilica of the Virgin of Guadalupe in Tepeyac. Taken from Robert Wilson, Mexico and Its Religion *(London: Sampson Low, Son, and Co., 1856). Courtesy of Mandeville Special Collections Library, University of California, San Diego.*

CHAPTER EIGHT

Routes to Respectability

Confraternities and Men of African Descent in New Spain

Nicole von Germeten

An elderly African man called Juan Roque lay in bed in a small house in Mexico City. The year was 1629. Roque's daughter and a notary with pen and paper in hand sat near him, along with several elderly African friends gathered around the room. As Roque spoke quietly to the notary in Spanish, occasionally his companions spoke to each other, all in the same African language. "I want to be buried in my parish church or in the hospital I supported," said Roque, and the notary dutifully recorded that Roque requested burial in the Santa Veracruz church, or the hospital of the Immaculate Conception, both near the center of the city.[1] Roque continued, smiling weakly at his friends, "The men and women in my confraternity must walk with my body when it is buried, along with twelve priests and the confraternity of the Holy Sacrament. I leave this last group twenty pesos in alms in exchange for their presence. My funeral must have a requiem Mass, communion and a deacon present. I also want sixty-four masses to be said for my soul and the soul of my deceased wife, Isabel." The notary asked if Roque had any special request for the locations of the masses for his soul: "I want them divided between the hospitals of the city, with twenty in the Carmelite convent," he replied. After listening to the notary read back his last will and testament, Roque leaned back, and his friends came forward, reassuring him of their prayers for his soul and congratulating him on this well-organized document that would surely lessen his time in purgatory.

This chapter explains how African men and men descended from Africans immersed themselves in the institution of the religious brotherhood, or confraternity.[2] Two life stories are reconstructed: that of the African Juan Roque, and that of Diego Durán, a mulato master architect who lived from 1721 to 1795 in the provincial town now called Morelia. These short biographies emphasize the social and religious world of the confraternity. Both men used Catholic institutions to increase their personal status in urban society, and both were prosperous and respected among their peers. Their lives demonstrate how the viceregal church successfully drew in a wide range of society and how active participation in Catholic public ceremony was fundamental to social status. Rather than rebel against or reject their conversion to Christianity in New Spain, Roque and Durán embraced confraternities.

It would be extremely difficult to know exactly what Africans believed or felt about their conversion to Christianity or their transplanted lives in the Americas because they tended not to leave written accounts of the experience. Instead, evidence left behind by religious institutions in which they took an active part allows historians to reconstruct their public lives. Confraternity records and testaments hint at inner experience and elucidate Afro-Mexican social activity within the church. Although Africans did not necessarily consider each other as sharing religious beliefs or experiences, their confraternities suggest that they sought a communal experience of worship and belief in their new home. Accordingly, this essay focuses on the material and social implications of their participation in the Catholic religion and its institutions.

Among the social options of the time, confraternities competed with bathhouses, bars selling pulque, gambling houses, and brothels. Dances organized by poorer people of Indian or African ancestry also happened frequently but were seen as somewhat suspect, because of their possible pagan element. By contrast, confraternities provided a legal, Catholic, and customary way for people to socialize during the frequent fiestas, funerals of members, organizational meetings, feasts, and even dances. Although they could be excuses for drinking and revelry, these events were tolerated by viceregal authorities because they were connected to devotion to a saint and protected under church auspices. Confraternities had an annual fiesta on the saint's official holiday and staged processions during Lent and on Corpus Christi. When large numbers of people marched in these parades, they felt the saint was being honored properly and the town as a whole put its religious devotion on display.

Because people of African descent were barred by Mexican church law from becoming priests, friars, or nuns, they took part in church life as parishioners and confraternity members. Mine workers, craftsmen, and domestic servants organized confraternities and held leadership roles, although they would have generally held no other positions of authority in the colonial world. While Spanish men, simultaneously involved in town government, led the richest confraternities, slaves, Indians, and women led other confraternities.

Confraternities with leaders described as blacks or mulatos were usually poor but required members to have at least a small amount of disposable income. Perhaps the possibility for blacks and mulatos to earn wages as miners, agricultural workers, and tradesmen explains why confraternities have been documented mainly in larger towns and cities, especially those that depended on a mining or hacienda economy. People of African descent may have organized religious brotherhoods in smaller agricultural settlements, but if so, they left little or no evidence of the confraternities' modest activities.

Slaves and poor people of African descent did not often have access to hospitals or other kinds of social welfare and depended on confraternities to help them through financial difficulties. When a town lacked a charity hospital, confraternities provided limited home health care for members. Like burial insurance today, confraternities guaranteed a church burial for members who paid their dues. Unlike the indigenous people of Mexico, people of African descent did not have ancient geographic and communal links to where they lived, nor did they often have multigenerational lineage ties with the people they knew in New Spain, as was the case for Spaniards. Confraternities personalized their experience of Christianity and created an extensive new family.

Confraternities brought local society together but also separated out certain groups. The wealthiest and most powerful people in each town controlled the most important confraternity, usually dedicated to the

Eucharist and based in the main church of the town. But other groups wanted to protect their special interests, and this was acceptable, especially to clergy who wanted to reach out to Indians or Africans. Like other immigrants, people of African descent living in New Spain sought connections among people who shared their cultural background as a step in the process of adapting to living in a new setting. Africans and mulatos formed confraternities with membership made up of their peers, and they were not the only immigrants to New Spain who tried to protect the exclusivity of their brotherhoods. For example, the famous Basque confraternity dedicated to the Virgin of Aránzazu was founded in Mexico in 1671 and had strict rules regarding benefits for Basque immigrants only.

Juan Roque and the Zape Confraternity

Who were Juan Roque and his friends? Africans were brought to New Spain from the time of the conquistadors to the late seventeenth century. Some were slaves brought directly from western Africa to the port of Veracruz; they knew little about Catholicism, the Spanish language, or Hispanic culture. Other slaves came from Angola or Congo, at this time under Portuguese control, and had some exposure to Christianity in Africa due to Portuguese missionary efforts in this region. Others came in the entourages of Spaniards, serving as servants or domestic slaves. These Africans may have already lived in Spain or other parts of the Indies and had a sophisticated understanding of Hispanic society.

Although only a minority of slaves managed to buy their freedom, this was a possibility within the Spanish legal tradition. Some slaves were also freed in their masters' testaments. By taking advantage of their masters' patronage or communal support including confraternities or simply through their own talents and hard work, some slaves became financially successful property owners.

Juan Roque and the men and women from the area where he was born in Africa founded an exclusive confraternity. Describing themselves as part of the Zape *nación* (the term used in the colonial era to designate African regions), they founded their brotherhood in the Mexico City hospital of the Limpia Concepción (or, Immaculate Conception), a charitable hospital patronized by the Marqués del Valle, the title of nobility granted to Hernán Cortés and his descendants.[3]

The Zapes were brought to New Spain as slaves mainly in the six-teenth century from what is now coastal Sierra Leone in West Africa. By the end of the 1500s, Zapes declined as a percentage of the slaves brought to New Spain after the Portuguese united with the Spanish crown in 1580. Spaniards now had more open and legal access to Portuguese slav-ing ventures. Because of the fifteenth-century Portuguese imperial expan-sion to central Africa, the union of Portugal and Spain resulted in a numeric domination of Congo and Angolan slaves sold in seventeenth-century New Spain. Therefore most Zape slaves arrived in the Hispanic world much earlier than the more numerous Angolan slaves. By 1600 some Zapes in Mexico City had either been given their freedom by their masters or had bought their way out of slavery and had sufficient social status and wealth to found their own confraternity. Their desire to pre-serve their separate Zape identity was intertwined with their long-term residence and relative success in the Hispanic world of Mexico City.

In the 1600s the Zapes struggled through financial fluctuations to maintain their confraternity's financial autonomy and Zape leadership. The confraternity of the Limpia Concepción was far from wealthy and petitioned to be relieved of the twelve-peso fee they had to pay a priest for permission to have their fiesta in 1600.[4] When one of the prosperous founders of Limpia Concepción, Juan Roque, died in 1629, he endowed the group with a property in the San Hipólito barrio worth sixty pesos.[5] This was probably a modest one-story house, but rental income from this property did offer the confraternity a small yearly income, which might be enough to pay for perhaps one or two masses to be said in honor of the members' souls. However, this legacy did not come to the confraternity uncontested. Although Roque's wishes were stated as common knowledge among the Zape community, the priest Joseph de Peñafiel had taken direct control of the rents of the house (which added up to twenty-four pesos after four years rented to a Spanish woman), probably because he had been assigned to say the masses Roque requested. The Zape confra-ternity leaders wanted this rent returned to them, along with control of the house.

The Zape confraternity brothers and sisters doubted that the priest was actually carrying out Roque's bequest and appealed to Roque's uni-versal heir, his daughter Ana María, described as a "morena" or "negra libre" (or, a free black) married to a mulato tailor. When the priest refused to give the rent back to the Zape confraternity, the Zapes brought the case to court in 1634. By then, Ana María had also died, leaving no heirs. However, a few weeks before her death, she called on the members of the Zape confraternity to carry out her father's wishes regarding his house. Several members represented the confraternity in court and claimed that Ana María had told them her father meant to give the house to the confraternity to pay for pious works the confraternity could do for his soul.

Judging from his will, Ana's father Juan Roque was a prosperous man, able to afford numerous pious bequests. Less than five men or women of stated African heritage left instructions for such an elaborate funeral and procession in the records of Mexico City's seventeenth-century testaments. Given Roque's status as a free African, his funeral was extremely elaborate and elegant. His funeral Mass fit the normal pattern for wealthy residents of Mexico City in this era: a sung requiem Mass with a deacon and subdeacon present and an offering of communion. Roque also asked for ten masses to be said at special altars designated to lessen an individual's time in purgatory, twenty masses in the Carmelite convent, ten masses in the hospital of the Limpia Concepción, four masses in the Espíritu Santo hospital, ten masses in the Indian Hospital, and twenty masses generally for the souls in purgatory and the soul of his wife, the morena Isabel de Pereira. It is unknown why Roque chose these locations for his masses, although perhaps he wanted to donate to institutions he believed were especially worthy and sacred, spreading his bequests around in hopes that they would be heard and granted.

Even many Spaniards' wills did not include such extensive pious bequests, although in this era of devout religious practice, those who could afford to willingly paid for thousands of masses to lessen their personal time in purgatory, along with providing help for their already deceased friends and family. People who could pay the entry fees joined as many confraternities as possible; some testaments listed a dozen or more and occasionally testators simply said, "Check my records, and contact all confraternities I joined during my life to inform them of my death, so they can fulfill their obligations to me." Testators depended on confraternity members to come to their funeral and pray for their soul, hoping to gather a large community of believers whose numbers would demand attention from God and lead to less time in purgatory. For similar reasons, some people also chose burial in convents or monasteries, believing that proximity to holy communities would ease their concerns regarding the afterlife. Despite coming from Africa in his youth, Roque clearly shared these baroque religious beliefs and could afford to pay for what was termed at the time "a good death." He could die hoping for an eternity spent in paradise and also feel comforted by the social respect his funeral would generate in Mexico City.

How could Juan Roque go from slave to freedman with the wealth to pay for such a lavish funeral and impressive bequests? He was known to own property, but his profession is not known. The elaborate procession and Mass suggests that he may have been viewed as a more prominent man than most other Africans living in the capital, at least by those who took part in the ceremony. He may have been an important person before he left Africa or emerged as a Zape leader (literally leading some members of this nación in a confraternity) after spending time as a slave in Mexico. Roque was not a typical freedman, but his will suggests that some Africans were able to achieve high social status in seventeenth-century Mexico City. Zapes achieved respectability both among their peers and, to a limited degree, among Spanish authorities willing to recognize their confraternity as an independent organization of Africans from the Zape nación. The court case involving the Zape confraternity and Roque's will both mention other elderly Zape leaders. The Zape confraternity leaders' longevity attested to a decent standard of living. Because most Zapes came to New Spain before 1600, Roque and the other leaders of the confraternity had probably spent thirty years of their adult life in Mexico, gained freedom and some prosperity and formed a kind of elite or at least distinct group among other Africans. Juan Roque's will shows that a funeral with all the trappings of baroque religiosity combined with membership in a confraternity were one route to respectability open to men of African descent in New Spain.

For as long as possible, the Zapes controlled their confraternity. In all documentation generated in the dispute over Roque's bequest to the confraternity, the confraternity was referred to as "de morenos de la nación zape." At least ten individuals were mentioned in this case, all described as Zape and leaders of the confraternity. In 1644, another conflict arose over the possession of houses held as an endowment by the Zapes. Even at this later date, nine Zape men and four Zape women defended the rights of the confraternity, as leaders of an aging, decreasing group.[6] Although members had struggled for decades to maintain the confraternity's Zape identity, by the mid-seventeenth century, no Zapes had come to New Spain for generations and the current population was elderly. It was unlikely that they could

control the confraternity forever. Despite their two court cases and struggles to maintain an African/Zape identity, the confraternity did not survive
the seventeenth century. Conflicts over leadership, the aging Zape population, and intermarriage probably hastened the decline of this African brotherhood, and its members became part of the mass of Spanish-speaking
Mexico City residents. This pattern is already evident in Roque's daughter's
marriage to a mulato. Any children of this union probably did not feel compelled to emphasize their African heritage by continuing to support the
Zape confraternity. The organization disappeared from the record about
forty years after Roque's death.

Diego Durán and the Rosary Confraternity

Outside Mexico City, few Africans achieved Juan Roque's level of success
and ability to maintain associations with Africa through confraternity membership. But African ties were not the only way for people of African descent
to make social connections in New Spain. By the mid-sixteenth century, a
large group of people in New Spain were called *mulatos*. This term referred
to their mixed Spanish and African parentage and insultingly alluded to
mules, the supposedly sterile offspring of a donkey and a horse. As the conquerors and rulers of America, Spaniards were on top of New Spain's social
and racial hierarchy, with Indians in a lesser, childlike position. The Spanish
viewed Africans as necessary for the hard labor of building an empire, but
also as a disruptive force, especially when they had children with Spaniards
or Indians. Despite the racial hierarchy of New Spain, some Africans and
mulatos became free men and achieved prosperity in New Spain, often as
skilled urban craftsmen. Diego Durán exemplifies this kind of successful
free man of African descent whose social connections were created by confraternity ties. Both Roque and Durán placed great importance on their
confraternities but at very different times and places. Whereas Roque's confraternity emphasized African ethnicity, Durán's confraternity dedicated to
the rosary had a free mulato membership of mainly craftsmen and artisans
completely immersed in the Hispanic urban world.

Existing from the late sixteenth to at least the mid-nineteenth century, the confraternity of Our Lady of the Rosary was the longest-lasting
and most prominent confraternity in Valladolid. Today called Morelia,
Valladolid was a moderately large city and the seat of the diocese of
Michoacán, a region northwest of Mexico City. The history of the mulato

branch of Our Lady of the Rosary mirrors the rise in respectability among mulatos in eighteenth-century Valladolid and parallels the ascent of people of African descent through Hispanic society from slave status to members of a plebeian class of tradesmen. Throughout the colonial period, members of Valladolid's mulato confraternity were prominent leaders of their own social group. But these leaders still worked within an organization officially labeled and generally referred to as "Rosary of the mulatos." Until Mexican independence from Spain and the elimination of formal racial labels, free blacks were labeled in such a way that reiterated the racial divisions of colonial society and their supposed inferiority.

Rosary confraternities supported a strong traditional belief in the rosary, one of the most popular confraternity advocations in New Spain. Although the Dominican order usually sponsored devotion to the rosary, convents of other orders as well as parish churches throughout Mexico often served as headquarters for a rosary confraternity, founded in imitation of the original in the Dominican convent in Mexico City. Valladolid did not have a Dominican convent, but some time during the sixteenth century the institutionalized devotion to the rosary began.

The early years of the rosary confraternity in Valladolid are shrouded in mystery, although the organization had a permanent location in the Franciscan church and a connection with a prominent Spanish confraternity. The earliest historical record of the confraternity appears in a book from 1681 that dates the confraternity's founding in 1586 in the monastery of San Francisco.[7] In 1681, the members decided they needed to separate the "confraternities of Spanish, Indians, and mulatos," thus ratifying a long-standing unofficial racial division. At this stage, the division of the confraternity into two *gremios* (or, corporate groups) was made explicit. Instead of sharing an altar, the Spanish began to worship Our Lady of the Rosary at the altar that

> is in the main chapel of this church on the right side next
> to the priest's seats, and designated for the guild of mulatos,
> mestizos and Indians is the altar of Our Lady of the Rosary
> that is in the body of the church immediately to the right
> of the main chapel.[8]

If, prior to 1681, the entire confraternity worshiped the rosary at one altar, the division between the two branches of the confraternity stressed different positions in the church depending on racial labels. The Spaniards had a superior position in the main chapel, which made sense to them since they probably funded its construction. As the confraternity became more prominent and wealthy, Spanish members wanted to impose a more elite membership, even though, or perhaps because, non-Spanish members were active and numerous.

Throughout the seventeenth and eighteenth centuries the Spanish Confraternity of the Rosary grew in wealth but declined in numbers. The members of the elite confraternity had separated themselves from their lower-status members, but their financial domination did not lead to obvious spiritual or social dominance. They functioned more as a behind-the-scenes investment partnership than as a public and social brotherhood. The wealthy Spanish confraternity owned extensive urban properties and rural haciendas, making money from rent and agricultural production. Only a few members managed these investments, more like a modern board of directors than a festive religious brotherhood. Their large income paid for expenses in the Franciscan church, including more than a thousand pounds of wax per year for candles.

The development and history of the mulato Confraternity of the Rosary took a distinct path from its elite Spanish counterpart. The mulato confraternity members were descended from urban and rural slaves and tried various schemes to make money when they faced financial difficulties. They owned a few low-rent properties and tried to make a modest income by selling cheese produced on a farm outside the city. It was up to ambitious men like Diego Durán to generate income and gain status for the confraternity, helping it survive into the independence period.

A 1633 constitution established the long tradition of the mulato Confraternity of the Rosary.[9] In this document, confraternity members presented their version of their history. The 1633 officials, including Bartolomé Pérez and Juan Biafara, whose name indicates African birth, stated that the confraternity was founded fifty years before. The 1633 officials were labeled morenos, mulatos, and mestizos, and these early leaders claimed inspiration from the rosary confraternity in Mexico City. At this time, the confraternity had no rents, and depended entirely on alms, with the bishop's consent. The constitution suggested that new members give some donation to support the confraternity, whatever they could manage. The masses paid for by the mulato confraternity were much less impressive than those of their Spanish counterpart. The constitution said that the confraternity had to give the Franciscan convent one peso a week for a Sunday Mass, and twenty pesos for the celebrations on each of the Virgin's four feast days. The confraternity also celebrated the fiesta of the rosary and promised a Mass for every dead confraternity brother, with mandatory attendance by members, guaranteeing members a sense of security because they could count on their confraternity brothers to pray for their release from purgatory. There was also a weekly confraternity procession that reinforced their solidarity as devotees of the rosary.

As did many other confraternities in the diocese of Michoacán, the Confraternity of the Rosary was not ashamed to emphasize its poverty and humility in an attempt to appeal to the bishop's pity and to gain his consent for alms gathering outside the city of Valladolid. For example, in 1664 and 1667, its members petitioned the bishop for permission, detailing various aspects and causes of their poverty: no rents; inability to pay expenses; no inventory; a lack of alms. In a 1679 petition they went even further:

> This confraternity always has been sustained by alms begged
> for outside this jurisdiction with the license of the bishops
> and the most illustrious council, because within the city and
> the jurisdiction they cannot collect sufficient alms for the
> ornaments and wax of the most holy Virgin nor for her masses
> nor anniversaries said for the souls of the *poor slaves our fathers*
> and for the succor of the sick that we attend to and for the
> wax at the funerals of the poor that we attend punctually and
> devotedly. [Emphasis added.][10]

This petition not only presented their piety, charitable activities, and poverty, but also sought pity from the bishop for the souls of their "poor slave fathers," although free mulatos, blacks, and mestizos, along with a few slaves, were actually the words used to describe the early leaders of the confraternity. Although charitable concerns drew in the bishop's interest, an emphasis on humble slaves reminded him of the connection between low social status and piety, granting their founders a Christlike humility. Even in this time of Baroque ritual ostentation, the poor and humble had symbolic importance as part of both the social and spiritual hierarchy. By contrast, in this petition, members emphasized the fact that their *fathers*, not themselves, were slaves.

Diego Durán was the most effective and ambitious leader of the
mulato confraternity. A master architect known for his contributions to
the repair of Valladolid's aqueduct and work on the cathedral, his leadership, skill at a trade—in this case an elevated one—and connections with
the Hispanic world helped him achieve a level of renown rare for a mulato
in the colonial era. Although he was always called a mulato, the Durán
family heritage was Indian and African—the African side from Pénjamo,
a small town in the modern state of Guanajuato where Diego Durán's
paternal ancestors probably worked as agricultural slaves. Late in the
1600s, Durán's maternal great-grandparents moved into Valladolid. The
grandfather Lucas and an uncle, Juan, were both reputable architects,
called "oficiales de arquitectura" or "oficiales de alarife [building]." Both
Lucas Durán and Diego Durán were credited with being the leading
architects of the Valladolid cathedral, working from 1704 to around 1744.
Diego Durán also worked on the hospital of San Juan de Dios and other
buildings in and around the city.[11]

Diego's mother María Nicolasa Durán, described as an *india*, married
his father, a free mulato from Pénjamo, in 1717. When Diego was born in
1721, his parents were both called free mulatos. This kind of racial label-
ing was fluid at the time and depended often on the whim of the government or ecclesiastical official who was describing the person during their
encounter with colonial bureaucracy. Durán inherited the race label of
mulato and took the name of his mother and his reputable maternal
grandfather, gaining his inheritance and status through his maternal relatives. Diego was lucky to know several generations of his mother's family and to have their support for his success.

Durán's personal life also shows his success and prosperity. Three times
a widower, he married in 1742, 1749, 1764, and 1765. His first two wives
were labeled mulatas, the third Spanish, and the fourth mestiza. Durán's
first three wives succumbed to the dangers of childbirth, which threatened
all eighteenth-century women. After the death of his third wife, Durán was
left with only one daughter. With his fourth wife, Durán had six living children. Only this fourth wife brought him a significant dowry, consisting of
three large urban houses.[12] Because women frequently died in childbirth, it
was common for affluent men of African descent (and perhaps most other
men in New Spain) to marry several times. Durán's longevity and wealth
made him desirable many times over as a husband. His determination to
remarry shows his desire to pass on his wealth to offspring, just as he

benefited from the trade knowledge of his ancestors. The continuation of his legacy may have been an important factor motivating Durán, who had nine children, with six survivors, with his last wife, who survived him.

Durán effectively moved up the social ladder of New Spain both through ambitious work and his connections with the Catholic Church in the form of the Confraternity of the Rosary. Durán became a wealthy man, especially for a mulato, and later in life lived in a house worth more than four thousand pesos, a castle compared to the small house worth only sixty pesos that Juan Roque donated to the Zape confraternity in the 1600s. His connections, established throughout his long lifetime and gained through his skilled profession and urban property ownership, were complex. Durán appears regularly in property transactions and loans after the mid-eighteenth century, especially in the 1770s, when he worked most avidly to increase the status of the confraternity.

His contact with the confraternity leadership began in 1743, when his uncle Juan Durán served as a *diputado* (deputy) in the confraternity. Durán did not hold office until 1746 at the age of twenty-five. He worked his way up from deputy to financial officer, to the highest office of mayordomo in 1750. Several men served with Durán, forming a powerful clique, including Tomás Huerta, another builder, Onofre Martínez, Sebastián Cortés, and Nicolás Rangel. These men, all skilled craftsmen like Durán, shared important family connections: for example, Martínez was a witness at Durán's third and fourth marriages.[13] As mayordomo, Durán immediately tripled the income of the confraternity, bringing it close to one thousand pesos annually, instituting more ambitious property development (including purchasing and renovating) and alms-collecting projects. Durán not only accepted Catholicism but also actively promoted it through confraternity expansion, benefiting himself, his fellow confraternity brothers, and the Confraternity of the Rosary itself. Similar to Juan Roque, Durán seemed eager to become an active participant in the material and spiritual Catholic world. But both Durán and his confraternity shared a nagging mulato label that would not disappear: until after the end of the colonial era, it was labeled "de los mulatos." Durán's own life showed the success possible for a mulato in eighteenth-century Valladolid, but he was never addressed as don or even señor, testifying to the limits of his rise.

People of African descent were able to improve their lives in eighteenth-century Valladolid, and the corporate religion of the confraternity was one of the primary vectors of this communal identity and improvements. Yet these improvements were fragile, and those who had this racial designation faced discrete limits in their social and professional ascent. For example, no person known to be of African descent was ever addressed as "don" in Valladolid, although they tried to work around this limitation in their public reputation. The use of the title don implied good lineage and was used in addressing prominent Spaniards and Indian noblemen, but very rarely even the most wealthy and distinguished Afro-Mexicans. Nevertheless, a pattern existed in Valladolid in the eighteenth century of calling prominent mestizos and mulatos by the title *maestro*. This title, meaning "master," was a concession to their personal dignity, which they achieved through the route of skills in workmanship, not through great wealth or lineage. Most of the confraternity leaders could claim this title, and it was used constantly in reference to Durán and other leaders. Whether these titles were official and connected to a guild or were simply used to show respect is unknown, but a trip to Mexico City would have been necessary to pass an examination to become a master architect, and there is little evidence for the existence of strong guilds in Valladolid. The title maestro was emphasized in the context of confraternity business to enhance the brothers' respectability, in hopes that this honor would continue into other spheres of society and compensate for the impossibility of access to don status. The concern over titles and their repetition reveals that these men wanted to generate some kind of deference and had internalized the Spanish obsession with titles.

Durán's ambitious plans came to light soon after he took power over the confraternity. In 1753, he attempted to move the altar of the confraternity to a better location in the Franciscan church.[14] Since 1681, the mulato confraternity had been relegated to a small "extremely uncomfortable" area on the side of the church. Durán and other confraternity leaders hoped the Franciscans would allow them to expand their altar and bury members in a new chapel. Durán claimed expansion and a more lavish chapel would lead to greater veneration of their image of the Virgin. Because the area in which Durán wanted to expand was a chapel that already sheltered the permanent illumination of the Holy Sacrament, Durán suggested that the confraternity assume this cost—a cost that he estimated at fifty pesos annually, another *cargo* (responsibility) which would bring glory to the confraternity by demonstrating communal faith and honor of the greatest symbol of Catholic belief. The Franciscan provincial approved the moving of confraternity's chapel, but he scoffed at the suggestion that they could pay for the oil for the lamp, noting that this serious undertaking could not be given to a confraternity that did not have access to secure principal worth more than one thousand pesos. The friar observed that the mulato confraternity was taking in more and more alms but that its future was uncertain. Nevertheless, Durán continued with his plan and produced evidence that his confraternity did in fact own several properties. This presumption irritated the friar, who decided that the altar should not be moved because it would disrupt graves. Durán had, however, already started the building and complained that he now had to pay three hundred pesos of his own money for the work. Ultimately, Durán achieved his goals, including the new chapel and payment for the illumination of the Host.

Durán's other reforms included a 1754 idea that the confraternity, with the participation of two friars, should have a monthly illuminated procession around the convent, reciting the rosary. Thus, Durán's ambitious plans emphasized the mulato confraternity's connection to the Franciscan order, their community spirit, their desire to lavishly honor the Eucharist, have burials in an enviable position near a sacred area of the church, and elevate the confraternity's status in the town. These changes benefited Durán's personal reputation but also revealed him to be an enthusiastic, devout participant in the Catholic religion and local Spanish society.

Although the material splendor of baroque Catholicism was theoretically less popular by the late 1700s, the Confraternity of the Rosary continued increasing its physical displays of religious devotion in an effort to attain a more elevated position in Valladolid confraternal life. Claiming, as most confraternity petitions did, that the suggested changes would lead to "greater decency, worship, and adornment" of the Virgin, confraternity members requested permission to fashion a new crown for their image and to buy a new banner for the confraternity.[15] The confraternity brothers told the bishop that their saint had many jewels, clothing, and ornaments, but her crown was of an unsuitable, cheap material. They wanted a new crown of gold and silver, inlaid with several jewels already in their possession, including three hundred eighty pesos worth of gold, emeralds, pearls, and rubies, a decent amount for a confraternity of mulatos. The bishop approved of this desire to increase the displayed wealth of the image of rosary through the purchase of a crown worth around fifty-eight pesos. These new accoutrements openly represented the wealth and success of the eighteenth-century rosary and its morally righteous and socially acceptable devotion to the Virgin Mary.

Diego Durán was an ambitious man who made enemies in life, but he defended his own integrity to the end, demonstrating a special vehemence when his role as a confraternity patron was challenged. As an old man, Durán may have feared his own mortality and valued his record of the religious commitment he had shown in life as a powerful tool in achieving his personal salvation. Just prior to his death in 1795, officials of the confraternity rebelled against his power, challenging some of his accounting practices and claiming Durán owed money to the confraternity. Although these officials were careful to begin the petition to the bishop with respectful words for Durán, mentioning his integrity and long-term concern for confraternity interests, they claimed Durán owed 150 pesos in rents and fees to the confraternity. The aged Durán responded to these accusations, blaming the loss of the confraternity's income and goods on another confraternity brother. At the end of his life, one can discern Durán's voice in this petition:

> The facility with which the [leader of the petition]
> and his accomplices throw suspicion on my conduct is
> reprehensible and inexcusable. It is well known in this
> city that for more than twenty-five years, since 1776,
> I have led this confraternity as majordomo, taking care
> of all expenses from the past and present. After so many
> years, I left my successor one thousand pesos, incontestable
> proof of my great care and the pains I took in conserving
> this confraternity and adding to its alms and rents.[16]

The result of the case was a review of the confraternity's accounts, but Durán died a few months later without producing them.

After Durán's death the case over the accounts continued and became more vituperative.[17] The petitioners seemed to blame all their problems on Durán when he could no longer protest or protect his reputation. Factions clearly formed around the members for and against the Durán family, led by Diego's fourth, surviving wife and their daughter, who were his main heirs. One of the first complaints made was that Durán ordered the confraternity to pay thirteen pesos for the funeral of his adopted daughter who had never paid confraternity dues. Confusion and conflict mounted because Durán owed the confraternity money, and it was said that the "adopted" daughter was actually an illegitimate child. Although the shaky hand of his final accounts shows Durán did some confraternity work during his final illness, his heirs said this was done conscientiously, and they claimed to owe the Confraternity of the Rosary only eighty pesos of the one hundred fifty originally demanded.

Without Durán's strong leadership, the confraternity broke down quickly into factions that threatened to tear apart all the organization had achieved in the eighteenth century. However, Durán helped make the confraternity strong enough to last the eighteenth and early nineteenth centuries at a time when many other confraternities were falling apart. He achieved this although he never received unqualified recognition or status in society.

The poor but popular mulato Confraternity of the Rosary survived the first half of the nineteenth century, while the powerful and rich Spanish Confraternity of the Rosary faded away. Membership in the Spanish confraternity was so exclusive that even most people of Spanish descent in Valladolid did not belong. By contrast, the mulato group always had a wider membership, and the family connections that maintained it through other difficult periods continued to exist after Mexican independence from Spain.[18] Members and leaders of the mulato confraternity may have had a greater interest in confraternities after independence, because of their dependence on charitable burials and the promise of social stability offered by confraternity membership. Government financial policies in the final years of the colonial era, which required confraternities to call in outstanding loans, may have threatened the wealth of the Spanish confraternity, and it may have also lost properties when haciendas were sacked in the war for independence from Spain. After the 1820s, race labels of the colonial period were abolished. Officially, if not practically, the overt racial barriers to prominence for this and other colonial Afro-Mexican confraternities were also abolished. Confraternity of the Rosary, previously called *de mulatos*, flourished until the mid-1800s and even reemerged at the end of the nineteenth century.

Although the Confraternity of the Rosary and its members could never completely shed the burdens of the colonial racial hierarchy, the confraternity's leaders worked toward giving their confraternity a higher profile in Valladolid. With the official end of racial hierarchies, people who had previously been officially labeled mulato were now ready to take up positions of leadership that had been impossible for them to hold in the colonial period. The centuries-long process of Hispanization of African slaves had reached its final stage in Valladolid. Mexico's early years as a nation may have offered new opportunities for confraternity leaders who had long ago chosen to embrace the values of Hispanic society.

In both Mexico City and Valladolid, Africans and mulatos succeeded in forming groups designated for their own interests. Mexico City residents of all social groups experienced a more intense atmosphere of public, confraternal life, which declined rapidly during the eighteenth century. Reports in the capital from the end of the colonial period testify that confraternities led by Africans and their descendants had deteriorated long before. By contrast, in Valladolid, mulatos could financially support and organize their confraternities into the mid-nineteenth century. An individual's confraternal experience in New Spain was influenced by race. The term *mulato*, suggesting a Spanish-speaker of mixed descent, implies integration into colonial society. This label was much more common in the eighteenth century than "black" or slave. Confraternities did not maintain the label "black" or references to African cultures such as Zape into the eighteenth century. In fact, confraternities led by Spaniards associated with regions in Spain and certain advocations of the Virgin were more concerned about holding onto a connection between the Old and New Worlds than Afro-Mexican confraternities. Afro-Mexican confraternities also lacked ties to a specific locale, characteristic of Indian rural confraternities. Accordingly, a confraternity referred to as de los mulatos, in contrast to Spanish confraternities that emphasized ties to Spain, or Indian confraternities that may have helped maintain social connections based on geographic location, more closely approximates an institution formed entirely out of a New World identity and the colonial experience.

NOTES

1. Juan Roque's last will and testament is preserved in the Archivo General de la Nación, Mexico City (hereafter, AGN), Bienes Nacionales, vol. 1175, exp. 11. Thanks to my colleagues at Oregon State University, Paul Kopperman, Maureen Healy, and Ron Doel, for their excellent suggestions on this work.

2. See the previous chapter by Brian Larkin for more information on confraternities.

3. AGN, Bienes Nacionales, vol. 1175, exp. 11.

4. AGN, Bienes Nacionales, vol. 78, exp. 81.

5. This entire section taken from a long case in AGN, Bienes Nacionales, vol. 1175, exp. 11.

6. At this time the renters of the houses included a widow, a mulata, and five female slaves.

7. Casa de Morelos, Cofradías, Siglo XVII, Parroquial Disciplinar Cofradías Asientos, caja 1, exp. 1, Libro de Cofradía de Nuestra Señora de Rosario.

8. Casa de Morelos, Cofradías, Siglo XVII, Parroquial Disciplinar Cofradías Asientos, caja 1, exp. 1, Libro de Cofradía de Nuestra Señora de Rosario.

9. Casa de Morelos, Parroquial, Disciplinar, Cofradías Asientos, caja 1246, leg. 9.

10. Casa de Morelos, Parroquial, Disciplinar, Cofradías Licencias y Solicitudes, caja 7.

11. Moisés Guzmán Pérez, "El Maestro Diego Durán y la arquitectura scolonial en Valladolid de Michoacán, siglo XVIII," in *Arquitectura, comercia, ilustración y poder en Valladolid de Michoacán* (Mexico: INAH, 1993).

12. Ibid., 29.

13. Latter Day Saints Microfilm Collection, Roll #644854.

14. Casa de Morelos, Diocesano, Justicia, Procesos Contenciosos, Cofradías, caja 582.

15. Casa de Morelos, Parroquial, Disciplinar, Cofradías Solicitudes, caja 1267, leg. 16.

16. Casa de Morelos, Diocesano, Justicia, Procesos Contenciosos, Cofradías, caja 596.

17. Casa de Morelos, Diocesano, Justicia, Procesos Legales, caja 925.

18. Casa de Morelos, Parroquial, Disciplinar, Cofradías Asientos, caja 1248.

S. JUAN NEPOMUCENO.
Abogado de la Honra, y Fama.

Nava Sc.

año. 1767

FIGURE 21. Juan de Nepomuceno

Taken from Devocionario mexicano. Pequeños grabado novohispanos, *introducción de Alicia Gojman (Mexico: Backal Editores, 1998). Courtesy of Backal Editores.*

CHAPTER NINE

Voices from a Living Hell

Slavery, Death, and Salvation in a Mexican Obraje

JAVIER VILLA-FLORES

In 1659, Francisco Sangley, a slave from the Philippines, was stripped naked and held down by four men in the *obraje* (textile workshop) of Melchor Díaz de Posadas in Coyoacán, southwest of Mexico City, while Fernando Díaz, Melchor's son, whipped him. Francisco begged his tormentors to end the beating for the sake of the Virgin Mary and all the saints, but since they had no intention to set him free, the slave renounced the Holy Trinity to force them to stop.[1] Infuriated by these words, Fernando Díaz de Posadas put a stick in Francisco's mouth and roared in anger: "Do you think that because you renounce God we will denounce you to the Holy Office? I have permission of the Holy Office to punish you!" This was of course a lie, but many other slaves of this obraje also experienced in their own flesh the brutal consequences of resorting to the Christian pantheon to be freed from their master's son's whip. Around February 1660, Fernando Díaz and his overseers whipped the mulato Ramón González in the *tapuchinga* (spinning room) because he did not finish his wool assignment. Having unsuccessfully begged to be spared for the sake of God, Holy Mary, and all the saints, González raised his eyes to a crucifix hanging on one of the walls and implored: "Oh Christ crucified, will you not come down [from] the cross to favor me?" Fernando Díaz kicked him in the mouth and retorted in anger, "Dog! Nobody can stop the beating but me! [Those] saints are worth nothing here! It is the *tequio* [the daily load assigned] that is important!" The whipping continued for more than one hour.[2]

What prompted Fernando Díaz to react with such anger to his slaves' pleadings to stop "for the sake of God" and to claim he had proper jurisdiction to punish his slaves when they blasphemed? Why did Francisco believe he could force his master to drop the whip by renouncing the Holy Trinity? The actions of both masters and slaves in this case were part of a common pattern in sixteenth- and seventeenth-century New Spain. As victims of cruelty and mistreatment, black slaves renounced God and His saints while being beaten to provoke the intervention of the Inquisition as a way to be freed, at least momentarily, from the harsh working conditions they endured. The slaves' chances to be brought before the Inquisition were highly improved, of course, if beyond appealing to the master's Christian conscience, they drew the attention of a wider audience composed of neighbors, bystanders, and witnesses of various kinds, who often expressed concern over the dangers awaiting the Christian community if blasphemers were not punished. For slaveholders, taking their slaves to the Inquisition to be tried for blasphemy had important disadvantages. These included paying for the stay of their slaves in prison—which could represent a hefty sum in a lengthy trial—and losing their labor power during the slaves' time in jail. If it were so ordered by the Inquisition, a slaveholder had to sell a slave; since an unruly slave could decrease in market value, the slaveholder would experience an economic loss in selling a bondsman that had been tried by the Holy Office.

For their part, slaves found such relief from a masters' hand to the extent that they could place the responsibility for the crime committed on their masters and establish their own good faith. Facing the Holy Tribunal, black slaves tried to place responsibility for blasphemies proffered on their owners by stating that they had been "forced" to blaspheme and "lose their soul" on account of their masters' brutal chastisement. To the slaveholders' dismay, black slaves sometimes succeeded in obtaining from the Inquisition an order to transfer them to another location and a new master because their salvation was endangered by continuous physical abuse. In this way, claiming a Christian identity allowed bondsmen to resist their masters by drawing the attention of the Holy Office and thus obtaining the protection that judicial courts rarely granted. Moreover, inquisitional judges and theologians often concluded that slaves who renounced God or the saints because of whipping could not be held responsible for blasphemy or apostasy. This derived from the idea of some jurists that blasphemy that did not reflect one's true belief but was the result of torture or pain did not merit punishment.[3]

In claiming to lose their souls at the hands of the owners of their bodies, black slaves made political use of the Christian doctrine of salvation that was tantamount to a reversal of the colonial discourse that justified slavery in general. Indeed, from the very beginning of the Atlantic slave traffic, spreading Christian faith among heathen Africans constituted the main argument advanced by emerging European powers to justify the initial enslavement of Africans and the continuous enslavement of those already converted. Since church doctrine deemed Africans' bodies to be mere containers of their precious souls, theologians and jurists found defensible the forced migration of slaves to Europe and the Americas in order to set them free from the "bonds of sin." Saint Paul wrote to the Romans, "Now that you have been set free from sin and have become *slaves of God*, the return you get is sanctification and its end, eternal life" (Romans 6:20–22); thus, true freedom only exists in "enslavement" to the Christian God. Admittedly, not all theologians believed that freedom of the soul had to be paid for by servitude of the body, but most agreed with Francisco de Vitoria's famous dictum (1546): "If treated humanely, it would be better for them [the Africans] to be slaves among Christians than free in their own lands [for] . . . it is the greatest fortune to become Christians."[4]

But could slavery be understood as "humane treatment," especially when as an institution it rested on coercion and violence? Early in the colonial period, the Spanish crown fleshed out this notion by legislating in decrees and ordinances that all masters should feed and clothe their slaves adequately and not punish them with cruelty. In cases of extreme abuse slaves could be sold to another master.[5] Significantly, both state and church predicated the notion of "humane treatment" for slaves on the fact that they also "shared" their masters' religion. At the same time, colonial authorities preached submission and obedience for slaves, justifying slavery through Scripture and urging them to serve their masters in good will.[6] Inquisitorial records against slave blasphemers show, however, that contrary to the authorities' expectations, the adoption of a Christian identity by slaves could represent a powerful tool of resistance against their masters' excesses.

Although many of the slaves tried by the Inquisition on blasphemy charges were employed as domestic servants, a significant number of all cases involving Afro-Mexican slaves originated in obrajes in Mexico City, Los Ángeles (Puebla), Coyoacán, and other urban areas.[7] This is hardly surprising, since obrajes enjoyed a well-earned reputation as sordid premises in which "the work was hard, food and living conditions were unsatisfactory, and physical abuse was a commonplace."[8] The nightmarish repute of these textile workshops drew the attention of authorities, and in 1596 King Philip II ordered viceregal inspections of them to curb abuses. This injunction notwithstanding, news of excesses continued to reach both ecclesiastical and religious authorities. Only two years after Philip's decree, in May 1598, the inquisitional commissary Melchior Márquez de Amarilla reported that the continuous mistreatment meted out to the slaves of the obraje owned by Gabriel de Castro in Los Ángeles, Puebla, was a motive of constant scandal in the neighborhood, for God was daily blasphemed because of the cruelty with which they were chastised.[9] That same year, Viceroy Luis de Velasco, *hijo* (literally, "son" or the younger; his father had also been viceroy of New Spain, thus the two are distinguished as father and son) commissioned Vasco López de Vivero to inspect all obrajes in Mexico City and within a ten-league radius. Included in this area was the Cortés family's territory in Toluca, Coyoacán, and Tacubaya, which up to this moment had been exempt from inspections due to its special jurisdictional status as part of the estate of the Marqués del Valle, thus constituting a haven of abusive *obrajeros* (owners or operators of obrajes).[10] Unfortunately, López de Vivero and the obrajeros reached a "friendly agreement," and it was not until the winter of 1660 that the Audiencia finally commissioned a rigorous inspection of six obrajes in Coyoacán to be headed by *oidor* (Audiencia judge) Dr. Andrés Sánchez de Ocampo. Particularly gruesome among them was the labor regime of the obraje of Melchor Díaz de Posada, which Sánchez de Ocampo visited on November 12, 1660.[11]

Based on an analysis of the two-day inspection and several inquisitorial proceedings against some of Díaz's slaves for blasphemy, this essay explores the ambivalences of the politics of salvation in a colonial setting by analyzing the contrasting ways in which masters and slaves understood and made use of Christian dogma to negotiate the harshness of slavery as an institution. As the slaves gambled their bodies and souls before the Holy Office, other tales of corruption, death, and violence in colonial Mexico unfolded.[12]

Life and Death in a Mexican Obraje

Like many other obrajes, the Díaz de Posadas's workshop relied on a heterogeneous work force of coerced and indentured labor. Free workers, mostly Indians, had been attracted to the obraje by means of wage advances, loans, and exploitative contracts that kept them in the textile mill for years.[13] The Díaz de Posadas family also took advantage of the government's policy of putting criminals and vagabonds to work, and their relationship with royal magistrates and local authorities gave them access to a cheap and steady supply of workers. The obraje served as a place of detention instead of the old and insecure public jails of the area.[14] But slaves of African and Philippine origin provided the vast majority of the workshop's labor force, for obrajeros were expected to replace Indian workers with bondsmen following a royal decree issued on this regard in 1602.[15]

Life in an obraje was notoriously violent, cruel, and demeaning. Food was constantly in short supply for the workers: the colonial authorities ordered obrajeros to feed their workers minimal amounts of tortillas and meat, but even those rules were violated frequently. The work itself was physically demanding and mostly carried out in noisome, unventilated rooms known as the *emborrizo* (carding room) and the tapuchinga. Convict workers wore leg irons and punishment for any infraction, such as failing to work quickly enough, elicited fierce beatings.

Brutal as these beatings were, most slaves somehow survived; unfortunately, this was not always the case. For example, in 1658, the year Nicolás Bazán arrived in the workshop, a fourteen-year mulato boy known as Frasquillo was brutally beaten on orders of Fernando Díaz de Posadas (a member of the obraje owner's family) because he did not finish his assigned amount of spun wool. While four men held him down, transforming his body into a human cross, two more hit the young man two hundred times with switches of quince and a whip of leather from the back of his knees up his body. After reviving the unconscious slave with a pitcher of cold water, his torturers resumed the beating. Later, they took Frasquillo to the dormitory where male slaves were locked at the end of day. He was found dead the following day, and his body was secretly buried at night outside the obraje on orders of Fernando Díaz.[16] In these circumstances, only the intervention of a higher authority could make a difference in the lives of the slaves, workers, and prisoners of this infamous mill.

In the fall of 1660, Melchor Díaz de Posadas heard rumors that the Audiencia of Mexico was about to send a magistrate to conduct a detailed inspection of the obrajes of Coyoacán in full defiance of the Marqués del Valle's authority over this jurisdiction. In the few months preceding the *visita* (a judicial investigation), Díaz ordered his overseers to treat his workers well and suspend the usually harsh punishment administered to them. It was not until mid-November, however, that Sánchez de Ocampo was finally commissioned to inspect the six obrajes in Coyoacán. Learning that the visita was to take place on the twelfth, the obrajero released several workers who had been illegally imprisoned and "instructed" them to declare, if interrogated by the oidor, that they had never been coerced to stay in the obraje, threatening them with beatings if they failed to comply.[17]

The oidor Sánchez de Ocampo and his constable Benito Delgado arrived in the morning to start a two-day inspection of the establishment. Appointed by the royal government to observe the working and living conditions of this and other textile mills, Sánchez de Ocampo ordered the main door to be closed from the inside and the key given to Delgado so that no one could leave the establishment before the inspection was completed. Moving from room to room, the inspecting judge questioned the workers and received direct reports and complaints regarding past and present abuses. Indeed, in spite of the obrajero's threats, several workers took the opportunity to complain to the inspector about brutal mistreatment, excessive workload, and lack of food.

The following day, the oidor learned about several cases of illegal imprisonment and decreed the immediate liberation of those held. In the afternoon, a free mulato named Juan Bautista approached don Andrés to let him know about the horrible death of the young slave Loya, also known as Frasquillo. Further testimony was given by the slave Gerónimo de Vergara, who asked for mercy on his knees for, as was clear from the loud threats of his nervous master, he would be harshly punished if he declared what he knew on this matter. The oidor reassured him by stating out loud that neither he nor any of the other slaves interviewed would be punished. The detailed description he now heard about the killing and secret burial of Frasquillo painted an even more dreadful image of the working and living conditions in this obraje. After Vergara concluded his deposition, the oidor ordered Constable Delgado and Captain Diego Martínez de la Carra to transfer him to the obraje of Juan de Olivares because he likely faced reprisal if he remained.[18]

Although Sánchez de Ocampo officially concluded his visita on November 3, he decided to return to the obraje on November 15 to see if there was anything else that could be remedied. He had barely entered the premises when Nicolás Bazán approached him stating that he had things to declare. Since Melchor Díaz was present at the moment, the oidor ordered him to leave, so that Bazán would not feel intimidated by his master. Bazán stated under oath that in a period of less than four months he had been given "more than fourteen thousand lashes" because he had been falsely accused of plotting the murder of one of the mayordomos. Since he also testified about the deaths of slaves Frasquillo and Juana del Buen Suceso, the oidor ordered his transfer to the obraje of Pedro de Sierra. That very day Sánchez de Ocampo prohibited Fernando de Posadas from acting as a mayordomo of the mill.[19] Given the large number of irregularities found by the oidor, the Audiencia of Mexico instructed don Antonio to continue with the inspection of the obraje on December 20. At a time when the price of a male slave ranged between 300 and 500 pesos, Melchor Díaz was ordered to pay 283 pesos toward the salaries and expenses of the inspector and his ministers.[20] Fearing the consequences of a bad report for his still unlicensed mill, Melchor Díaz concentrated his efforts in the following days not only on retrieving his workers who had been transferred or liberated by don Andrés but also on pressuring the two most damaging witnesses, the slaves Gerónimo de Vergara and Nicolás Bazán, into retracting their declarations. This proved to be a most difficult task, and as the obrajero was about to learn, his problems with the colonial authorities were just about to take a complicating turn.

"Turning on" the Inquisitorial Machine

A couple of weeks after the oidor's inspection, on November 29, 1660, the obrajero Juan Gallardo de Céspedes appeared before the inquisitor Bernardo de la Higuera y Amarilla in the Holy Office's headquarters in Mexico City. In his testimony, Gallardo reported that fifteen days before, a young worker of Díaz de Posadas, the free mulato Juanillo, alias "el noble," had been transferred to his obraje on orders of the oidor don Andrés Sánchez de Ocampo. In the afternoon of that same day, Juanillo told Gallardo about the cruelty with which Melchor Díaz and his son Fernando punished the slaves in the obraje. In particular, and this was the reason of Gallardo's presence at the Holy Office, Juanillo not only described to the obrajero the cruel chastisement of the slave Ramón González but also the outburst of Fernando Díaz when González asked

Christ to intervene on his favor: "Nobody can stop the beating but me!" On December 11, Constable Benito Delgado also reported in the Holy Office to have learned about Díaz's blasphemous utterances from Gerónimo de Vergara on the day he took the slave to the obraje of Juan de Olivares under mandate of Sánchez de Ocampo.[21]

Summoned by the inquisitor on December 15, 1660, Gerónimo de Vergara told Bernardo de la Higuera that ten months before, around seven or eight at night, Fernando Díaz de Posadas went to the tapuchinga where people were carding and spinning wool to get a report on the workloads of the slaves. Since he was not satisfied with the production, Díaz de Posadas whipped Vergara and other slaves. "As a dessert," the voracious master ordered four slaves to grab Ramón González by the feet and hands while two more whipped him for more than an hour. Everybody was scandalized to see him punished for such a long time. Even more scandalous, however, was the blasphemous reaction of the ruthless master to González's pleading. But Vergara not only denounced Fernando Díaz de Posadas as a blasphemer; he also told of several occasions in which the slaveholder's violent excesses led his slaves to renounce God, as was the case of Nicolás Bazán, Francisco Sangley, and others who blasphemed in an attempt to stop the beatings.[22]

In denouncing the slaves Nicolás Bazán and Francisco Sangley for blasphemy, Gerónimo de Vergara created momentous consequences not only for Melchor Díaz's son, but also for his family's business, for he would be forced to bring his slaves before the Holy Office. But the inquisitorial machine rarely moved expeditiously, and months elapsed before Melchor Díaz's slaves were brought to the Holy Office to testify about Fernando's blasphemous speech and about their own renunciations of the Christian God. Probably ignoring the inquisitorial inquiries at this point, Melchor Díaz concentrated his energies on convincing his slaves to withdraw their testimony to the obraje inspector.

In the case of Nicolás Bazán, the pressure started while he was still in the textile mill of Pedro de Sierra. Probably urged by Melchor Díaz, the Dominican friar Martín Rueda traveled from his convent at San Jacinto to the Sierra obraje to talk with Bazán in mid-November 1660. Taking him to the storeroom of the obraje, Rueda asked Bazán to take back what he declared against Melchor Díaz and his son in his testimony before Sánchez de Ocampo. The cleric tried to convince Bazán by promising him, on behalf of his master, that he would be transferred wherever he wished. Unmoved by this proposition, Bazán answered that he could not detract his statement to the inspector because everything he had said to the oidor was true and all things done to Christians in the obraje were "great offenses against God Our Lord."

Similarly, a Mercedarian known as fray Felipe, a brother-in-law of Pedro de Sierra and also chaplain at his mill, approached Bazán using a different strategy. Appealing to the Christian ideals of charity and spiritual fraternity, fray Felipe asked Bazán to take back his declaration, for "it is of good slaves to give a hand to their masters when they are under great duress [*caídos y en trabajos*]." The Mercedarian further assured Bazán that he would "deserve a lot from God" if he acted as he was advised. Bazán responded that he could not deny anything, lest he risk damnation. At this moment, the mayordomo of Sierra's mill, Alonso Jiménez, told Bazán again that Melchor Díaz promised not only to transfer him wherever he pleased but also to give him any kind of food he wanted if he acceded to his petition. Knowing that Bazán had manifested no interests in his proposition and was determined not to change his statement, Melchor Díaz sent two reales (*tomines*), bread, and tobacco to Bazán with a free mulato named Andrés Gavilán. Pretending to give Bazán advice on his own, Gavilán told him to declare that he was drunk when he was interviewed by the oidor, or that he had testified falsely because he had been assigned too much work, or even perhaps that Vergara misadvised him. Further increasing the pressure on Bazán, the surgeon of Coyoacán, Joseph Carrillo, visited him in Sierra's mill and asked the slave if he had received the two reales sent by Díaz de Posadas. Upon Bazán's affirmative response, Carrillo told him to feel free to ask for whatever he needed from the shopkeeper of Pedro de Sierra's store in the obraje. Bazán, however, did not ask for anything.[23]

Some time later, Nicolás Bazán asked Pedro de Sierra's mayordomo, Antonio de Ballesteros, to take him to the Holy Office because he had something to declare. The assistant to the obraje, Pedro Hernández, mocked Bazán and attempted to discourage him by saying, "What do you have to say at the Inquisition? You're a slave and you'll die a slave." Alonso Jiménez, another assistant to the obraje, went even further: "Let the fire of Christ be sent to the mulatto that dares to testify against his master! He should be tied to a stick with a target drawn on his heart, so that one could teach oneself to shoot with an harquebus!" Ballesteros also tried to intimidate Bazán by saying that Díaz de Posadas had instructed him to administer Bazán one hundred lashes a day until the slave himself asked to be returned to his master. In spite of their dismissive and threatening attitude toward Bazán, it was clear that the assistants of Pedro de Sierra were concerned about the possible intervention of the Holy Office, for they notified Melchor Díaz immediately about this troubling new development.[24]

On June 17, 1661, after more than seven months of being away, don Andrés Sánchez de Ocampo ordered the corregidor don Julián Poblete de Espinosa to transfer Nicolás Bazán and Gerónimo de Vergara back to the obraje of Díaz de Posadas. Knowing of the possibility of reprisals by their master, the oidor warned Díaz not to beat them or inflict any kind of chastisement on them, lest he lose his workshop.[25] The slaves were transferred two days later, on Sunday, June 19. When Bazán arrived at the obraje late in the afternoon, he was urged by the corregidor, in the presence of the chief constable (*alguacil mayor*), the notary, and some other authorities of Coyoacán, to throw himself at the feet of his master and ask for forgiveness. Bazán responded that he had done nothing that required forgiveness, since he did not testify falsely against Díaz. The corregidor pressed Bazán to ask for pardon and to kiss the hands of his master, the obrajero, presumably as a gesture of submission. Bazán finally kissed the hands of Melchor and his son but refused to ask for forgiveness. One hour later Melchor Díaz summoned him to the storeroom. The obrajero reproached Bazán for giving false testimony to the oidor and defiling his honor and told him that it was clear that the inspector had promised freedom to all those who declared against him.[26] This was of course not true. The obrajeros may not have feared God, but they certainly feared social consequences.

It is unknown if Gerónimo de Vergara, like Nicolás Bazán, received similar threats, promises, or gifts from Melchor Díaz and his friends while at the obraje of Juan de Olivares, though this was likely. It is certain, however, that after his arrival at the obraje, Vergara was also urged to show comparable gestures of submission and ask for forgiveness while throwing himself at the feet of his master. Vergara did so because the lieutenant who took him back to the obraje promised to intercede on his behalf before Díaz de Posadas. Ironically, it was the ruthless master who was begging Vergara by the end of the day. Taking his slave aside after all had gone to sleep, Melchor Díaz pleaded with Vergara to declare to the oidor that everything he had said previously was false, that his memory had failed him at the moment of the inspection, or even perhaps that he had been wrongly advised by others.[27] While Díaz de Posadas desperately pressed his slaves into changing their testimony to the oidor, inquisitors Francisco Estrada and Juan de Mañozca made a decision that would seriously complicate the issue for the obrajero.

On June 20, 1661, having revised the available evidence, the inquisitors resumed their investigation about the blasphemous excesses of Díaz's son by ordering the slave Ramón González brought before the Holy Office. Fearing the worst, Fernando Díaz summoned González to the storeroom before taking him to the Holy Office's headquarters. Upon entering the room, González found Melchor Díaz sitting on a chair and Fernando Díaz standing close to his father. While Fernando asked him not to testify against him, Melchor feigned a more dismissive attitude by telling his slave to go to the Inquisition and say everything he knew about them. The owner claimed he did not care what was said and ordered the slave to take a cloak for the trip. Half an hour later, González was summoned again to the storeroom. "Come here," said Fernando Díaz, "do you remember the night I whipped you? Didn't you ask Christ to descend from the cross to help you? What did I answer to you?" González said he did not remember. Fernando Díaz replied in anger: "Come here, drunk dog! Didn't I tell you that Christ would not come down from the cross to make a miracle for you?" Cautiously, González admitted that it might have happened that way, but he did not remember. "Go with God and say whatever you please," said an impatient Díaz. "What do you think? I don't care what you say." When González was about to depart, however, Fernando Díaz gave him two half reales and promised him his freedom if he watched what he said at the Holy Office.[28]

Moreover, since it was now clear that both Nicolás Bazán and Gerónimo de Vergara would also be summoned to the Holy Office, Melchor Díaz decided to make a preemptive move that same day by writing a letter to the inquisitors. Acting as a good Catholic, Díaz informed the inquisitors that Bazán claimed to have something to declare before the Holy Office, but he questioned both the slave's honesty and his intentions. Díaz stated that both Bazán and Vergara had been sold to him as habitual liars and asserted that they had plotted with his (Díaz's) enemies to testify against him, his son, and his overseers during the recent inspection of his mill by the oidor don Antonio Sánchez. The slaves had testified against him, Díaz explained, because the oidor had promised them their freedom. As a consequence, he had been deprived of the work of Bazán and Vergara for seven months. Bazán in particular had stained his

reputation and caused great scandal among his slaves by summoning up
the demons, pretending to be mad, stabbing his overseers, and stating
great lies such as that Díaz gave him fourteen thousand lashes and had
killed and buried a young slave. Melchor Díaz was particularly concerned
about the effects of this whole affair on his authority among his slaves.
Indeed, ever since they had seen that one of their number had been able
to denounce him falsely without being punished for it, "every slave is now
in need of an overseer." He thus concluded by asking for an exemplary
punishment for Bazán so that God might be served and his family's reputation cleared.[29] That night, the Spanish overseer Francisco Flores took
both the mulato slave Ramón González and the letter to the Holy Office.
On the road, the overseer told González he only had to contradict "these
dogs" (Bazán and Vergara) and instructed him never to declare against his
master. As a reward, he promised González he would not be forced to
work anymore.[30]

It is unknown what went through the mind of Ramón González while
he was being carried to Mexico City, but the promise of freedom probably had an intoxicating effect on the thirty-year-old mulato. Born a slave,
Ramón had spent more than six years in the obraje since his owner, the
widow Ana González de Godoy, deposited him in the mill to earn three
pesos a month for her. During that period, González became one of the
slaves most constantly beaten and abused, his scarred skin being frequently marked by switches and whips and burned with hot sugar. That
night, however, as he entered the Holy Office's jail, González had probably already decided to take his chances by testifying on behalf of Melchor
and Fernando Díaz de Posadas.

Prison Conversations

The following day, on June 21, 1661, Ramón González faced the inquisitor Francisco Estrada y Escobedo. Although he first claimed not to know
why he had been summoned by the Holy Office, González later declared
that he had been beaten the previous year in the Díaz de Posadas obraje
because he had not completed his workload. He remembered asking
Fernando Díaz several times to stop the punishment for the sake of
Christ, His Holy Mother, and some saints, and to have implored while
looking at a crucifix: "Oh my Lord Jesus Christ come down the cross and
help me." Seeing that the chastisement continued, González later asked

Díaz to leave him alone "for the sake of the bones of his [Díaz's] mother." Fernando Díaz allegedly told González that he was a fool in expecting this new plea would make him stop, for he did not end the beating before when he was asked to do it for the sake of Jesus and the Virgin Mary themselves. Díaz thus continued the punishment until he decided to stop "out of his fair grace." Since González's declaration clearly contradicted the statement of Gerónimo de Vergara, the inquisitor urged him to declare the whole truth without fear since nobody would know what he said at the Holy Office. Testimony as a point of law was supposed to be entirely secret and depending on the scrupulousness of the inquisitor, it often was protected.

Having heard the content of the accusations against Fernando Díaz, Ramón González asserted that all the charges were a lie and even identified Gerónimo de Vergara as the author of such false testimony. González intimated that Vergara had something to gain since he had been brought to the Inquisition in a sedan chair six months before, or so González was allegedly told. In contrast, González himself had been repeatedly punished with switches of quince, whips, and hot sugar applied to his skin—a kind of punishment, he assured Estrada, used only on him—and never falsely accused either Fernando Díaz de Posadas or his father. Besides, González further stated, Vergara was a mulato of bad lineage and a liar with a bad tongue and worse habits who was now accusing "a saint" (Fernando Díaz). González also related how Vergara threw himself at the feet of Melchor Díaz asking for his mercy on the day he was brought to the obraje. According to González, the beatific master forgave Vergara for declaring falsely to the oidor and even blessing him.

The inquisitor Estrada continued by asking Ramón González if he had been influenced in any way by Fernando or Melchor Díaz to declare in their favor at the Holy Office. González asserted that Fernando Díaz himself had instructed him simply to tell the truth, "even if it was against him."[31] At the conclusion of the hearing, Estrada made a highly unusual gesture (and an illegal one): the inquisitor took two reales from his pocket and gave them to González, praising him for not declaring against his own master.[32] That night, after returning to his prison, González gave a report of his declarations to the overseer Francisco Flores through the jail's window. Finding his testimony satisfactory, Flores gave González two more reales and instructed him not to inform the inquisitor about the other slaves that had renounced God in the obraje. In the following days,

González received a new shirt, a blanket, a hat, tobacco, and more money as a reward. Even the Augustinian friar Pedro Díaz, the other son of Melchor Díaz de Posadas, came to the window of González's prison to commend the slave and to tell him that Melchor had already released him from servitude on account of his performance before the Holy Office.[33]

For his part, Gerónimo de Vergara stuck firmly to his version of the horrid events. Interrogated by Estrada immediately after Ramón González's hearing on June 21, Vergara assured the inquisitor that he had told the truth six months before and even mentioned other slaves who witnessed the beating of González and the blasphemous exchange with Fernando Díaz. If a different version had reached the Holy Office, he suggested, it probably was because Melchor Díaz instructed the informants to lie. To exemplify Díaz's maneuvering with his slaves, Vergara related how the obrajero had unsuccessfully begged him to retract his declaration to the oidor. Vergara confessed, however, to have asked Melchor Díaz for forgiveness, but it was only because he did not want to be mistreated, not because he lied to the oidor. After the hearing, Estrada ordered Constable Fernando Hurtado to take Vergara to the Holy Office's prison where both he and González were to receive two reales worth of food every day.[34]

In the meantime, pending his imminent call to the Holy Office, Nicolás Bazán was treated to a desperate mixture of promises, threats, and warnings in the obraje. "What do you have to say at the Inquisition?" the overseer Francisco Flores asked Bazán one day in the store room. "Wouldn't it be better if I brought you a confessor so you can unload your conscience instead of exposing yourself to be punished at the Holy Office?" Claiming that the inquisitors knew that slaves always testify falsely against their master, Flores told Bazán that he risked being burned at the Holy Office, or at least a punishment of two hundred lashes. He praised Ramón González as a model of conduct and advised Bazán to ask Melchor Díaz on his knees for forgiveness. The obrajero entered the room at this point in the conversation and hurled in anger: "What is this little Jewish dog thinking? That I haven't told those Lords [the inquisitors] about his rogueries and iniquities? They told me that there would be no men of honor in the Indies had they given credit to the word of such dogs!"[35] Melchor's profound irritation not only stemmed from the obvious fact that his authority over his slaves in the mill could be severely undermined by the Inquisition's willingness to hear their testimony against him and his family. Most significantly, the obrajero saw in this entire affair a threat to the colonial social order in which black slaves should be at the bottom, for they were generally deemed vile and infamous.

Nicolás Bazán was summoned to the Holy Office on July 13, 1661. The next day, the overseers Francisco Flores and Juan de León took him to Mexico City. It was around six in the morning when they arrived to the Inquisition's headquarters. Recognizing Francisco Flores, Ramón González asked him through the prison window why he was there so early. Learning that Bazán had been summoned to the Inquisition, González exclaimed, while looking at Bazán: "These cuckold dogs that come to testify against their master!" Like Melchor's outburst of the previous day, González's sexual epithet was aimed at depicting Bazán as a creature without honor, though this time as an emasculated male. Before leaving, Flores instructed González to stick with his version of the events and promised the slave that he himself would emancipate him. Bazán did not enter the prison until much later, however, for he was taken upstairs to have his first hearing. When Bazán finally returned, González threatened him: "Brother, I will break the bones of he who dares to testify against me." Bazán simply replied that he had come to the Holy Office to ask for justice for himself and his fellow bondsmen (*compañeros*). As expected, this was just the first of many fights over this subject among the slaves. In the tense following days, Bazán would bitterly reproach González for being a false witness and not declaring honestly about Fernando Díaz's excesses.[36]

Between July 14 and September 12, 1661, Nicolás Bazán rendered a spectacular account of the violent regimen of work that reigned in the obraje to the inquisitor Francisco de Estrada. Nicolás Bazán declared that Fernando Díaz committed many excesses against the slaves that included administering between ten and twelve thousand lashes a day, burning them with hot sugar, and placing sticks in their mouths as gags. He described in detail the brutal beating of Francisco Sangley and Fernando Díaz's response when Sangley renounced God to stop the punishment he was receiving: "I have permission of the Holy Office to punish you!" Bazán also informed Estrada about the killings of Gerónimo de Vergara's wife and Frasquillo, the beating of Ramón González, and the blasphemous response of Díaz to González's plea to Christ to intervene in his favor. Bazán also declared how he himself had been beaten on orders of Fernando Díaz de Posadas to a point close to death. After he got better, he continued, his workload was increased by 50 percent. In addition, he

was forced to use a *gargantón*—a combination of collar and handcuffs—
that made it very difficult for him to eat. The punishment inflicted by this
instrument was so rigorous, Bazán told the inquisitor, that "any Christian
[would be] in great danger of renouncing God and His just faith"—something he actually did according to other witnesses.

Local authorities knew about the brutality practiced in the obraje,
Bazán informed Estrada. They had decided not to intervene because they
were on excellent terms with Melchor Díaz. Bazán also told Estrada about
the multiple ways in which he had been pressured by friends, relatives,
and workers of Melchor Díaz first to retract his declaration to the oidor,
and then to testify in favor of Fernando Díaz at the Holy Office. In addition, Bazán told the inquisitor that González had been instructed to lie by
the overseer Francisco Flores who frequently came to the prison's window
to talk to González and to bring him clothes, food, and money on behalf
of Melchor Díaz. Fearing the cruel punishment that was awaiting him for
declaring against Díaz, Bazán implored on his knees at one of his hearings
not to be sent to the obraje, lest he be forced to despair and "lose his soul"
(by renouncing God). Finally, on September 12, Bazán concluded his last
session before Estrada by stressing that the torments suffered in
Coyoacán by "Christians redeemed by Christ's blood at the hands of fellow Christians [were so painful] that not even among Turks and Moors a
comparable martyrdom was endured."[37] In spite of the dramatic nature of
Bazán's appeal to the inquisitor to save his soul and spare his body as a fellow Christian, it was unlikely that Francisco de Estrada would feel moved
to intervene in his favor given the way Estrada rewarded Ramón's false
testimony. But if the presence of don Andrés Sánchez de Ocampo had
been needed to correct the excesses allowed by the local authorities of
Coyoacán, the intervention of a new protagonist in the Holy Office would
now be necessary to cut through the thick cobweb of corruption that
ranged from the inquisitor himself to the slave González and thus make
a way out for Vergara and Bazán.

The Inquisitor on Trial: Enter Pedro Medina Rico

On November 10, 1661, don Pedro Medina Rico, *visitador* (a royally
appointed judge-investigator with broad authority to impose law and seek
indictments of those who had failed to apply the law in the colonies) to the
Mexican Holy Office, took charge of the process. An illustrious attorney

and university professor in Córdoba and Seville, in Spain, Medina Rico had served the Spanish crown in various capacities such as visitador general of the Archdiocese of Seville, inquisitor of Seville, and visitador to the Inquisition in Cartagena de Indias (Colombia). Instructed to conduct a detailed inspection of the Mexican Inquisition in 1651, Medina Rico arrived in Mexico in 1654 to investigate multiple irregularities that included peculation, violation of rights of defendants, illegal confiscation of property, and general disregard of prescribed inquisitorial procedures. Before pressing charges against this institution, Medina Rico and his administrative deputy Marcos Alonso de Huydobro analyzed all Inquisition records from 1640 and 1657. They sent a list of charges to Madrid in 1658 and waited four years for a decision from the Supreme Council of the Inquisition. Interestingly, out of 175 indictments made by Medina, 111 corresponded to the inquisitor Francisco Estrada y Escobedo who was charged with peculation, among other things. While the visitador waited for the sentence from Madrid, he continued revising the hundreds of inquisitorial records until his return to Spain in 1669. In reviewing the inquisitorial proceedings involving Nicolás Bazán, Gerónimo de Vergara, and Ramón González, Medina Rico learned about the excesses practiced in the Díaz's obraje, the bribery of González, and the highly irregular communications between the prisoners and various messengers of Melchor Díaz. After inspecting the prison of the Holy Office and gathering additional evidence of such conversations from other inmates and from Bazán himself, Medina Rico ordered the transferal of Bazán, González, and Vergara to the more secluded *cárceles secretas* (secret prisons) to guarantee that the slaves could not be prevented from telling the truth.[38]

On January 25, 1662, Nicolás Bazán informed the visitador about the exchange of money between the inquisitor Francisco de Estrada and Ramón González. Medina Rico decided to interrogate the prison's constable (*secretario del secreto*), Captain Martín Ibáñez de Guadiana, on February 1, 1662, in this respect, but the officer asserted that he had not witnessed such a thing. One month later, on March 16, 1662, in the company of inquisitors Bernardo de la Higuera and Juan de Mañozca, the visitador decreed the immediate release of Bazán. Since returning Bazán to his master could clearly endanger his life, Medina Rico ordered that the slave be sold to a different master of good condition and completely unrelated to Melchor Díaz. In addition, his new master could not employ him in the countryside or in a textile or sugar mill (*ingenio*), or any other place of hard work. Pending Bazán's sale, the slave was to be kept in the prison of the Holy Office at Melchor Díaz's expense, who was also expected to pay an unspecified amount toward the costs of Bazán's whole stay in jail. On May 17, 1662, Estrada himself was condemned by the Supreme Council in Madrid to return thirty-six hundred pesos to the Holy Treasury for money, jewels he had purloined, and three hundred pesos in fines. The records do not indicate what became of Gerónimo de Vergara, but it is likely that the visitador also released him without charges. For his part, Ramón González had to wait two more years in a cell for his case to be concluded. Since he persisted in denying the evidence accumulated against him, the inquisitors decided to torture him *in caput alienum*, that is, to force him to denounce his accomplices. When they were conducting him to the chamber of torture González finally broke and gave a full confession on May 20, 1664. He was sentenced on October 23, 1664, to appear naked to the waist, with a rope and a gag, and a hat (*coroza*) with the inscription "false witness" at the Auto de Fe of that year. In addition, he was to receive two hundred lashes and be sold to another master in an obraje or ingenio, where he was expected to serve "in perpetuity." González implored for a diminution of the penalty, but this only increased his sentence another two hundred lashes.[39] This was indeed a sad ending for a slave considered by his fellow bondsmen as the most consistently brutalized by Fernando Díaz.

The Inquisition apparently never tried Fernando Díaz de Posadas (probably because the charges for blasphemy had been lodged by his own slaves, whose word was not deemed as valuable as that of a free man). His father finally received a license to operate his obraje on May 5, 1662, upon the payment of 250 pesos, which covered half of its cost, and the promise of paying the rest within six months.[40] The family apparently remained in business for a long time. Upon Melchor Díaz de Posadas's death on October 18, 1682, his widow Juana de Agurto and his sons took charge of the obraje.[41] More than twenty years later, in 1706, some Indian workers charged a Juan de Posadas of abusing them in Coyoacán. By that time, however, the visitas had been transformed into "perfunctory legal rituals," for inspectors often held simultaneous appointments as magistrates of the Audiencia of Mexico and judges of criminal and civil matters within the estate of the Marqués del Valle.[42]

By the end of the seventeenth century slaves found it increasingly difficult to draw the attention of the Holy Office to their miserable condition by blaspheming while being punished by their masters. Christian slaveholding societies varied considerably regarding the existence of legal constraints on the masters and the overall treatment of slaves, but the bondsmen's liability to physical punishment was commonly held as a crucial element of slavery as a condition. Like all colonial authorities, the Holy Office utilized Christianity as a means to exact conformity and submission from bondsmen under the promise of future redemption. However, Afro-Mexicans were often able to resist their masters by declaring to share their masters' faith before the Mexican Inquisition. Claiming to possess a Christian identity, slaves held their masters responsible for provoking their blasphemies and putting at risk the salvation of their souls. In this sense, slaves used their "integration" into the Christian community to fight the abuses deriving from their marginality in the slaveholders' society. As time went on, the Inquisition grew weary of this strategy of mitigating the harshness of slavery as an institution. Knowing that their interventions undermined the masters' authority, undoubtedly a crucial issue in a slave society, the inquisitors increasingly refused to intervene on behalf of the slaves. Equally important in this respect was the Holy Office's growing resistance to commit its time and resources in these often lengthy and burdensome trials.[43] The combination of these two institutional changes deprived the slaves of two important avenues to escape, if only temporarily, the living hell of the obrajes.

NOTES

1. Many thanks to Paul Vanderwood, Andrew Fisher, Bruce Tyler, María De La Torre, and Martin Nesvig for comments and suggestions on previous drafts. Research for this chapter was made possible by the generous support of the Huntington Library through a Mrs. Francis J. Weber Research Fellowship in Roman Catholic History, and UCMexus research grant.

2. Huntington Library, HM 35131, vol. 37, part I, fs. 17, 19v.

3. Solange Alberro, "Negros y mulatos en los documentos inquisitoriales: Rechazo e integración," in *El trabajo y los trabajadores en la historia de México*, ed. Elsa C. Frost et al. (Mexico: El Colegio de México; University of Arizona Press, 1979), 158–60. A notable example of this jurisprudential view is found in the commentaries of Francisco Peña on the *Directorium Inquisitorum* of Nicolai Eymeric (Venice: apud Marcum Antonium Zalterium, 1595), the medieval inquisitional manual.

4. Francisco de Vitoria, *Political Writings*, ed. Anthony Pagden and Jeremy Lawrance (New York: Cambridge University Press, 1991), 335.

5. Colin A. Palmer, *Slaves of the White God: Blacks in Mexico, 1570–1650* (Cambridge, MA: Harvard University Press, 1976), 120–21.

6. On scriptural justification of slavery, see Albert J. Raboteau, *Slave Religion: The "Invisible" Institution" in the Antebellum South* (New York: Oxford University Press, 1993).

7. See Javier Villa-Flores, "To Lose One's Soul: Blasphemy and Slavery in New Spain, 1596–1664," *Hispanic American Hisotrical Review* 82 (2002).

8. Charles Gibson, *The Aztecs Under Spanish Rule: A History of the Indians of the Valley of Mexico, 1519–1810* (Stanford, CA: Stanford University, 1964), 243.

9. Archivo General de la Nación (hereafter AGN), Inquisición, vol. 147, exp. 2.

10. Successful supervision and control by royal inspectors proved difficult to accomplish because of the scattering of the workshops in the territory. Viceroy Gaspar de Zúñiga y Acevedo (Count of Monterrey) attempted to solve the problem of surveillance by ordering the obrajeros to relocate their workshops within the four selected areas of Mexico City, Puebla, Oaxaca, and Valladolid (present-day Morelia). The obraje owners resisted the plan so fiercely, however, that the decree was almost never enforced. Many obrajeros resolved to move to different areas of the Cortés's estate such as Xochimilco, Tacubaya, Cuernavaca, Toluca, and Coyoacán to escape viceregal supervision. See Richard E. Greenleaf, "Viceregal Power and the Obrajes of the Cortés Estate, 1595–1708," *Hispanic American Historical Review* 48 (1968): 368–70.

11. Greenleaf, "Viceregal Power."

12. This paper is based on the 1660 report by don Andrés Sánchez de Ocampo, the Inquisition records involving the slaves Nicolás Bazán, Ramón González, and Gerónimo de Vergara, and the reports of prison conversations included in the trial of Lucas de Araujo and Nicolás Bazán. The report of Andrés Sánchez de Ocampo's visita is included in the documents published by Edmundo O'Gorman under the title "El trabajo industrial en la Nueva España a mediados del siglo XVII: Visita a los obrajes de paños en la jurisdicción de Coyoacán, 1660," *Boletín del Archivo General de la Nación* XI (1940). The information on the slaves was obtained from the following sources: Huntington Library, HM 35131, vol. 37, part I, fs. 1–50v and unfoliated pages of the same document, AGN, Inquisición, vol. 583, exp. 4, fs. 390–519, and AGN, Inquisición, vol. 583, exp. 5, fs. 520–68v.

13. O'Gorman, "El trabajo industrial," 43–73.

14. See O'Gorman, "El trabajo industrial," passim; Samuel Kagan, "Penal Servitude in New Spain: The Colonial Textile Industry" (Ph.D. dissertation, City University of New York, 1977), 121. The fact that this obraje was a closed shop did not mean that its workers were entirely isolated. Indeed, many workers retained contacts with surrounding Nahua communities of Coyoacán and even established sexual unions that contributed to the process of increasing racial miscegenation in New Spain. Indeed, marriages across racial lines became usual. For instance, Benito de la Cruz, a *chino* slave of Melchor Díaz de Posadas, married the Indian Francisca Magdalena. Similarly, Francisco de la Cruz, another chino slave, had been married for ten years to María de la O, a free mulata. Mestizos Juan Antonio and Juan Chico married Indian women from San Agustín and San Jacinto respectively, and the chino Ventura Rodríguez married the Indian Ana María de la Concepción. See O'Gorman, "El trabajo industrial," 44, 52, 60–61, 51.

15. Gonzalo Aguirre Beltrán, "La esclavitud en los obrajes novoespañoles," in *La heterodoxia recuperada. En torno a Angel Palerm*, ed. Susana Glantz (Mexico: Fondo de Cultura Económica, 1987), 256 n. 10.

16. Huntington Library, HM 35131, vol. 37, part I, fs. 16v, 21, 23. This was not, however, the first time that a slave had lost his life in an obraje. Only a few months later, Juana del Buen Suceso, the wife of slave Gerónimo de Vergara, bled to death as a result of a fierce beating she received from the overseers

17. O'Gorman, "El trabajo industrial," 49, 70–72.

18. Ibid., 51, 54–55.

19. Ibid., 61–64.

20. Ibid., 92–93.

21. Huntington Library, HM 35131, vol. 37, part I, fs. 3–4v.

22. Huntington Library, HM 35131, vol. 37, part I, fs. 7–7v.

23. Huntington Library, HM 35131, vol. 37, part I, fs. 21–22, 47.

24. Huntington Library, HM 35131, vol. 37, part I, fs. 16–16v, 43v.

25. O'Gorman, "El trabajo industrial," 95.

26. Huntington Library, HM 35131, vol. 37, part I, f. 22v.

27. Huntington Library, HM 35131, vol. 37, part I, f. 14.

28. AGN, Inquisición, vol. 583, exp. 4. fs. 390–519.

29. Huntington Library, HM 35131, vol. 37, part I, fs. 35–36.

30. AGN, Inquisición, vol. 583, exp.4, fs. 390–519.

31. Huntington Library, HM 35131, vol. 37, part I, fs. 10–11v.

32. Huntington Library, HM 35131, vol. 37, part I, fs. 47v–48; AGN, Inquisición, vol. 583, exp. 4, f. 456.

33. Huntington Library, HM 35131, vol. 37, part I, f. 27.

34. Huntington Library, HM 35131, vol. 37, part I, f. 14.

35. Huntington Library, HM 35131, vol. 37, part I, fs. 48–48v.

36. The angry exchange between Nicolás Bazán and Ramón González was witnessed by prison inmates Philippine slave Lucas de Araujo and a man named Cristóbal de la Cruz who shared the same prison cell with the Afro-Mexican slaves. See Huntington Library, HM 35131, vol. 37, part I, fs. 36v, 42. See also AGN, Inquisición, vol. 583, exp. 5, f. 533v.

37. Huntington Library, HM 35131, vol. 37, part I, fs. 16–27.

38. Richard Greenleaf, "The Great Visitas of the Mexican Holy Office 1645–1669," *The Americas* 64 (1988); Huntington Library, HM 35131, vol. 37, part I, f. 37

39. Greenleaf, "Great Visitas," 418. Huntington Library, HM 35095, *Abecedario de Relaxados, reconciliados y penitenciados*, 300v–301; HM 35131 (unfoliated pages); AGN, Inquisición, vol. 583, exp. 4, f. 519.

40. Silvio Zavala and María Castelo, *Fuentes para la historia del trabajo*, 8 vols. (Mexico: Fondo de Cultura Económica, 1945), 8:41.

Araceli Reynoso Medina, "Esclavos y condenados: Trabajo y etnicidad en el obraje de Posadas," in *El rostro colectivo de la nación mexicana*, ed. María Guadalupe Chávez Carvajal (Morelia: Universidad Michoacana de San Nicolás de Hidalgo, 1997).

41. O'Gorman, "El trabajo industrial," 101, 123–24.

42. For a good example of this change of attitude, see the letter written by weary prosecutor Andrés de Cabalca to the Holy Office in 1663 in AGN, Inquisición, exp. 502, f. 385. Huntington Library, HM 35131, vol. 37, part I, fs. 16–27. Greenleaf, "Great Visitas," 418. Huntington Library, HM 35131, vol. 37, part I, f. 37. Huntington Library, HM 35095, *Abecedario de Relaxados, reconciliados y penitenciados*, 300v–301; HM 35131 (unfoliated pages), AGN, Inquisición, vol. 583, exp. 4, f. 519.

FIGURE 22. Santa Gertrudis

Taken from Die XVI novembris. Officium in festo Sanctae
Gertrudis Magnae *(Mexico: Herederos de la Viuda de Francisco
Rodríguez Lupercio, 1721).*

CHAPTER TEN

Catholicisms

WILLIAM CHRISTIAN JR.

Catholicism has become the prime example of catholicism. Because it has a center, a centrally controlled hierarchy, a set of dogmas, and a common ritual core, Catholics and non-Catholics alike tend to think of Catholicism as one thing, so that, at least before Mass was said in the vernacular, you could step out of it in Uganda and into it in Vietnam without missing a beat.[1] The original adjective *catholic*, from the Latin *catholicus*, universal, is a synonym for all-inclusive and far ranging and an antonym for local and particular. A number of Web dictionary definitions make this antilocal connotation explicit: "free from provincial prejudices or attachments." "Catholic" and "catholic" were mutually reinforced in meaning as one of the world's oldest ongoing organizations spread over the planet.

Because of the ideology of unity and centralization, most Catholics would say all Catholicism is the same, but in fact what they think is true Catholicism tends to be their own variety, not someone else's. Because historians or ethnographers of Catholicism as it is practiced tend to study one particular country, they are often unaware of the considerable differences in practices, beliefs, and devotional styles from country to country.

Hence pointing to regional differences and variations, asking just how catholic Catholicism has been, questions a central tenet of the faith.

There were periods in the last two thousand years in which church and secular authorities made concerted efforts to maintain a certain homogeneity of doctrine and practice, expelling individuals and groups to this end. But in fact the process of evangelization has generally allowed for an assimilation of local procedures and an accommodation to local holy places and times. Campaigns to destroy idols and abolish superstitions have tended to run out of steam as other priorities come to the fore, allowing the targeted practices and beliefs to reassert themselves.[2]

Protestantism has generally demanded a complete disengagement from the notion of grace invested in objects, images, or places. This disengagement was one of the fundamental ways that Protestants cut themselves free from their Catholic roots, and Protestant missionaries applied it radically outside of Europe in both Catholic and non-Catholic areas, requiring a kind of new persona from converts, many of whom themselves have been eager to change.[3] In contrast, the use of shrines, images, and relics provided Catholicism with procedures and practices that could mesh with those of preexisting religions, providing an easier and less demanding transition and opening the possibility of hybridization.[4]

Local variation in Catholicism has its place in canon law. As in many other legal systems, including the Roman law operant in much of Europe until the seventeenth century, Roman Catholic canon law leaves ample room for customary practice that accumulates at all levels.[5] Scholars refer to this process of accumulation of varying norms as legal polycentricity, and this concept applies especially well to the layered customs of the Catholic Church, where the "consuetudine" of medieval monasteries—that is, the rules of particular monasteries in addition to the general rules of the order—could run to several volumes and synodal constitutions supplement canon legislation of dioceses.[6]

Custom has legal force at the parish level as well. In the early modern parish record books in the Nansa Valley of Cantabria (and I have no reason to suppose otherwise elsewhere in Spain), parish priests, say every fifty years or so, wrote down the "usos y costumbres" of their particular parish. These texts, in fact customary rules, would have been for the benefit of subsequent priests. Those I read included customs, among others, for masses, death masses, and death offerings, many of which the parish priest had a vested interest in maintaining. Much customary law in Catholicism as a whole similarly refers to practices involving the liturgy, prayer, and the reception of the sacraments.[7] Such rules, binding on inhabitants as household members, applied as well for communal religious vows, which formed part of the town's secular unwritten laws.

Canon lawyers have devoted much attention to the relation of customary law to universal canon law, with special attention to conflicts between the two. Some have gone so far as to say that when new written canon law conflicts with customary practice, the custom takes precedent unless explicitly and specifically abrogated.[8] Canon law has admitted different definitions of how long a custom must be in place to be considered to have force, but the time span most agreed-on is fixed at forty years. Considered in this light, the flexibility of bishops and parish clergy in the application of Conciliar doctrine, whether that of the Council of Trent or the Second Vatican Council, has been grounded in a body of long and respectable doctrine. On the one hand, there is a kind of systemic foot-dragging entropy in Catholicism, which acts as a long-term impediment on central authority and its efforts to standardize and purify the religion of local variation. While common to most systems, it is exacerbated in Catholicism by its multicultural and geographic variety. But in addition there is a kind of intrinsic, historical decentralization, born out of the process of co-optive evangelization that grants custom legal respect.

The place of custom in canon law is congruent with its place in Spanish law. In the *Siete Partidas*, Alfonso X defines usage and custom and specifies their power: custom is usage consecrated over time (he specifies ten to twenty years), reasonable, not contrary to the law of God, not antagonistic to government, not against natural law or the common good, but approved by the lord of the land during that time. It can be used to interpret law, and it can even annul ancient laws made before it.[9] In practice, until the eighteenth century Spain was a patchwork of local microlegal concessions and exceptions, both regionally (kingdoms, *fueros*, *usus terrae* of districts, *señoríos*), and also on a town-by-town basis. Its legal code still includes an appendix of regional civil laws.[10]

When the late 1580s the Jesuit historian and ethnographer José de Acosta wrote, "As a general rule, one can say that whatever of the Indians' customary practices can be permitted (when their old errors are not mixed in), it is good to do so and in accord with the advice of Pope Saint Gregory, seeing to it that their festivals and celebrations are directed to the honor of God and the saints whose days are being celebrated." He used the phrase "costumbres y usos." Acosta enhances the dignity of the Indians' customs by his explicit reference to Gregory the Great's respect for usos and costumbres in the Christianization of Europe. But for Acosta and his contemporary readers, the concept of "usos and costumbres" already came with dignity, for it applied as well to their own localities, to, say, Acosta's hometown of Medina del Campo.[11] Parish usos y costumbres run parallel with, and sometimes overlap, the secular usos and costumbres of villages, towns, and cities, which, in Spain at least, have a similar legal status as practices that continue unless expressly prohibited at a higher level, and even then tend to stubbornly reappear.

The statement in the *Partidas* that custom is a way to interpret law points to the broader distinction between written law and practice. All legislation is inevitably limited in its application by local conditions, local beliefs, and local practices, and it is just as important to know "law in action"—how the law is enforced locally by local officials and by inhabitants in general—as it is to know the law on the books. The convictions and vigor of the enforcers and the accumulated habits of the community help set the normal parameters for practice, in religious as well as secular matters.[12]

Much of the force and success of custom will be invisible to the historian. The promulgation of rules and the campaigns to enforce them leaves a coherent, consolidated paper trail; the stubborn and quiet nonobservance of these rules, or the gradual reversion to earlier custom, will leave a trail that is scattered and fitful at best, requiring slow, "scattered," cumulative research. Cases that reach Rome may generally have been resolved in favor of written rule over custom.[13] But what of the customs no one challenged, that simply continued, evolved, or died without directly entering the legal record?[14]

Within the Roman rite, the similarities and differences of contemporaneous liturgical practice among villages, regions, and countries has yet to be studied. Such a comparison would have to include not only ritual texts but also ritual performance. The same liturgy can been abbreviated, rushed, drawn out. Casual observation indicates that sections of the Mass are granted radically different salience and are accorded radically different amounts of attention. Sermons can be nonexistent or of dramatic importance. Although all masses will include the consecration of bread and wine, the ceremony at, say, Solesmes, will differ radically from that at an improvised altar on an Irish island, or a shrine in the Philippines. And there are major variations within and, more systematically, between national Catholic subcultures.[15]

The study of variation in Catholicism as practiced, historically or in the present, is in its infancy. Mary Lee Nolan and Sidney Nolan found remarkable differences among contemporary pilgrimage and shrine sites, especially between Irish Catholicism, which has marked the Catholicism of most of the English-speaking world, and Catholicism of Mediterranean origin.[16] Although it is true that most of the shrines studied by the Nolans were already in place by the end of the early modern period, for the medieval or early modern period there has been little or no comparative work by historians. Thematic works tend to look for trends across countries, glossing over differences between them. One reason is that, while it is evident that some practices exist in a given place, it is difficult to ascertain that they do not exist. A serious transgression in one country, worthy of synodal constitutions, Inquisition campaigns, concerted attacks by missionaries, or serial extirpations, may be so tolerated in another that it shows up only incidentally in written documents. Rare practices and devotions that approach the line of transgression we may hear about. Common practices, however idiosyncratic, that are well within the permitted will be less easy to find.

From my observation and acquaintance with historical documents, a systematic difference seems to hold between those Catholicisms that coexist with Protestantism (Ireland, the United Kingdom, France, Germany, Switzerland, Netherlands, the United States) and those of Italy, Spain, Portugal, and Latin America, where, at least until recently, Protestantism was not a competitor. In the former group, as if affected by the competition, the tone since Trent has been more rigorist and rule-bound, the religion more creed-oriented. In the latter group, Catholicism is more at home in its holy places, relaxed with its fiestas, and orthodoxy is rarely an issue; there belief and the creed tend to be pro forma. Some of these differences may have preceded the Protestant-Catholic rift.

Another dynamic surely develops when evangelizing Catholicism is faced with a local religious system that is even more image-, place-, and time-bound than Catholicism. On the face of it, one would expect missionaries from the Northern European tier to be less tolerant of these practices than those from the lower tier, although in Mexico, at least, idolatry was an issue for all of them in the sixteenth and early seventeenth centuries. The particular role of custom in canon and Spanish law provided great flexibility when confronted with the radically different *usos* and *costumbres* of the Indian populations of the Americas. A disposition of Charles V of August 6, 1555, permitted that the laws and customs of the indigenous population, so long as they did not conflict with Catholic religion or the laws of the Indies, should be kept and enforced.[17] In conflicts with the Mexican legal system, local Indian customary authorities still invoke the phrase "usos y costumbres" with a weight and heft that Alfonso X and Gregory the Great would have recognized.[18]

If the Catholic Church is indeed "a decentralized, collective, articulated process that serves the spiritual needs of Catholics and perpetuates itself, a community of memory with a particular purpose," then the local manifestation of the religion is that which combines the common memory of Christ and his passion with that of a set of people and their territory.[19] It is only part of the story, however, as these people are well aware they are part of something worldwide, with an articulated structure, agreed-on saints, and a visible head. That is, while they are Catholics of a particular breed, they tend to think of themselves as Catholics pure and simple, as what we could think of as the common denominator of all the Catholicisms. They are connected to the wider system by a host of circulating human agents (members of religious orders, bishops and Vatican diplomats, visionaries and prophets), as well as words, ideas, and images (by print, visual media, and now, the Internet) that maintain the network's articulation. But they will be well aware of the margin for local variation throughout Catholicism.

There are thus two elements to the local side of Catholicism in Mexico: on the part of criollos of Spanish descent the adaptation of a Spanish system of holy times and places to the Mexican landscape (the outcome of this process, as described by Antonio Rubial García in this book, is essentially similar to that in Spain); and on the part of Indian communities and the clergy that serve them the melding of indigenous holy places, deities, and times with those of Spanish Catholicism. These processes of adaptation and melding are continuous and dynamic. They are periodically stimulated by creative entrepreneurs who found or revitalize shrines, promote new saints, devotions, and brotherhoods, or anchor religion to place through vision or inspiration. They are affected by periods of control in the form of anti-idolatry campaigns and the Inquisition, and by waves of transnational enthusiasts, like, say, a newly arrived group of Spanish Franciscans at the College of San Fernando. They are rooted also in a systemic localist entropy, manifest in the people of Nativitas who do not want their image to go to Mexico City and the archdiocese that wants to have enthusiasm centralized and under control. But both localist entropy and centralizing authority, based on the built-in respect of Spanish and canon law for usage and custom, have contributed to making new Catholicisms in the New World.

NOTES

1. I am grateful for the comments and suggestions of Webb Keane, Sia Akermark, Greg Alexander, María José del Río, Lauren Edelman, Jacqueline Jung, Osvaldo Pardo, William Taylor, and Ignasi Terradas, and for the hospitality of the Center for Advanced Study in the Behavioral Sciences, Stanford.

2. Kenneth Mills, *Idolatry and its Enemies; Colonial Andean Religion and Extirpation, 1640–1750* (Princeton, NJ: Princeton University Press, 1987); Francisco Fajardo Spínola, *Hechicería y brujería en Canarias en la Edad Moderna* (Las Palmas de Gran Canaria, Spain: Cabildo Insular de Gran Canaria, 1991 [1992]); James Lockhart, *The Nahuas After the Conquest: A Social and Cultural History of the Indians of Central Mexico, Sixteenth Through Eighteenth Centuries* (Stanford, CA: Stanford University Press, 1992), 257–60; William B. Taylor, *Magistrates of the Sacred, Priests and Parishioners in Eighteenth-Century Mexico* (Stanford, CA: Stanford University Press, 1996), 66–67.

3. Webb Keane, "Christian Global" (lecture at the Dept. of Anthropology, Stanford University, Mar. 1, 2004); see also his "Sincerity, 'Modernity,' and the Protestants," *Cultural Anthropology*, 17 (2002); and Fenella Cannell, ed., *The Anthropology of Christianity* (Durham, NC: Duke University Press, forthcoming).

4. For the transfer of indigenous fiestas to Catholic ones in Mexico, see Solange Alberro, *El águila y la cruz, orígenes religiosos de la conciencia criolla, México, siglos XVI–XVII* (Mexico: El Colegio de Mexico; Fondo de Cultura Económica, 1999), 16–50.

5. On the rise of customary law constitutionalism and natural law as challenges to the old Roman ius commune, see James Q. Whitman, *The Legacy of Roman Law in the German Romantic Era; Historical Vision and Legal Change* (Princeton, NJ: Princeton University Press, 1990), 44–52, 116–20. I thank Greg Alexander for this reference.

6. I am grateful to Sia Akermark for introducing me to this concept.

7. José Ángel Fernández Arruti, "La costumbre en la nueva codificación canónica," in *Le Nouveau Code de Droit Canonique / The New Code of Canon Law. Proceedings of the 5th International Congress of Canon Law, organized by Saint Paul University and held at the University of Ottawa, August 19–25, 1984,* ed. M. Thériault and J. Thorn (Ottawa: Faculty of Canon Law, University of Saint Paul, 1986), 1:159–83, 164.

8. Boniface VIII in the thirteenth century: "A subsequent general law does not abrogate a prior contrary particular and reasonable custom, without a specific derogation," similar to c. 28 of current canon law (all cited in Fernández Arruti, "La costumbre en la nueva codificación canónica," 165).

9. Title 2 of Partida 1, *Las Siete Partidas*, trans. Samuel Parsons Scott (Philadelphia: University of Pennsylvania Press, 2001), 1:10–13. The editor in a footnote draws the parallel with Isidore of Seville's *Etymologies,* lib. V, cap. 3: "Mos est vetustate probata consuetudo, sive lex non scripta" [Usage is a custom tested by time, or an unwritten law], and Gratian: "Consuetudo autem est jus quoddam moribus institutum quod pro lege suscipitur, cum deficit lex" [Custom is a certain kind of law established by practice which is taken for law when a law is lacking]. Cf. John P. McIntyre, *Customary Law in the Corpus Iuris Canonici* (San Francisco: Mellen Research University Press, 1990), 81–86. On the convergence of divine and human law in medieval Spain, Francisco Tomás y Valiente, *Manual de Historia del Derecho Español,* 4th ed. (Madrid: Tecnos, 1997), 134–36.

10. See Woodrow Borah, *Justice by Insurance: The General Indian Court of Colonial Mexico and the Legal Aides of the Half-Real* (Berkeley: University of California Press, 1983), 1–11, 33.

11. "Generalmente, es digno de admitir que lo que pudiere dejar a los indios de sus costumbres y usos (no habiendo mezcla de sus errores antiguos), es bien dejallo y conforme al consejo de San Gregorio papa, procurando que sus fiestas y regocijos se encaminen al honor de Dios y de los santos cuyas fiestas celebran." Padre Joseph de Acosta, *Historia natural y moral de las Indias* (Mexico: Porrúa, 1962), libro VI, cap. 28, 312, cited in Alberro, *El águila y la cruz,* 45.

12. For a contemporary case study set in the United States, see Robert C. Ellickson, *Order Without Law: How Neighbors Settle Disputes* (Cambridge, MA: Harvard University Press, 1991).

13. See the examples in René Wehrlé, *De la coûtume dans le droit canonique; essai historique s'étendant des origines de l'église au pontificat de Pie XI.* [Thèse pour le Doctorat de Droit (Sciences Juridiques), Université de Paris, Faculté de Droit] (Paris: Librairie de Recueil Sirey, 1928), 372–77, from Marie Dominique Bouix, *Tractatus de principiis iuris canonici*, 2nd ed. (Paris: Perisse Frères, [1862]). On reasonable custom in the sixteenth century, see Wehrlé, *De la coûtume dans le droit canonique*, 274–78.

14. Such matters may enter the legal record incidentally in other ways: in civil trials, in notarial archives, and in criminal proceedings. There is rich material on religious festivals in early modern Toledo in criminal proceedings, since fiestas were often the setting for public fights and disputes; see Fernando Martínez Gil and Alfredo Rodríguez González, "La fiesta en el Mundo Rural. Siglos XVII y XVIII," in Palma Martínez-Burgos García and Alfredo Rodríguez González, *La Fiesta en el mundo hispánico* (Toledo: Universidad de Castilla-La Mancha, 2000).

15. For historical variation of liturgical practices, see Pierre-Marie Gy, "L'inculturation de la liturgie occidental," in his *La liturgie dans l'histoire* (Paris: Editions Saint-Paul; Editions du Cerf, 1990). I am indebted to Osvaldo Pardo for this reference. Pardo describes substantially different ideas about the sacraments and how they should be applied in Mexico among Spanish theologians in *The Origins of Mexican Catholicism: Nahua Rituals and Christian Sacraments in Sixteenth Century Mexico* (Ann Arbor: University of Michigan Press, 2004), passim, referring to "a misguided and still rather pervasive view of Christian theology as a uniform and monolithic system" (14).

16. Mary Lee Nolan and Sidney Nolan, *Christian Pilgrimage in Modern Western Europe* (Chapel Hill: University of North Carolina Press, 1989); Mary Lee Nolan, "Irish Pilgrimage: The Different Tradition," *Annals of the Association of American Geographers* 73 (1983).

17. Tomás y Valiente, *Manual de Historia del Derecho Español*, 341; this reconfirmed decrees of 1530 and 1542, cf. Borah, *Justice by Insurance*, 28–33, who writes that in practice, native law gradually gave way before Spanish law. But see also Jorge Alberto González Galván, *El estado y las etnias nacionales en México: La relación entre el derecho estatal y el derecho consuetudinario* (Mexico: UNAM, 1995), 92–93. Víctor Tau Anzoátegui, in *El poder de la costumbre; Estudios sobre el Derecho Consuetudinario en América latina hasta la Emancipación* (Buenos Aires: Instituto de Investigaciones de Historia del Derecho, 2001), describes the decline of the legal force of custom at the end of the eighteenth century.

18. See examples in Jorge Alberto González Galván, *El derecho consuetudinario de las culturas indígenas de México: Notas de un caso: los Nayerij* (Mexico: UNAM, 1994), 74–87; also Jane Fishburne Collier, *Law and Social Change in Zinacantan* (Stanford, CA: Stanford University Press, 1973); José de Jesús Orozco Henriques, *El Derecho constitucional consuetudinario* (Mexico: UNAM, 1983); and for Latin America in general, Rodolfo Stavenhagen and Diego Iturralde, eds., *Entre la Ley y la costumbre: El derecho consuetudinario indígena en América Latina* (Mexico: Instituto Indigenista Interamericano; Instituto Interamericano de Derechos Humanos, 1990). This respect for indigenous custom was a subset of Spanish respect for local variation in general. Charles R. Cutter writes, "Respect for local particularism, even when *contra legem*, has been perhaps the most overlooked dimension of the Spanish colonial legal system" (*The Legal Culture of Northern New Spain 1700–1810* [Albuquerque: University of New Mexico Press, 1995], 34–35, also 38, 75, 143). Indian invocations of "usos y costumbres" were less effective in the later eighteenth century, when they came up against the Bourbon *regla fija*.

19. William A. Christian Jr., *Visionaries: The Spanish Republic and the Reign of Christ* (Berkeley: University of California Press, 1996), 400.

Glossary

Alcalde: judge and administrator on a local and/or municipal level, exercising basic civil and criminal justice

Altepetl: basic community unit in pre-Hispanic central Mexico, primarily among Mexica/Nahua ethnic groupings

Audiencia: the highest criminal and civil court in the Spanish empire; an Audiencia was composed of judges called oidores who acted as both judge and legislator

Aztec: a nineteenth-century invention, referring to the inhabitants and empire of the Valley of Mexico in the early sixteenth century when the Spaniards arrived; technically this was the Mexica empire, but modern historians often employ the term Aztec because of its greater recognition

Bourbon: the royal house that ruled Spain in the eighteenth century after the end of the Hapsburg line; the Bourbons are also associated with instituting a wide-ranging, French-inspired, reform throughout the Spanish Americas

Bull: a papal pronouncement that carried with it the force of law

Cabildo: the local governing unit in the Spanish Americas exercising civil authority

Cacique: indigenous elite man who often served as administrator or governor in indigenous pueblos and communities and as intermediary with royal officials

Casta: caste, referring to the racial-ethnic definition and status of a person in colonial society

Castizo/a: person of mixed ethnicity, with one parent criollo/a and one mestizo/a

Catechesis: training in (Catholic) doctrine and the articles of the faith of the Catholic Church

Christocentric: Christ-centered; the term refers to a type of religious devotion that is focused heavily on Christ and less on saints and their images

Cofradía: a confraternity, a religious lay brotherhood whose principal activities were social welfare, burying the dead, and celebrating religious festivals; they were also important corporate units in which people could assert social prominence

Corpus Christi: the body of Christ; also a major festival celebrating the body of Christ

Criollo/a: someone of exclusively Spanish background born in Mexico or elsewhere in the Americas; the term often has a negative connotation, since it was often assumed that birth in the Americas made one genetically inferior

Diocesan: the church associated with the bishop and his administrative structure; a diocese, or bishopric, was the larger unit of the Catholic Church's structure, which composed various parishes and doctrinas; diocesan therefore refers to authority of the diocese itself; it also refers to the clergy that were associated with the diocese, in distinction to the mendicant clergy, or the friars

Doctrina: a protoparish, or a small administrative and physical grouping of Indians in the Mexican countryside for the purpose of conversion and teaching; also a short treatise on Catholic doctrine and the various articles of the faith, commandments, virtues, vices, and sacraments

Don/doña: an honorific title implying respect or aristocratic birth; in the early colonial period it referred to Spaniards of noble birth; by the eighteenth century the meaning had shifted to imply respect or social prestige and was not necessarily the result of aristocratic background

Español: Spanish, or Spaniards, referring to a person from Spain

Eucharist: the sacrament of communion, represented in the bread or wafer that symbolized the body of Christ

Fiesta: a feast or party; in the context of religion it refers to the feast day of a saint or a particular Virgin Mary, such as the Virgin of Guadalupe, or Christ

Fiscal: prosecutor

Fray/friar: monk; in the case of Mexico, often a missionary

Hacienda: a large rural estate often associated with grants of land and Indians after the conquest

Hispanization: the process of making Indians Spanish through religious indoctrination, language acquisition and training, and the learning of Spanish law, custom, and government

Iberia: the peninsula of far Western Europe, including present-day Portugal and Spain; Iberian refers to customs, language, law, or religion common to both Portugal and Spain

Indio/a: Indian; a legal term meaning someone of exclusively indigenous background and as such subject to different laws and administrative control in colonial Mexico

Inquisition: a religious court established in 1478 in Spain and in 1527 in Mexico to investigate and punish heresy, bigamy, blasphemy, and other sin-crimes against the church

Marian: devotion to the Virgin Mary, referring to the cult surrounding her image and veneration

Marqués: a title of nobility in the Spanish Empire; that is, a marquis

Mascarada: a public celebration of baroque culture involving masked performers and frequently the reading of poetry or theatrical pieces

Mayordomo: an administrator of funds and physical property; a superintendent

Mestizo/a: an ethnic and legal term referring to someone of mixed Spanish and Indian background

Mexica: refers to both an ethno-linguistic group also called the Nahua or Aztecs; the empire associated with this group coming to prominence in the fourteenth century in the Valley of Mexico and coming to form the central group to dominate an empire called the triple Alliance, centered in Tenochtitlan, present-day Mexico City

Moreno/a: an ethnic but not legal term referring to skin color and/or ethnicity, meaning dark but not necessarily wholly Indian, sometimes also meaning black African

Mulato/a: an ethnic and legal term referring to someone of mixed Spanish and African (and sometimes Indian) background

Nación: a nation or ethno-linguistic group

Nahua: an ethnic-linguistic group of central Mexico

Nahuatl: the dominant native language of central Mexico at the time of the conquest

Negro/a: an ethnic and legal term referring to someone of exclusively (or close to) African background

New Spain: the viceroyalty that covered, through to the eighteenth century, the territory from New Mexico to Nicaragua; a viceroyalty was the largest administrative unit in the Spanish empire, overseen by a viceroy (*virrey*), or the vicarious king

Nopal: cactus native to Mexico, associated with Mexica origin mythology; also a staple food item in both pre-Hispanic and colonial societies

Oidor: judge of the Audiencia, the high court

Otomí: a native pre-Hispanic language and ethnic group, principally from north of the Valley of Mexico in the current states of San Luis Potosí, Querétaro, and Guanajuato

Pardo/a: an ethnic term meaning "black" or African, much like Negro

Parish: the basic administrative unit of the Catholic Church on the local level

Peninsular: a Spanish person born in Spain

Peso: a standard unit of currency in colonial Mexico, equal in value to eight reales; originally, the term meant *peso de ocho*, or piece of eight, to refer to the eight pieces of reales that it was worth

Pueblo: small indigenous town, usually rural, associated with the altepetl in geographic boundaries

Pulque: the fermented juice of the agave cactus, used in pre-Hispanic Mexico for ceremonial purposes and in the colonial period more as an intoxicant

Real: a standard unit of currency in colonial Mexico, equal to one-eighth of a peso

Reconquest: the military process by which Spanish kingdoms retook the Iberian Peninsula from North African/Muslim rule

Regal: royal

Relic: a piece of a saint's body, such as a bone, revered as possessing holy properties symbolic of the saint as a whole or specifically associated with a part of the saint, or sometimes a part of the martyrdom of the saint or Christ, as in a piece of the Cross or Crown of Thorns

Sacrament: a holy rite in the Catholic Church imbued with sacral power and associated with salvation, such as communion, confession, or marriage; the rejection of a sacrament was generally understood to mean heresy

Sacristan: a person who had taken on "minor orders" but not necessarily a priest who was the physical custodian of a church

Scholasticism: a type of medieval Catholic thought associated with dialectical and/or syllogistic reasoning, reliance of other Catholic thinkers for authority, and heavily attacked by Protestant reformers like Luther as intellectual futile

Shrine: a physical building built to honor a saint but not always specifically a church where Mass was said

Syncretism: fusion of cultural behavior, beliefs, or attitudes

Tenochtitlan: the capital city of the Aztecs in the Valley of Mexico; site of the conquest of Mexico by Cortés

Texcoco: a city-state east of Tenochtitlan and the site of the first Franciscan conversion efforts

Theology: the study of God, religion, or Scripture broadly understood

Tlatelolco: a semi-independent city-state to the north of Tenochtitlan in the Valley of Mexico and a part of the Mexica Empire

Tonantzin: an Aztec mother goddess whose shrine was in Tepeyac, site of the current Basilica of the Virgin of Guadalupe, who eventually took on many characteristics of Tonatnzin

Vera cruz: the true cross

Viceroy/viceroyalty: the largest administrative unit in the Spanish
 Empire; a viceroyalty was a kind of miniature kingdom within
 a kingdom, administered by a viceroy, who was the king's physical
 representative; technically, New Spain was never a colony but
 rather a viceroyalty with all the same rights, privileges, and
 authority as other viceroyalties, such as those in Spain

Contributors

Christian, William, Jr., Ph.D., Sociology, University of Michigan; independent scholar. Author of numerous books on Spanish religious culture, including *Local Religion in Sixteenth-Century Spain* (Princeton, NJ: Princeton University Press, 1981); *Apparitions in Late Medieval and Renaissance Spain* (Princeton, NJ: Princeton University Press, 1981); *Moving Crucifixes in Modern Spain* (Princeton, NJ: Princeton University Press, 1992); and *Visionaries: The Spanish Republic and the Reign of Christ* (Berkeley: University of California Press, 1996).

Eire, Carlos M. N. Ph.D., Religious Studies, Yale University; Riggs Professor of History and Religious Studies, Yale University. Author of *War Against the Idols: The Reformation of Worship from Erasmus to Calvin* (Cambridge: Cambridge University Press, 1986); and *From Madrid to Purgatory: The Art and Craft of Dying in Sixteenth-Century Spain* (Cambridge: Cambridge University Press, 1995). He received the National Book Award in nonfiction in 2003 for his memoir *Waiting for Snow in Cuba: Confessions of a Cuban Boy* (New York: Free Press, 2002).

Larkin, Brian. Ph.D., History, University of Texas, Austin; Assistant Professor of History, St. John's University, Minnesota. Author of "The Splendor of Worship: Baroque Catholicism, Religious Reform, and Last Wills and Testaments in Eighteenth-Century Mexico City," *Colonial Latin American Historical Review* (1999).

Nesvig, Martin Austin. Ph.D., History, Yale University; Assistant Professor of History, University of Miami. Dissertation: "Pearls Before Swine: Theory and Practice of Censorship in New Spain, 1527–1640." Author of "The Difficult Terrain of Latin American Homosexuality," *Hispanic American Historical Review* (2001); and "Heterodoxia popular e Inquisición diocesana en Michoacán, siglo XVI," *Tzintzun* (2004).

Osowski, Edward W. Ph.D., History, Penn State University; independent scholar living in Montreal and a Nahuatl expert; his dissertation "Saints of the Republic: Nahua Religious Obligations in Central Mexico, 1692–1810," is currently being considered by Stanford University Press.

Rubial García, Antonio. Ph.D., Philosophy, Universidad de Sevilla; Ph.D., History, Universidad Autónoma de México (UNAM); Profesor Titular, UNAM. Author of numerous books on religion in colonial Mexico, including *El convento agustino y la sociedad colonial (1533-1630)* (Mexico: UNAM, 1989); *La plaza, el palacio y el convento. La ciudad de México en el siglo XVII* (Mexico: Conaculta, 1998); *La santidad controvertida* (Mexico: UNAM; Fondo de Cultura Económica, 1999); and *Evangelización de Mesoamérica* (Mexico: Conaculta, 2002).

Tavárez, David. Ph.D., History and Anthropology, University of Chicago; Assistant Professor of History, Vassar College, New York. Author of "La idolatría letrada," *Historia Mexicana* (1999); "Idolatry as an Ontological Question," *Journal of Early Modern History* (2002); and "The Passion According to the Wooden Drum," *The Americas* (2006). Coauthor of *Chimalpahin and the* Conquest of Mexico *by Francisco López de Gómara* (Norman: University of Oklahoma Press, 2007).

Taylor, William B. Ph.D., History, University of Michigan; Muriel McKevitt Sonne Chair in History, University of California, Berkeley. Author of numerous works, including *Landlord and Peasant in Colonial Oaxaca* (Stanford, CA: Stanford University Press, 1972); *Drinking, Homicide, and Rebellion in Colonial Mexican Villages* (Stanford, CA: Stanford University Press, 1979; Spanish ed., Mexico, 1987); and

Magistrates of the Sacred: Priests and Parishioners in Eighteenth-Century Mexico (Stanford, CA: Stanford University Press, 1996). Coeditor, with Kenneth Mills, *Colonial Spanish America: A Sourcebook* (Wilmington, DE: Scholarly Resources, 1998).

Villa-Flores, Javier. Ph.D., History, University of California, San Diego; Assistant Professor of History, University of Illinois, Chicago. Author of *Carlo Ginzburg, el historiador como teórico* (Guadalajara: Universidad de Guadalajara, 1995); and "'To Lose One's Soul': Blasphemy and Slavery in New Spain, 1596–1669," *Hispanic American Historical Review* (2002).

Von Germeten, Nicole. Ph.D., History, University of California, Berkeley; Assistant Professor of History, Oregon State University. Author of the forthcoming *Black Blood Brothers* (Gainesville: University of Florida Press, 2006); and "Death in Black and White," *Colonial Latin American Historical Review* (forthcoming).

Index

absolution, 71, 128–29, 134

Acosta, José de, 261–62

African, Africans, xxi, xxv, 14, 20, 82, 99, 127, 128, 130, 136, 179, 215–28, 232, 236-237, 239, 249

Alberro, Solange, xxi, xxvii (n4)

Alcalde, 93, 111 (n9), 122–23, 126–35, 139 (n16), 163–67

Alfonso X, 261, 264

All Saints Day, xxi, 48, 65

alms (limosnas), xxv, 51, 105-106, 114 (n29), 156-158, 160-169, 172–74, 178–81, 196, 198, 200, 215, 224-225, 227, 229–30

ancestral devotions, xxi, 27-28, 65, 121, 124–26, 132, 134–37

apostles, 41, 50, 57–59

altepetl, 126, 158-160, 171, 174–75, 177–82, 269, 272

Anne, St., 41, 47

Anthony, St., of Padua, 41, 54, 161

anthropology, anthropologists, xix, 2–3, 13, 44, 79, 83, 121

anticlericalism, xvii–xviii

archdiocese (in general). *See* diocese

audiencia, 50, 53, 71, 76, 105, 107, 111 (n8), 114 (n21), 155, 238–39, 241, 252

Augustine, St., 41, 83

Augustinians, xvii, xxi, 41–42, 45, 65–66, 70–72, 83, 86 (n11), 248

auto de fe, 132, 252

Ave Maria, 74

Baptism, 38, 41, 57, 59, 65–66, 79, 83, 128, 136, 141 (n28)

baroque, 14, 20, 55, 221, 225, 229, 271

Bartholomew, St., 41, 47

Bernard, St., of Siena, 41, 51

Bible, 10, 73–75

biblical, 41, 51, 81

bishops, xvi, xx, xxiv, xxvi, 17, 21, 50, 62, 65–66, 68–69, 71–73, 75–76, 78, 80, 84, 85 (n4), 103, 105–8, 112 (n11, n13, n17, n18), 115 (n33), 122–24, 132–33, 137, 139 (n16), 140 (n19), 149, 173–175, 179, 191, 194, 197–200, 206, 221 (n26), 224–25, 229–30, 261, 264

blasphemy, xxv, 12, 23, 236–38, 242–45, 248–53, 271

Bourbon (dynasty), 110 (n6), 158, 175, 210 (n18), 268 (n18)

burial, 189, 193–95, 200–8, 215, 217, 220, 229, 231, 239–40, 246

cabildo, 46–47, 49–51, 53

cacique, 47, 56, 78, 127, 129, 136, 142 (n38), 167

calmecac, 77

Calvin, Jean, 10–12

canonization, xvii, 41, 52–53, 57

278